Corporate Social Responsibility in Asia

Corporate social responsibility (CSR) is an important issue in contemporary business, management and politics, especially since the launch of the United Nations Global Compact in 2000 as an initiative to encourage businesses worldwide to adopt sustainable and socially responsible policies, and to report on them. This book examines the theory and practice of CSR in Asia. The philosophical and ideological underpinnings of CSR are rooted in Anglo-American and European principles of liberal democratic rights, justice and societal structures. This book not only considers the impact of Western CSR practices in Asia, but also provides much needed Asian perspectives on this issue. It investigates the operation of CSR in different countries across Asia, including China, Japan, Malaysia, Thailand and Bangladesh – comparing the different meanings given to CSR, and the varying degrees of success experienced in different national contexts. This book argues if CSR is ever to revolutionize the *manner* in which we trade then it needs to open itself up to the full variety of social responsibility as it occurs around the world. The book re-maps and refines debates about CSR as a global phenomenon, and will be of great value to professionals making strategic decisions in the global business environment.

Kyoko Fukukawa is a Senior Lecturer at Bradford University School of Management, UK. She was a Fellow of the Japan Foundation in 2006, investigating CSR practices in Japan, and co-edited the special issue of *Journal of Business Ethics* on corporate identity, ethics and CSR (2007).

Routledge International Business in Asia Series
Series editor: Hafiz Mirza
Bradford University School of Management

The primary aim of this series is to publish original, high-quality, research-level work, by both new and established scholars in the West and East, on all aspects of international business in Asia. Works of synthesis, reference books and edited collections will also be considered. Submissions from prospective authors are welcomed, and should in the first instance be sent to the series editor: Professor Hafiz Mirza, Bradford University School of Management, Emm Lane, Bradford BD9 4JL. Email: h.r.mirza@bradford.ac.uk.

1 **The Future of Foreign Investment in Southeast Asia**
Edited by Nick J. Freeman and Frank L. Bartels

2 **Multinationals and Asia**
Organizational and institutional relationships
Edited by Axele Giroud, Alexander T. Mohr and Deli Yang

3 **Multinationals and Economic Growth in East Asia**
Foreign direct investment, corporate strategies and national economic development
Edited by Shujiro Urata, Chia Siow Yue and Fukunari Kimura

4 **Changes in Japanese Employment Practices**
Beyond the Japanese model
Arjan B. Keizer

5 **Corporate Social Responsibility in Asia**
Edited by Kyoko Fukukawa

Corporate Social Responsibility in Asia

Edited by Kyoko Fukukawa

Routledge
Taylor & Francis Group

LONDON AND NEW YORK

To Luli, and her friends

First published 2010 by Routledge
2 Park Square, Milton Park, Abingdon, Oxon, OX14 4RN

Simultaneously published in the USA and Canada
by Routledge
711 Third Avenue, New York, NY 10017

Routledge is an imprint of the Taylor & Francis Group, an informa business

First issued in paperback 2011

Typeset in Times New Roman by Pindar NZ, Auckland, New Zealand

British Library Cataloguing in Publication Data
A catalogue record for this book is available from the British Library

Library of Congress Cataloging in Publication Data
Library of Congress Cataloging-in-Publication Data
Corporate social responsibility in Asia / edited by Kyoko Fukukawa.
    p. cm. — (Routledge international business in Asia series ; 5)
    Includes bibliographical references and index.
    1. Social responsibility of business—Asia. I. Fukukawa, Kyoko.
    HD60.5.A78C67 2010
    658.4'08—dc22   2009022984

ISBN 10: 0-415-45935-4 (hbk)
ISBN 10: 0-415-67304-6 (pbk)
ISBN 10: 0-203-86421-2 (ebk)

ISBN 13: 978-0-415-45935-8 (hbk)
ISBN 13: 978-0-415-67304-4 (pbk)
ISBN 13: 978-0-203-86421-0 (ebk)

The editor of this collection concludes her introduction by remarking that "This book hopes to offer – if only in a very modest fashion – something towards the development of a new 'world literature' on CSR". One can only congratulate her for hitting the nail right on the head. The essays reflect the editor's commitment to pluralism, pragmatism and a deeply respectful appreciation of the complexity of individuals and communities. In a world in which oversimplification is celebrated nearly as much in the world of scholarship as in broadcast media, it is refreshing to read a manuscript that celebrates complexity. Fukukawa's collection is a fine contribution to understanding the variety of forms of CSR across our planet and the importance of drawing on this rich resource to create a sustainable system of trade for all the planet's inhabitants.

Alex C. Michalos, Ph.D., F.R.S.C.
Chancellor
Director, Institute for Social Research and Evaluation
Professor Emeritus, Political Science
University of Northern British Columbia
Editor-in-Chief for *Journal of Business Ethics*

Two of the rising BRIC economies of the twenty-first century are in the Asia-Pacific region. India is the world's largest democracy; China is the largest country in the world and totalitarian and increasingly dominating the global economy; Russia and Brazil are struggling to shape their destinies as very different democracies. In the meantime Japan, still the world's second largest economy, is trying to maintain its economic and intellectual dominance. All Asian economies present different CSR perspectives shaped by their colonial and non-colonial experiences, and by their ethnic and religious diversities. This is a very useful and timely book, edited by one of the growing scholars in this area who has collected a great range of writers in one volume. A 'must-buy' for anyone interested in CSR, capitalism and sustainable enterprise in the 21st century.

Malcolm McIntosh
Professor of Sustainable Enterprise, Asia-Pacific Centre for Sustainable
Enterprise, Griffith Business School, Brisbane, Australia

Dr Fukukawa has put together a book that delivers far more than it promises. Upon seeing the title, I expected a delineation of CSR in Asian countries and how it differs from practice in the West. Indeed, it does this, at least for five countries, but it also re-visits the very basic questions of what is the purpose of CSR and what should it be, as well as what should be the relationship between business and society in today's "hot, flat, and crowded" world. The book is a must read for all of us who have a serious interest in the philosophy and practice of CSR.

Edmund R. Gray
Professor of Management and Chair of the Department of Management,
Loyola Marymount University, USA

Recently CSR has become so widely accepted and so rarely questioned, that we risk losing sight of its origins and implications. For Asian companies, the Western values and philosophies that underpin conventional CSR thinking are different to those from their own cultures and traditions. The implications of this simple observation, in an increasingly globalized business world, have barely begun to be explored by researchers. This book pulls together a range of expert contributions to reveal how an appreciation of CSR from an Asian perspective may be the key to a more ethical and sustainable global economy in the 21st century.

Professor Ken Peattie,
Director, BRASS Research Centre, Cardiff University

Contents

Illustrations and tables

List of figures

List of tables

Notes on contributors

John Elkington is a co-founder of Environmental Data Services (1978), SustainAbility (1987) and Volans (2008: www.volans.com). His 17 books include *Cannibals with Forks* (1997) and *The Power of Unreasonable People* (2008). *BusinessWeek* has described him as 'a Dean of the corporate responsibility movement for three decades'.

Abdullah Al Faruq is a Lecturer of Marketing in the School of Business of North South University, Bangladesh. He received his Bachelor in Business Administration degree from North South University and Masters degree in International Business and Management from the University of Bradford, UK. Prior to his present post as a Lecturer, Abdullah Faruq was involved in the corporate sector of Bangladesh for more than three years. His research interests include sports marketing, brand management and business ethics.

Kyoko Fukukawa is a Senior Lecturer in Marketing at Bradford University School of Management, UK. She is researching in corporate social responsibility (CSR) and ethical decision-making in consumption and business practices. She was a Japanese Studies Fellow of the Japan Foundation in 2006, during which time she conducted research on multinational companies to examine the communication and practice of CSR in Japan. She co-edited a special issue of the *Journal of Business Ethics* on corporate identity, ethics and CSR (2007, 76(1)).

Roszaini Haniffa is Professor of Accounting and the Head of Accounting and Finance Group at Bradford University School of Management, UK. She previously taught at University of Exeter, UK. She has published papers in *Abacus*, *Accounting, Auditing and Accountability Journal*, *Journal of Accounting and Public Policy*, *Journal of Business Finance and Accounting*, *Journal of Business Ethics*, *Accounting Business Research* and many other international peer-reviewed journals. Her research interests focus on corporate social responsibility reporting, corporate governance, accounting ethics, international accounting and the Islamic perspective of accounting. Ros has reviewed papers and is a member on the editorial board of several journals. She has supervised and acted as external examiner for a number of PhD students.

Samia Ferdous Hoque is a Lecturer of Business Ethics and International Business in the School of Business of North South University, Bangladesh. She received her Bachelor in Business Administration degree from North South University and Masters degree in International Business and Management from the University of Bradford, UK. Her research interests include business ethics, intellectual property management and consumer behavior.

Mohammad Hudaib is a Senior Lecturer in Accounting at the Essex Business School, UK. He has previously taught at Exeter University and Bradford University School of Management and prior to his teaching career, was an auditor in Saudi Arabia. He has published papers on auditing and corporate governance in *Accounting, Auditing and Accountability Journal, Journal of Business Finance and Accounting, Journal of Business Ethics* and *Journal of International Accounting, Auditing and Taxation*. His current research interests include auditing, Islamic perspective of accounting, accounting theory and ethics.

John Kidd is Professor and Honorary Research Fellow at Aston Business School, UK. He is author and co-author of many books and articles and his research lies in the overlap of technological and human factors in information and communication systems, especially those that have a global reach. These interactions form the hub of his studies of knowledge management and organizational learning in strategic alliances of multinational firms, where there are many cultural influences at work, and where ultimately trust is needed between the partners.

Nooch Kuasirikun is a Lecturer in Accounting at the Nottingham University Business School. Her research areas are social and environmental accounting, CSR and accounting history in Asia, with a main focus on Thailand. She has published in the *European Accounting Journal, Accounting, Auditing and Accountability Journal, Critical Perspectives on Accounting Journal* and *Accounting, Organizations and Society Journal*.

Frank-Jürgen Richter is the President of Horasis: The Global Visions Community. He is also a Senior Advisor to the leadership of corporations from Asia, Europe and North America. Prior to founding Horasis, Dr Richter was a Director at the World Economic Forum in charge of Asian affairs. During that time he developed an extensive experience and knowledge on the world's economic, business and political scene and its key players. Under his leadership, the forum's summits in Asia and the Asian part of 'Davos' have evolved to facilitate the exchange of expertise between leaders in business, government and civil society. Today, Horasis is the world's leading strategic advisor on long term scenarios related to globalization, systemic risk and Asian business holding frequent China/Europe business symposia.

William E. Shafer is an Associate Professor in the Department of Accountancy at Lingnan University in Hong Kong. His primary research interests are professionalism and ethics in accounting and corporate social and environmental responsibility. His publications have appeared in a variety of academic and professional journals, including *Accounting, Organizations and Society, Accounting, Auditing & Accountability Journal, Auditing: A Journal of Practice & Theory, Accounting Horizons, Business Ethics Quarterly, Journal of Business Ethics, Journal of Accountancy* and *The CPA Journal.*

Kanji Tanimoto is Professor of the Graduate School of Commerce and Management, Hitotsubashi University, Japan. He is also a representative director of Social Innovation Japan (NPO, Tokyo) and supervisor of Morningstar-SRI Index Japan. His research interests include business and society, CSR and social enterprise. He has published a number of books as well as of numerous papers on the corporate-social system in Japan and socially responsible investment.

Acknowledgements

First and foremost, I would like to thank all of my contributors, without whom there would obviously be no book. Although we may only have managed to gather around a virtual round-table, I do very much appreciate the opportunity I have had to hear – and bring together – everyone's thoughts and ideas on this complex subject. I am grateful for the help of all those at Routledge, particularly Peter Sowden and Tom Bates, and special thanks to Hafiz Mirza, series editor for Routledge International Business in Asia, for the support given right from the start on receiving my original proposal. Thanks also to Sunil Manghani for elucidating on issues of critical theory, in particular arguments related to the 'end of history'.

Foreword

Anyone who has worked in a number of Asian countries knows how different they can be from the rest of the world – and, in key respects, from each other. Kyoko Fukukawa has done us all a great service by pulling together nine authoritative contributors to explore how the corporate social responsibility (CSR) agenda is defined and addressed in such countries as China, Japan, Thailand, Malaysia and Bangladesh.

At the heart of this book, as observed in the editor's opening chapter, is the age-old tension 'within capitalism between efficiency and morality'. The notion that CSR provides key actors within capitalism with a moral compass is fine as far as it goes, but the uncomfortable fact is that there are various forms of capitalism at work in the world today. They are at different stages of their evolution. They define corporate responsibility in different ways. There is a variable gap between the rhetoric used and the market reality. And, creating a degree of background noise wherever you find yourself, the CSR agenda itself is often dogged by an unhelpful degree of complexity.

That has not stopped the agenda enjoying booms and – to some extent – busts in Asian countries that have been most exposed to globalizing supply chains and the issues that move hearts and minds in customer countries. But there is a nucleus of new mindsets, models and tools here that will form part of the genetic make-up of twenty-first century capitalism.

Meanwhile, as the economic downturn accelerated through 2009, the background noise intensified considerably – and there was a growing sense of unease that we may be seeing a parallel acceleration in the long-predicted shift of economic and critical mass to Asia. If this turns out to be an accurate forecast, then we are going to need all the political and market intelligence we can get our hands on, plus the brain power to make sense of it all.

The six chapters of this book provide a tremendously useful series of briefings not only on CSR but also on business mindsets generally across Asia. My role is not to recycle the ideas between these covers, but to open the door and invite you in, welcoming you to what I hope – and believe – you will find an insightful survey of two of the most critical trends of the new century: the rise of Asia and the parallel rise of the corporate responsibility, accountability and sustainability agendas.

Since co-founding SustainAbility in 1987, I have often worked in Asia, sometimes for government agencies and for business. Increasingly, however, I have also been interested in tracking down and supporting social and environmental entrepreneurs – people who are building their entire business models around the creation of social and/or environmental value. And the critical importance of understanding what is going on in different parts of Asia was underscored for me by work we have just finished at Volans, the new company several of us formed early in 2008, on what we call the 'Phoenix Economy' – which will rise from the ashes of the now-collapsing twentieth century economic order. Based in London and Singapore, Volans supports trailblazing innovators and entrepreneurs to do more, better, faster.

And their efforts could not be more timely. Charles Darwin lives on, we conclude in our report *The Phoenix Economy*, at least in the sense that natural selection pressures are working across global markets in powerful new ways. In 2009, we seem to be at one of those infrequent economic tipping points, also experienced in years like 1919, 1929, 1939 and 1989. Among other things, the current economic discontinuity is forcing a profound reassessment of public and private sector investment in areas such as corporate responsibility and sustainable development – all at a time when climate change and global inequalities are reaching critical limits and demanding urgent attention. The uncomfortable reality is that we still have a great deal to do if the new century's challenges are to be addressed effectively, in time and at the necessary scale.

It may be understandable, but disproportionate effort continues to be lavished by governments in the older industrial nations on shoring up the dinosaurs of the old order, rather than investing in the new pioneers, who are working hard – and often against the odds – to incubate and scale market solutions essential for a sustainable future.

Drawing on surveys of innovators and entrepreneurs around the world, we concluded that:

- The economic crisis has shaken confidence in old priorities, mindsets, incentives and investments, which are seen as increasingly bankrupt. This has helped to create a growing public and political appetite for an alternative paradigm, driven by a very different set of sustainable values, priorities and targets. To date, however, most initiatives have been driven by short-term panic rather than by any clear-sighted, long-term vision of how our economic priorities must evolve.
- Any market transformation must be based on scalable solutions that bridge the micro-macro divide. This will require entrepreneurial successes at five key stages of business and market development: (1) breakthrough insight; (2) experimentation; (3) enterprise development; (4) creation of alliances and replication of success and ultimately (5) mass market infiltration, involving economic and institutional transformations.
- Entrepreneurs – like all businesses – face increasingly tough financial challenges, but there is evidence that this is helping to drive necessary adaption. Many of our survey respondents anticipate new funding flowing into key

sustainability ventures from a variety of sources, including 'green new deal' investment programs launched by governments. But these same entrepreneurs must now also develop the political 'voice' and presence to ensure their views and proposed solutions carry weight and build the necessary momentum to achieve scale and impact.

• Strikingly, in spite of the anticipated growth in markets for social and environmental solutions, timely, reliable and affordable market research is still generally lacking, particularly in emerging economies, leaving many entrepreneurs ill-served when it comes to building their business case.

These conclusions are as true of the countries covered in the following pages as of those in Europe and North America, but the risks of allowing Asian development patterns to mimic the worst of Western patterns are clear. China, for example, has been described as a 'carbon copy' of some of the most climate-destabilizing elements of Western economies, from which so much of this activity has been outsourced or offshored. Corporate responsibility and citizenship are necessary conditions of progress, but if we are to create a global economy able to sustain a forecast human population of 9–10 billion some time this century we face a fundamental design challenge – how to adapt existing economic and business models to the new realities, and how to create new ones. Bear that in mind as you read what follows.

John Elkington
Founder and Director, Volans, and Founder, SustainAbility

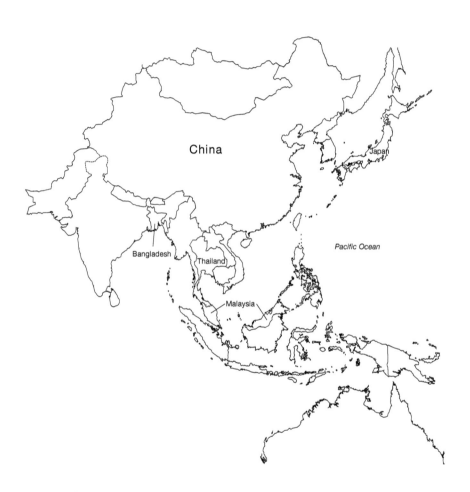

China

Japan

Pacific Ocean

Bangladesh

Thailand

Malaysia

Introduction

Global crossroads – corporate social responsibility in Asia

Kyoko Fukukawa

Corporate social responsibility (CSR) is a concept and practice that has been applied and adapted to a wide variety of business contexts, crisscrossing economic, political, cultural and social boundaries. Nevertheless, the definition and development of the concept has arguably been based upon a predominantly Western-led discourse. In an attempt to redress this imbalance, this book offers a series of alternative or at least supplementary perspectives; so placing CSR at something of a crossroads, both in terms of its philosophical conceptualization and its actual historical, political and cultural development within a global context. Specifically, the book provides five studies of the impact and significance of CSR in different South and East Asian countries: China, Japan, Thailand, Malaysia and Bangladesh; and concludes with a final chapter acting as something of a theoretical intervention.

An interest in and awareness of CSR and its activity steadily grew over the first decade of the twenty-first century, epitomized perhaps by an article in the *Harvard Business Review* in 2008, 'It's Time to Make Management a True Profession'; with the tagline: 'A rigorous code of ethics will make you a better manager. Society will benefit too.' (Khurana and Nohria 2008). The authors suggest that 'business leaders must embrace a way of looking at their role that goes beyond their responsibility to the shareholder to include a civic and personal commitment to their duty as institutional custodians' (p. 70). It is a view that coincides with an argument by Nakano (2007), who advocates for corporate conscience-based governance, with the establishment of business ethics based upon the shared values of a corporation and its stakeholders; in the pursuit of which, a corporation will invariably go beyond any legal framework, and rather abide by a self-espoused code of ethics. Interestingly, however, Khurana and Nohria (2008: 75) point out that in extreme cases, appealing to a 'corporate conscience' is not always beneficial. They cite the case of Japanese corporations unable to make short-term decisions to lay off employees and banks refusing to write off loans, which can be said to have contributed to the downturn of the Japanese economy in the 1990s. Of course, there is nothing new in a tension existing within capitalism between efficiency and morality, though the idea of CSR is that it is a force for good operating from *within* the very mechanics of commerce. The extent to which this is true remains open to debate.

The recent interest in CSR – as a 'tool' to help capitalism maintain its social compass – has not only been a feature of Western economies, but has also been set against the backdrop of relative growth and prosperity in those Western countries. In the time between first devising this book and actually producing the final manuscript the state of the global economy altered dramatically. Indeed, it fractured. A period of sustained growth suddenly burst following a collapse in confidence at the banks. The 'credit crunch', prompted by a crisis in the ethically questionable subprime mortgage market in the US, prompted a global recession and even talk of a depression. Inevitably, in the time between the book being published, distributed and being in your hands right now, things will no doubt look very different again. However, a substantial shift would seem to have occurred with regards to how we think about the 'health' of capitalism and the global economy.

It was incumbent upon world leaders to be seen to respond to the economic crisis, which led to unprecedented government bail outs of the financial sector – the very sector we would normally associate as the dynamic engine of unfettered capitalism. This seemingly 'topsy-turvy' occurrence engendered cross-party consensus in many cases, and crucially prompted a whole new set of questions about the management of national, regional and global economies. The British Prime Minister, Gordon Brown, called on a global consensus for a 'stronger and more just' world order; he urged we use the

> worldwide economic downturn as an opportunity to thoroughly reform international financial institutions and create a new "truly global society" … [to seek] agreement on a world trade deal and reform of the international financial system based on principles of "transparency, integrity, responsibility, sound banking practice and global governance with co-ordination across borders".
>
> (The *Telegraph*, 11 November 2008)

Similarly, Barack Obama, taking up office as the 44th US president, faced with the country's worst economic failure in decades, used his inauguration speech to signal the need for a new order of economic vigilance:

> The question we ask today is not whether our government is too big or too small, but whether it works […] And those of us who manage the public's dollars will be held to account – to spend wisely, reform bad habits, and do our business in the light of day – because only then can we restore the vital trust between a people and their government. […] Nor is the question before us whether the market is a force for good or ill. Its power to generate wealth and expand freedom is unmatched, but this crisis has reminded us that without a watchful eye, the market can spin out of control – that a nation cannot prosper long when it favours only the prosperous. The success of our economy has always depended not just on the size of our gross domestic product, but on the reach of our prosperity; on the ability to extend opportunity to every willing heart – not out of charity, but because it is the surest route to our common good.
>
> (Barack Obama, Inaugural Presidential Speech, 20 January 2009. Source: BBC News website)

Reich (2007) would argue it is only through the mechanism of the democratic political process, whether through government intervention or changes to the law, that we will see corporations pursue the public interest as well as their own. He would no doubt applaud various measures applied at the start of 2009 to prevent short-dealer trading and the capping of bonuses for those executives working at banks receiving government bail outs. Yet, he would also argue far more needs to be done in order to redress imbalances in the system. His thesis of 'supercapitalism' is that since the 1970s, due to major technological advances and deregulation of the global markets, we have witnessed an irreversible intensification of competition. As Michalos (2008) puts it: 'Supercapitalism is something like capitalism on steroids, finally delivering on the textbook promises of consumer and investor sovereignty'. Reich is highly skeptical of CSR. He does not discount the sincerity of those engaged in CSR, nor does he suggest it has no positive impact at all, but given CSR goes on outside of the democratic process his view is that it has little or no effect in changing the rules of the game (Reich 2007: 168). He can only see the same worn formula applies:

> corporate initiatives that ... generate higher profits and higher returns for investors, are not socially virtuous. They're just good management practices that should – and given the competitive pressures of supercapitalism, will – be undertaken regardless of how much or how little they benefit society.
>
> (Reich 2007: 173)

At his keynote address to the Second World Business Ethics Forum in Hong Kong in 2008, the editor-in-chief of the *Journal of Business Ethics*, Alex Michalos, presented a strong critique of Reich's thesis. In the pages of Reich's book, 'not only motives,' Michalos suggests,

> But human agency itself has practically disappeared, replaced by the hidden hand of the monster of supercapitalism, delivering the goods as theoretically promised. However, supposing that motives are essential components of any plausible analysis of human action, one must ask, Why can't the agent for a company be motivated by profits and moral virtue at the same time?
>
> (Michalos 2008)

Michalos challenges Reich's argument that one can never 'do well and do good at the same time' (Reich 2007: 171). In particular, Michalos takes issue in the way Reich pitches against a so-called 'efficiency argument for CSR', which leads to the conclusion that 'since governments fail to compel big corporations to act because they are themselves manipulated by the corporations ... the only remaining course of action, dealing directly with corporations, must also be the most efficient' (Michalos 2008). On one level, the difference between Michalos and Reich can seem to be a tussle between a pragmatic, liberal approach and a more instrumentalist, regulatory one. Yet, it goes deeper than that. Michalos, when he asks why we can't 'do well' *and* 'do good' is interjecting from a different philosophical position.

He is not simply asserting that businesses are more equipped than governments to make changes to society and the environment, but rather argues it does not make sense to see their actions in some kind of moral vacuum, and/or to privilege governments and political, legal processes with such capacity. The 'monster' of supercapitalism becomes a very singular target, which potentially takes our eye off the fact that levers for change (and barriers against change) exist in more multifarious and complex sites.

These problems are further nuanced when considering CSR in the context of Asia. In a series of interviews with CSR managers at multinational companies in Japan, for example, Fukukawa and Teramoto (2009) show how it is easy to consider Japan to be lagging behind in its understanding and adoption of CSR, due to the fact that policies and reporting do not necessarily occur in the formal manner one might expect. This would seem to play out a certain arrogance of companies fitting with Reich's assessment of supercapitalism. Yet, Fukukawa and Teramoto's study provides a far more subtle and revealing picture. Rather than wish to 'celebrate' CSR as some new business tool, a number of corporations would appear to see it as an exercise in labelling that already goes on in the company. As the authors put it: 'The overriding suggestion is that CSR will only be said to be working when we no longer have to say it is working, or name activities specifically as CSR' (Fukukawa and Teramoto 2009: 139). In respect of the debate between Reich and Michalos, this would seem to be a case where morality is existing *within* the parameters of corporate life. These firms are seemingly wrestling with the needs of 'doing well' and 'doing good', though there are questions remaining about how (and whether it is necessary) to make such activity visible. Without visibility, it is easy to see how Reich's concerns of a supercapitalist system come to the fore, but that does not necessarily mean such concerns are entirely valid.

In the business arena opinions range and responses are often divided. For example, the chairman of the Nippon Steel Corporation, Akio Mimura, has bemoaned government intervention in the wake of the economic slowdown. His view is that seeking help from the government is 'a shame or embarrassing. Capitalism has its weakness ... however it is a well made system able to allocate resources effectively and motivate corporations and individuals. We do not have an alternative economic system which is better than that' (*Nikkei*:1, 31 December 2008). By contrast, Yuki Honda, writing in the *Asahi* newspaper, and drawing on the work of the Nobel Prize-winning economist, Paul Robin Krugman, who predicted the collapse of the subprime loan market and warned of a global financial crisis, argues simply, 'Stop the hell of the market ... Corporations do not have the stamina to stably support a society' (*Asahi*, 27 October 2008). For Khurana and Nohria, however, there needs to be some middle ground:

> ... it is clear that the extreme approaches won't work. The flaws in a dogmatic adherence to the doctrine of "maximize shareholder value to the extent permitted by law" have become very apparent. On the other hand, the stakeholder approach has drawbacks as well. [...] To succeed, a management code will have to steer a middle course between these two extremes so that we lose

neither the value-creating impetus of the shareholder concept nor the accountability inherent in the stakeholder approach.

(Khurana and Nohria 2008: 75)

Without doubt, complexity abounds in debates of CSR and its global purview.
Nevertheless, some things are clear. Regardless of the position one takes, whether
to intervene in markets or stand clear and let matters take their course, whether
one argues for or against state-ownership and bail outs or perhaps a revitalized
(super)capitalism, the relationship between businesses and society over recent
years has been put under the spotlight with ever greater scrutiny. Out of which
two things emerge. First, the idea of corporate social responsibility has become
more significant, and certainly ever more part of a general discourse. Secondly,
the global recession has again prompted concerns about globalization and the
trading relationships between nations. The premise of this book is that the 'voice'
of Asian countries has largely hitherto been ignored in debates about the global
economy and social responsibility, subsequently it is timely we begin to find ways
to broaden the spectrum of those in engaged in thinking about the future and ethics
of world trade and commerce.

CSR and its complexity

In the English-speaking domain, a great deal of research has accrued on the topic
of CSR. Key textbooks have appeared, long-standing, mainstream academic journals have published on the subject and specialist journals have sprung up, too. In
short, CSR has become both a fashionable and serious-minded area of research.
The general contemporary definition of CSR, as it pervades through all the literature, is of a business activity that can be said to enhance society, to be voluntary
in conduct (i.e. not required by law or due to governmental or industry coercion),
and to be at a distance from a corporation's profit-making activity. However, like
any jargonistic term that gains wide currency, there is the potential for a lot of
slippage in the scope of its meaning and the uses to which it is put. As Fukukawa
and Moon (2004: 46) note, for example, '[it is] increasingly hard to isolate CSR
from mainstream business and government regulation given the prominence of the
"business case" and government incentives through soft regulation'. Nevertheless,
they go on to point out that CSR is still distinctive by 'its focus on responsiveness
to and even anticipation of social agendas, and by increased attention to social
performance. (46).

However, as noted at the start of this introduction, the discourse and practice
of CSR – in bearing a global presence – has predominately been led by those in
Western contexts. Crucially, the philosophical and ideological underpinnings of
CSR remain rooted in Anglo-American and European principles of liberal democratic rights, justice and societal structures. Empirical studies of CSR have certainly
demonstrated its wider purview, with numerous studies giving a view upon its
operation in South and East Asian and Middle Eastern territories. Yet, even though
'local' insights can be drawn out of these various studies, the critical theoretical

and analytical frameworks tend not to advance beyond the Western-dominated literatures. Furthermore, from the point of view of putting this book together, it is worth noting there has been a definite lack of awareness and joined-up thinking in more general debates, particularly with those outside of academia. Though small in respect of other areas of business scholarship, there is a growing body of literature concerned with CSR and Asia. However, this work is largely only accessed via specialist journals, which are not necessarily available to the general reader. This book obviously cannot hope to be as comprehensive as this growing body of literature, but nonetheless seeks to provide a more immediate and contextualized series of debates.

Within the Western context, CSR can be seen to date back to the 1950s (for a concise overview see Maignan and Ferrell 2004). In its earliest manifestation, CSR was characterized by a sense of social obligation, which Bowen (1953: 6) notes meant 'to follow those lines of action which are desirable in terms of the objectives and values of our society'. Carroll (1979) provides a more specific, four-part model of CSR, categorized in terms of economic, legal, ethical, and philanthropic responsibility. Corporations have always held a responsibility to create economic value for their owners and, in addition, corporations have been under legal obligations to comply with existing laws. Today, these laws and frameworks have become more complex with the expansion of global markets and the development of large legal entities, such as the European Union. However, the ethical and philanthropic responsibilities present additional dimensions. Ethical responsibilities concern what is right, just and fair for any given corporation, but which crucially are not necessarily bound up with an existing legal framework. Ethical responsibilities, then, relate to broader social and cultural concerns and emergent interests, which may or may not be formalized at any given point, but which provide significant impetus for certain behaviour or changes in behaviour. Cultural historian Raymond Williams defined culture as a whole way of life or a 'structure of feeling' (1965: 64–88) – 'it is as firm and definite as "structure" suggests, yet it operates in the most delicate and least tangible parts of our activity' (64). This idea of a structured, learned set of behaviour and phenomena, combined with the more ambiguous, less formed notion of a 'feeling' is perhaps one way of thinking about the *process* of shaping social and cultural attitudes and the responses corporations make in the face of continued developments. Again, in the context of a global economy, the complexities of ethical responsibility, which inevitably differ and evolve from one country to another, only increases the need for vigilance on the behalf of a socially responsible corporation. Philanthropic or discretionary responsibilities present a further area of consideration. These arise out of the philosophical and ethical tradition of being concerned with what is 'good' for a society as a whole. Philanthropy – an activity that typically goes beyond a firm's core business or operation – has provided the justification for corporations to help improve the quality of life for different (and often underprivileged) parties and communities in society as well as engaging with ecological initiatives.

Of course, appellations of what is 'good' for society and the kinds of endeavour we might associate with CSR activity can never be viewed as ideologically neutral.

Where some believe CSR is a genuine reflection of corporate ethos in the global community, others suggest it is merely a marketing gimmick. Philosophically, we might understand these contested positions pivot around the problem of corporate *identity* – the idea that a corporation is somehow an entity and agent in and of itself; stemming from the fact that it is legally designated and culpable as an individual provider in society (separate from those who work and own the company). In challenging this notion of the corporation as possessing its own identity, Ashman and Winstanley (2007: 83–95) argue it is precisely the abstract nature of this construct that typically leads corporations to suffer the criticism that CSR activity is conducted simply to make firms look good, or even to take attention away from bad behavior. Their point is that although the 'practical utility' of socially responsible corporate practice is no doubt possible, the notion of corporate *beingness* is questionable. In other words, a question remains as to how a corporation (as an entity) can be said to do 'good' in society, without considering more deeply the values placed upon such attempts to do good – and how they are put there in the first place. Inevitably, this involves thinking about those who own and work for the corporation, but also beyond that, too. A significant area of interest that parallels debates around CSR is the notion of stakeholders.

However, even though it has become common to talk about 'stakeholder theory', ultimately there is no one single account. Nevertheless, 'each version generally adheres to the same basic principle, namely that corporations should heed the needs, interests, and influence of those affected by their policies' (Buchholz and Rosenthal 2005: 137). Importantly:

> in contrast to the traditional legal/economic perspective, which disregards all non-marketplace interaction and avows that the corporation's sole responsibility is to maximize its shareholders' wealth, stakeholder theory takes a more pragmatic stance that sees shareholders as one among multiple contributors to the firm. Consequently, the firm is viewed as a sort of trustee for the interests of its sundry stakeholders and its managers have a moral obligation (and an enlightened self-interest) in directing the activities of the firm to strike an appropriate balance among stakeholder interests.
>
> (Hay and Gray 1974, cited in Balmer *et al.* 2007: 10)

In a number of cases, the chapters in this book offer commentary on how the stakeholders and their interrelationships (both in local and global contexts) have significant bearing on the styles, possibilities and barriers to practicing CSR. All of which, however, is not without its problems and complexity, particularly given that the concept and role of the stakeholder is hard to pinpoint. Antonacopoulou and Méric (2005), for example, offer a critique of stakeholder theory by suggesting we look more closely at its ideological assumptions. Without wishing to 'dismiss the possibility that stakeholder theory as an ideology of caring relationships and interdependencies would add value' (30), they wish to point out that stakeholder theory – like theories of CSR – can too readily be considered value free. It is important, when engaging with these debates and applying key concepts such as the stakeholder and CSR more generally, to keep open other philosophical standpoints. So, for example, drawing on insights from feminist theory as well as Buchholz and Rosenthal's (2005) consideration of social pragmatism, which each attempts to broaden the field of understanding and interpretations, Wicks *et al.* (1994) present useful *relational* philosophies to critique (and decentre) the notion of the responsible corporate entity. A similar move is intended with this book, with each chapter in themselves opening up the complexities of CSR with respect to a specific Asian context, and in relation to the wider global environ.

Interestingly, the work by Wicks *et al.* (1994) can be said to mirror Maignan and Ferrell's (2004) observation of a more recent 'ethics-driven' view of CSR, which takes its bearings direct from philosophical debate and theory. So, for example, Balmer *et al.* (2007) conceptualize the corporation as *being* bound up in a community, to the point that it is 'neither an isolatable, discrete element in, nor an atomic building block of, a community' (Buchholz and Rosenthal 2005: 143). This book, in examining CSR in Asia in its variety (and with respect to globalization generally), does not seek to create any unified, theoretical understanding; if anything it wholeheartedly resists such a move. However, in attempting to broaden the canvas upon which we view the notion of CSR and its manifestations around the world, there is a certain 'culture-driven' view of CSR and, more crucially, an attempt to deepen our ethical understanding of engaging in CSR at a cultural level, as well as politically and economically. The context-specific studies in this book, then, can offer new bearings on how we work from (and against) current philosophical debate and theory.

CSR and Asia

There are various challenges facing scholars at the 'margin', not least issues relating to translation and potential inequities in global academic exchange. It is difficult, therefore, to 'identify a critical mass of research work that allows for informed judgements regarding the universality of theories developed primarily in the context of the "American-European" mainstream' (Walters 2001: 468). Yet, given increased global connectivity and the social responsibilities and dilemmas it brings, the importance and timeliness of looking beyond the 'centre' as a critical endeavor cannot be underestimated. Inquiring into CSR in the Asian context is one part of that process.

Rupp *et al.* (2006) make the case that bringing an Asian perspective into view is critical if any genuine advancement can be made to influence positive social change and environmental sustainability. The approach taken here is that there is no specific need to assert who is 'right' and 'wrong', or to make claims about who is progressive or who is lagging behind in the development of CSR. Each society has its own codes of conduct and specific needs and concerns. Importantly, we need to understand the factors that lead to differences in CSR practice and how specific contexts have their own opportunities and barriers. Asia has generally only been examined for its 'importing' of CSR practice and not considered for yielding any independent contribution to the discourse. This book encourages us to newly regard – not disregard – a part of the globe that hitherto has been relatively quiet on the subject. As will become apparent from reading the various contributions, a lot does go on in the name of (or at least aspiring towards a form of) CSR in Asian countries. In some cases, the importing of CSR has led to various structural changes in the business community, as we find, for example, with the professionalization of CSR in Japanese corporations. Whereas in China, it would seem the importing of dominant Western views and principles has unintended and not always positive effects. In Malaysia and Thailand there is direct engagement with CSR debates and practices, but implementation tends to be selective. In the case of Malaysia, it can be shown selection differs with the differing levels of society, from micro decision-making in companies through to governmental policies and procedures. However, with a country such as Bangladesh, despite internal and external interests and pressures to develop recognizable CSR policies, there is a great deal of remedial work required before companies can truly compete in the marketplace at the same time as being socially responsible.

As individual snapshots, the accounts in this book are revealing in themselves, commenting on the various complexities faced by individual countries and/or individual sectors within those countries. Equally, however, as we come to think about them in combination, with respect to the issues of global connectivity, we can begin to properly understand the point made by Rupp *et al.* (2006) that an Asian perspective is necessary to any real advancement in social change and environmental sustainability. CSR cannot remain a static approach. In itself, the term must come to interrogate the competing values and ideologies – since these differences already exist in the marketplace. In other words, it is not about leveling the playing field, as if CSR can ease the world economy into a neat and tidy 'one size fits all' approach, but rather to acknowledge and navigate the variety of pathways and hazards that are the very fabric of the *real* world economy.

Given the relatively limited research conducted on CSR specific to Asian contexts, it is not surprising theorization remains weak. The chapters here on Malaysia (Chapter 4) and Bangladesh (Chapter 5) are useful in that they present theoretical templates for possible application to other contexts. Nevertheless, there are a variety of existing perspectives worth noting. Frost (2006) deals with issues of exploitation, particularly in relation to the supply chain in Bangladesh, Vietnam, Cambodia and China. The chapter on Bangladesh provides a very good example of work in this area. Welford (2007) focuses on the structures of corporate governance in Asian countries. His work shows how family ties often compromise the independence of a corporation's board of governors. The chapters here on Japan, Thailand and Malaysia, in part, follow up on this and related observances and provide further nuance. More broadly speaking, taking a more systematic look at CSR issues in Asia, Chapple and Moon (2007) argue specifically that Asian business systems both have their own practices and challenges:

> Asian business systems have a variety of their own norms and practices for CSR. Some are long-standing and embedded, reflecting wider institutional and cultural phenomena, and others relatively new, reflecting adjustments to

globalization. Asian societies also yield some very different CSR contexts and challenges, such as poverty and wealth distribution, labour rates and standards, educational disparities, civil society organizations, bases of governmental power and legitimacy, corporate governance challenges, access to water and a vulnerability to natural disasters.

(Chapple and Moon 2007: 183)

Businesses in some Asian countries are clearly making attempts to 'adopt' the Western version of CSR practices in order to survive global competition, and others are exploring the way they adjust their practices to take account of the West vis-à-vis their own local principles. Either way, in addition to needing to consider stakeholders and supply chains from a global perspective, it is inevitable – not least given the specific conditions Chapple and Moon note above – a variety of 'ethics' exist within the Asian context. These can be usefully drawn out to show how they combine, thwart and modify what we formerly understand as CSR.

On the one hand, Miles (2006) considers it appropriate to apply Anglo-American corporate governance in Confucianist-oriented societies. Assuming the benefits of Anglo-American corporate governance, Miles describes an opportunistic view amongst younger generations, which in turn, he suggests, leads to a more receptive view towards Western values. Subsequently, the foundation is laid for the application of Anglo-American style corporate governance. The opening chapter here, which examines the import of the Western 'dominant social paradigm' in China takes issue with such unchallenged appropriation of Western values. Yet, in the case of Japan (discussed in Chapter 2), it would seem there is more of a case for an optimistic view. Of course, Japan, in its recent history, has been subject to a great deal of Americanization, which arguably allows for greater assimilation of Western values. By contrast, however, Nakano (2007), speaking specifically of the Japanese context, is critical of shareholder-centered governance as a means to establishing a compliance-style business ethic. Within a compliance-style system, which must abide by existing laws and legislation, managers are nonetheless obliged to make decisions in order to protect shareholders' rights and maximize their value. Against this, Nakano advocates corporate conscience-based governance with the establishment of a business ethic based upon the shared values of a corporation and its stakeholders, which he suggests is more characteristic of the Japanese business context. The system requires managers to determine their responsibilities by reflecting upon the expectations and demands of various stakeholders. Thus, in order to fulfil its responsibilities, a corporation needs to go beyond a legal framework. Thus, Nakano begins to help identify Japan's ambivalent relationship with the concept of CSR (see Fukukawa and Teramoto 2009). Nakano's critical stance, apart from obviously needing to be fleshed out differently according to each specific context, is an important reminder of a need to continue to think differently about CSR as it spreads across the world, and crucially, not to take it as a simple, singular idea.

In focusing on different areas of South and East Asia, the collection of essays presented here seek to play their part in a bid to redress the imbalance in our worldwide understanding of CSR; to deepen, enrich and even potentially unsettle the philosophical, political and practical pragmatic debates that involve all members of the international business community. Furthermore, with Asia being home to strong existing economies and aggressive emerging markets, an underlying concern of the book is the *future* of CSR: what form(s) can it take to be widely acceptable and properly observed? Is international agreement (e.g. ISO 26000) the solution and if so, what is the basis of such a standard? Each of the chapters offer some commentary (and possible new research agendas) on these or related issues as part of looking ahead to the future shape and significance of CSR.

Overview of contributions

A guiding image in devising this book was of a group of scholars from a range of Asian countries sitting down at a round-table to discuss the relevant issues. Inevitably, given the geographical ambitions of the book, it was perhaps better (at least for the environment) for this to be an imaginary round-table. However, it was not simply about bringing people together in one place at a specific time to hear their views, but also to initiate the prospects for an ongoing 'circle of discussion', in which differing views, ideas and arguments move on and return for reflection among those involved. The six contributions in this book are only some of the voices that need to be heard in a globally orientated discussion. Hopefully, however, they offer useful starting points and represent an important step in the process of 'norm generation'; whereby participants from a range of contexts, not least those other than from G8 countries, become established in the debates. The rationale behind such a process relates to the underlying concern that the concept of CSR has never produced any actual consensus, yet its activities have spread with tremendous speed across borders, beyond Western territories. Lockett *et al.* (2006: 118) suggest it is because of the 'highly permeable boundaries' of CSR that it is unlikely to achieve consensus. A particular problem when studying the subject is 'the strict dichotomy between empirical and theoretical research [which] may not fully capture the role which empirical work might play in theory building in CSR' (Lockett *et al.* 2006: 118). It is argued then:

> [the field] is not simply driven by rational or experimental practices but also by business, social and political agendas. In light of these qualifications, we conjecture that the field of CSR will be characterized by a lack of convergence and, therefore, the body of CSR research will remain fragmented in terms of empirics, theory and (non) normative orientation.
>
> (Lockett *et al.* 2006: 118)

Keeping these concerns in mind, the contributions to this book can be thought to provide insight into CSR in Asia, in terms of both contemporary and historical perspectives, and provide an exploratory blend of empirical and theoretical accounts. In each case the authors offer their own definitions of CSR and relevant analytical approaches. The chapters conclude with commentaries on possible future agendas for CSR, whether specific to the context of a single country, or more broadly in terms of global interests. In addition, each chapter provides a list of suitable further reading.

In the opening chapter, William Shafer examines the role and influence of the Western dominant social paradigm (DSP) in contemporary China. Studies in North America and Europe have found that environmental concern and attitudes towards environmental accountability are strongly influenced by individuals' commitment to the DSP. The DSP is usually characterized to include support for 'free markets', belief in the possibility and desirability of unlimited economic growth, commitment to limited government regulation of business, devotion to private property rights, emphasis on economic individualism and faith in the ability of science and technology to mitigate environmental problems. Although it is sometimes suggested this world view is unique to Western societies, in the current environment of neoliberalism and globalization, Shafer notes that there is an effort among certain economic elites to propagate this paradigm worldwide. The chapter raises an important question as to what extent this 'dominant' world view exists in developing countries such as China. For almost 30 years China has been in a state of 'transition' from a state-controlled to a market economy, which, as Shafer shows, suggests that fundamental shifts in social paradigms or world views should be occurring. Empirical studies have not directly addressed the extent to which the Western DSP has taken root in China, however, Chinese scholars have lamented the growing influence of neoliberalism and the world view encapsulated in the Western DSP in their country. In reviewing a variety of literature to assess the implications of the DSP concept in the context of China, Shafer argues that the Chinese people are highly susceptible to the influence of the Western DSP, but that its influence is producing particularly dysfunctional results due to a lack of adequate social, political and legal constraints on market behavior. Thus, Shafer marks a very important point that the effective translatability of concepts and practices from one context to another can never be guaranteed. Indeed, their migration can have adverse effects.

Kanji Tanimoto looks historically at the structural changes in corporate society and CSR in Japan. There was a boom in CSR activity in Japan from around 2003, during which time many leading corporations established specialist units for CSR, resulting in an increase in the publication of dedicated reports. The background to this boom relates to global pressures, the growing voice of stakeholders (rather than shareholders) who have increased demands for corporate accountability and gradual changes, since the beginning of the 1990s, in the structure of Japanese corporate society and the relationship between corporations and their stakeholders. Given that these factors have led corporations to respond more explicitly to CSR issues (and the Western rhetoric of CSR), Tanimoto considers three main aspects of Japanese CSR. First, an overview is given of how Japanese corporations understand the concept of CSR and how it relates to their system of management. Second, following the collapse of the bubble economy of the early 1990s, with subsequent changes occurring to the structure of the corporate-social system, a more complex understanding of the main stakeholders (notably, shareholders, employees and suppliers) is presented. Third, with the view to a more sustainable economic society, the chapter considers the continued challenges faced by Japanese corporate society and the future role of governmental policy and intervention.

In Chapter 3, Nooch Kuasirikun examines the perceptions of CSR and its adaptation amongst businesses in Thailand. The chapter considers the extent to which CSR activities reflect Thai social and environmental problems. Kuasirikun usefully draws upon key commentaries in Thai newspapers and government reports, providing a revealing portrait of the key concerns and debates currently occurring within the business community and its presentation within wider public discourse. Kuasirikun demonstrates that awareness of CSR among businesses in Thailand is undoubtedly growing, though its practice and implementation is rather selective.

Roszaini Haniffa and Mohammad Hudaib's empirical study of CSR disclosure in Malaysia finds that corporations are increasingly engaged in CSR due to both internal and external pressures to demonstrate accountability both locally and globally. They present a model based on multilevel constructs (supra, macro, meso and micro), which reflect the various pressures affecting corporate social and environmental disclosure (CSED) policy and practices. Using content analysis, their dependent variable consists of two measures of CSED: 'variety' and 'extent'. At the supra and macro levels, their findings indicate the importance of industry recognition, reporting awards and other forms of support and encouragement. At the meso level, size, profitability and boards dominated by non-executive directors appear to be significant, while at the micro level, boards dominated by Malay directors are significantly related to CSED. Taken together, the authors show how it is an assessment of factors at the various levels that can enhance our understanding of the forces influencing corporate accountability and transparency in the context of Malaysia. Haniffa and Hudaib's framework is encompassing of a variety of key issues of CSR disclosure, giving real potential for its applicability to other contexts, which in turn may aid comparative analysis across markets.

In the penultimate chapter, Samia Ferdous Hoque and Abdullah Al Faruq provide an account of the exploitation of labour in the Bangladeshi ready-made garment sector. Given Bangladesh's status as a developing country, the concept of CSR is relatively new in this context. In the ready-made garment sector in particular, the most important industry of the country, unethical practices are widespread, including poor wage provision, poor working conditions and sexual harassment. Yet, as we know, many of the garment factories in Bangladesh are producing products for well known corporations in the USA and Europe. Hence, these multinational companies are frequently criticized for playing a silent role in inhumane practices within the supply chains and thus indirectly encouraging exploitation. Foreign buyers place emphasis upon the benefits of low-cost production. In order to meet these demands, Bangladeshi suppliers try to keep their operating costs low by not providing a minimum wage, by undermining health and safety standards and by forcing workers to work overtime without proper compensation. By adopting this low-cost route, suppliers compete not only with other local garment factories but also with international competitors. However, as Hoque and Faruq point out, with the rise of ethical consumerism, multinationals are amalgamating socially responsible activities to ensure social, economical and environmental sustainability. Buyers are pressuring suppliers to comply with codes of conduct. They also highlight how there are completing concerns. Certain factors driven by foreign buyers and Bangladeshi suppliers, combined with some factors relating to the dictates of the Bangladeshi government, often make it difficult, even contradictory, to comply with codes of conduct. The chapter offers genuine insight, from within the country itself, into the kinds of difficulties being faced by a nation eager to develop its economic footing, but undermined by its place within the economic hierarchies of a global system. Within the context of the other chapters in the book, Hoque and Faruq's account of the ready-made garment sector in Bangladesh is an important reminder that however laudable CSR reporting might be, in some cases there are more fundamental problems needing to be overcome before any 'system' of transparency and accountability can even be envisaged.

In the final contribution to the book, John Kidd and Frank-Jürgen Richter present a theoretical discussion of a so-called 'virtuous circle' of CSR in the global context. They ask *which* circle and *whose* virtue is at stake or being applied. In doing so, the chapter illustrates the various confusions that can arise in forcing CSR practices derived and practiced elsewhere in the globe upon another region or country. They present a contrast between firms in China that are developing quickly (some already of a global standing) and those in Europe and the US that have had decades of hesitant learning about CSR. The authors warn the forces of globalization cause us all to operate unethically at times. For example, it is frequently the case that the notion of CSR is upheld as being important by those equally finding themselves buying fake goods, many of which are produced in China. One particular problem is that these fakes are often not detectable as they enter into a bona fide supply chain. They also suggest how too often in the Western press we see firms avow they are CSR compliant yet, in fact, operate using more dubious practices that are tailored for operation in different countries. The relativist argument is made that managers are adhering to local practices, despite their actions not being in accord with international or Western best practice. Hence, the authors' basic question: to whose virtuous circle ought we to adhere? An important argument they make is how notions of trust alter significantly from country to country, and particularly between 'East' and 'West' business practices. If there is to be a way to share in the critical debates over CSR policies and practices, Kidd and Richter suggest we need to find a means to re-invigorate trust between trading partners and company stakeholders and to come to a greater understanding of differing modes of trust. The chapter, then, brings us full circle, to the very issues of the translatability and migration of the concept of CSR that we find in Shafer's opening chapter on China.

A means to an end?

It is easy, amidst all the research, debates and reports on CSR, to lose sight of two straightforward questions. First, what are we trying to achieve through CSR, what is its ultimate goal? Secondly, when do we know it has been achieved, and/or who exactly has the right to say so? The study previously referred to, which involved a series of interviews with CSR managers at multinational companies in Japan (Fukukawa and Teramoto 2009), is insightful for the first of these questions. One manager in the study comments:

> We must make sure CSR management does not end as having been a tempo-rary boom or fad … If I put this in an extreme way [the phenomenon of CSR adaptation as a fad or trend] is the reason Japanese corporations established CSR promotion departments, as did my company. However, if we were to take CSR to its ultimate conclusion, I wonder, perhaps, it would make no sense for organizations to have such units or departments.
>
> (Fukukawa and Teramoto 2009: 139)

Given that CSR has become something of an 'industry' in itself (with books, journals, research centres, think tanks and whole careers – arguably my own – based on the subject) it is hard not to register a certain melancholy in the words of this manager. There does not appear to be an end in sight – no discourse seeks to eliminate itself. Cynically, we might say the only reason his department will close will be due to financial constraints, not because his job is done. Yet, equally, there is seemingly real wisdom expressed by this manager. We might indeed need to look for the disappearance of CSR to know that it has achieved what it set out to achieve.

Of course, the situation is greatly complicated by the second of the two ques-tions: who exactly has the right to determine when CSR has reached its end goal? In a piece written for the Japan Foundation, Malcolm McIntosh notes: 'In 1998 and 2003 we argued that if CSR meant anything it was a call for all enterprises to know themselves: to be able to articulate their role, scope and purpose to the wider world' (2008: 9–10). A growing and shared discourse in CSR, along with the establishment of specialist units within companies, as noted by the manager quoted above, would seem to suggest companies increasingly do 'know themselves' bet-ter. However, the arguments that come through the different chapters in this book demonstrate that we need to go further, to know of things and practices further afield. It is not just about a company being more aware of itself and more proac-tive in engaging in the world for the social good. It is also about knowing 'others', knowing how differing circumstances, contexts and needs are all constantly in flux. As Kidd and Richter (in Chapter 6) suggest, we need to 'trust in trusting' – being suggestive of an external reality that is as much part of ourselves. Of course, this is much harder to define; it means taking the plural in McIntosh's line 'to know themselves' literally. Any one entity is a site of plurality and subsequently we might be better to say there is no end to CSR, only many ends – like trailing threads of a garment still yet to fall off the production line in a factory in Bangladesh, but destined for a retail store in the West.

A more straightforward argument would be that, although CSR might benefit from minor improvements and adjustments here and there, its goal is essentially its profileration. This argument mirrors that of the spread of liberal democracy, as the best means to achieve effective distribution of wealth and prosperity. In a comparative study of US and Thai business people, Marta and Singhapakdi (2005) present a set of results as 'confirmation of Inglehart's claim ... that economic development moves countries in a common direction, no matter how divergent their cultures and histories. Fukuyama's (1992) much-debated hypothesis that history is directional and terminates in capitalist democracy finds some support here' (571). The argument then, which as they note fits with Fukuyama's (1989; 1992) thesis of an 'end of history', is that economic development is a more powerful factor in social development than cultural and political variables.

If we consider CSR to exist within and alongside mainstream capitalism, then we might find ourselves close to the remarks noted above for an 'efficiency argument of CSR' – that it is economic development and power that effects change. If, however, we consider CSR an external voice to capitalism, we end up with Reich's (2007) position that CSR makes little or no difference to the march of economic development. Fukuyama wrote his article on the 'end of history' in 1989, leading up to the fall of the Berlin Wall and the wholesale collapse of communism. It was an article about the larger narratives of communism, socialism and capitalism and with a very definite pronouncement that with the ideological end of history upon us it is liberal democracy that 'wins' out. Critics, such as Anderson (1992: 351–52), ask why it is that if the end of history really has arrived, 'it is essentially because the socialist experience is over'. What this fails to acknowledge, however, is that it is not that a socialist experience is effaced, but that the capitalist ideology is the only system that allows all other systems to compete within it. It is a master narrative, out of which one cannot step outside or beyond. Thus, as Manghani (2008) points out, 'the predicament is not so much that Fukuyama is right but that his argument is symptomatic of the cul-de-sac that "living without an alternative" places us in' (44). Added to which, however, he notes, 'it is easy to forget that the title of Fukuyama's article ends in a question mark, "The End of History?" ... as if to say: "the end of history – is this all we get?"' (Manghani 2008: 144). The point hits home only in the final paragraph of Fukuyama's original article: 'In the post-historical period there will be neither art nor philosophy, just the perpetual caretaking of the museum of human history ... Perhaps this very prospect of centuries of boredom at the end of history will serve to get history started once again?' (Fukuyama 1989: 18). The all too simplistic criticism levelled at Fukuyama is that history never did, and never will stop. His argument, however, is not that the *time* of history will come to a halt, just that the evolution of ideological history has entered its final phase. Yet, equally, his closing remarks would seem to unsettle his own thesis. On the one hand, we might view CSR as just a facet of the 'perpetual caretaking' that takes place at this ideological end point, in which capitalism has won out as the only alternative. In this sense, CSR is thought of as simply a means for capitalist democracy to incorporate or elucidate certain social values within its own system. On the other hand, if we take Fukuyama seriously that the prospects of 'centuries of boredom' might re-start (ideological) history, we could suggest CSR to pose something of a new beginning, or at least a new degree of complexity for the current 'end of history' of corporate business. In this respect CSR would mark something different about the order we live in.

If we turn to another seemingly teleological philosophy (or science), Darwinism, we can draw out a similar set of observations, but significantly we can come to the view that social mechanisms are part of (and have always been part of) the way in which we compete and trade. Klein (2003) notes how attempts to explain capitalism by social Darwinism has prompted a serious misconception. On the face of it, Darwinian natural selection comes to explain, in terms of human activity, how 'extreme competition will allow the most "fit" competitors to rise to the top and to survive in this "struggle for existence," and this process of dog-eat-dog competition leads to both material and social progress' (387). Yet, this does not equate well with those who argue natural selection is not so much about the survival of the fittest (and only the fittest), but the survival of a greater complexity in the gene pool (Gould 1997); added to which, 'the contemporary findings of neoDarwinists [show] that the behavior of monkeys and apes reveals a blend of competition and cooperation and, generally, a close connection to human moral development'(Klein 2003: 387). As Klein demonstrates, it is a view that sits well with the work of Adam Smith, who

> maintains that nature's wisdom, as seen in its harmony and balance, is displayed in economics and human nature. Competitive free enterprise, as a vehicle for exchange, functions within a cooperative context and exhibits virtues and values such as mutual help and benefit, trust, harmony, and friendship.
>
> (Klein 2003: 387)

I have a vivid memory of something my geography teacher asked my class in high school. 'Why,' he said, 'does the subject of geography exist? Why do we choose to study it?' Imagining the usual scene of a class of teenagers, no doubt wishing to be elsewhere having fun, this blunt question stopped everything for a moment. However, it was the answer he gave that really sticks in my mind. After a brief pause, he said very simply and quietly, '… because of love'. Of course, the class burst out laughing, but he continued: 'Dad loves mum. They love their children. They want to feed their children. Dad imagines if he can harvest lots of rice from the field, he can feed children and make them smile. That is why he wanted to know where water comes from, the best type of soils to grow things in and so on and so forth. It is love that bore the subject.' Despite this somewhat dramatic, overly romantic way of explaining things, there is something very significant to note. In all the complexity of our lives and its histories, we tend not to stop and ask what is at the root of all our discourses and disciplines. But, were we to ask, generally the answer could run along similar lines: that fundamentally there is something about human connectivity (even if it is the destruction of that connectivity) at the root of everything we do.

I return, then, to the remarks raised previously in relation to the debate between Reich's (2007) thesis of supercapitalism and Michalos, who maintains within current structures we can 'do well' at the same time as 'do good'. Similarly, his argument is not so much that we have now reached a point when it is possible, but that the potential has and always will be present – it is constitutive of our being social animals. He makes the case in an essay called 'The Best and Worst Argument for Business Ethics' (Michalos 1995), where he defends the claim that the institution of morality is necessary for community as follows:

> communities or societies cannot exist without a minimum sort of morality based on at least two moral principles, one proscribing killing people at will and the other proscribing lying to people. In other words, in order for a community to exist, people must, at the minimum, adhere to the principles of not indiscriminately killing people and lying to them. To see that such a minimum morality is necessary for community, imagine the opposite. Imagine a community in which people are told that they ought to kill people at will and to lie to everyone and anyone. Such a community would be short-lived, if it could even get started. If members of the community did what they ought to do, they would literally destroy each other in the worst case.
>
> (Michalos 1995: 55)

Reflecting on this argument in his keynote address at the World Business Ethics Forum in Hong Kong in 2008, Michalos makes a strong case of the importance of CSR:

> It is counter-productive for Reich or anyone else to abandon demands for corporate responsibility because the latter is necessary for human communities to exist and when the latter disappear, the monster of supercapitalism will have nothing left to feed on and not only the monster, but its more benign brother, capitalism itself will also disappear. ... It is less complicated (sophisticated) than the argument found in Marx and Engels ... about the bourgeoisie producing "its own grave-diggers", but it shares some natural affinities.
>
> (Michalos 2008)

If there is an 'end' to CSR it is one that is bound up in capitalism itself, a system which seemingly has no end to speak of. So, rather than seek to determine what those ends might be, we can more usefully put our attention on what it means 'for human communities to exist'. This book hopes to have taken a step in that direction, to consider 'alternatives' to how we currently map and understand the concept of CSR. It is about looking towards a greater complexity of CSR, not its rigidities. One of the observations that comes out of Robertson's (1995) much cited work on globalization is the curious fact that economies in the Far East have seemingly maintained principles of solidarity and communism, yet equally have proved to be highly competitive (and productive), willing to embrace capitalism wholeheartedly. We need to understand and *share* in the understanding of such phenomena. Indeed, acknowledging that solidarity and competition may well co-exist, is part of unpacking and illustrating Michalos' argument that 'doing well' need not preclude 'doing good'. This book, then, seeks to encourage a change of perspective in the critical analysis and worldly practice of CSR. Just as we can collectively celebrate feats of individual excellence at the Olympic Games, we need to keep ourselves open to an imaginary arena, or marketplace, in which to broker a better understanding and practice of social responsibility in a global context.

When Karl Marx and Friedrich Engels wrote *The Communist Manifesto* (first published in 1848) – probably the most well-known political manuscript of modern times, pronouncing the needs of a new global order based on social justice – the authors were taking a stand against the burgeoning capitalist world system. The *Manifesto* begins with that famous enigmatic line: 'A spectre is haunting Europe – the spectre of Communism.' The claim, if only a rhetorical one, was that although communism was feared across Europe, it was not understood; thus leading to a perceived urgency for communists to make their views known with a manifesto. Today, in the face of so-called supercapitalism might we dare to claim a spectre haunts the global economy, the spectre of CSR? Although hardly feared, and certainly not in opposition to the capitalist order, CSR (as a means towards a greater good) nonetheless courts suspicion and is often misunderstood or inadequately practiced. I can only suggest here an ironic gesture towards the writing of a CSR manifesto (not least since it is not clear who would rightly author such a document), but there is an important point at stake. Any significant development in CSR – as a genuine response to the current state of global business and society – must assume its proper global proportions; as foreseen by Marx and Engels over 150 years ago:

> All old-established national industries have been destroyed or are daily being destroyed. They are dislodged by new industries, whose introduction becomes a life and death question for all civilized nations, by industries that no longer work up indigenous raw material, but raw material drawn from the remotest zones; industries whose products are consumed, not only at home, but in every quarter of the globe. In place of the old wants, satisfied by the production of the country, we find new wants, requiring for their satisfaction the products of distant lands and climes. In place of the old local and national seclusion and self-sufficiency, we have intercourse in every direction, universal inter-dependence of nations. [...] National one-sidedness and narrow-mindedness become more and more impossible, and from the numerous national and local literatures, there arises a world literature.
>
> (Marx and Engels 1967: 83–84)

These 'dislodged' industries, new wants and the universal inter-dependence of nations are now, of course, our common, lived reality – so much so we hardly question the state we are in. Perhaps we cannot easily relate to the *sturm* and *drang* of the revolutionary times Marx and others lived through and now represent. But that need not undermine the force of today's pragmatism. It is no longer an ideological struggle between grand narratives such as communism and capitalism that need concern us, but rather how – at our present end of ideological history – we can better understand capitalism, if not get it to operate better, too. Crucially, if CSR is ever to 'revolutionize' the *manner* in which we trade (in the ethical, rather than technical sense of the word), then it is surely going to need to open itself up to the full variety of social responsibility as it occurs around the world. This book hopes to offer – if only in a very modest fashion – something towards the development of a new 'world literature' on CSR.

References

Anderson, P. (1992) *A Zone of Engagement*. London: Verso.

Antonacopoulou, E.P. and J. Méric. (2005) 'A Critique of Stake-holder Theory: Management Science of a Sophisticated Ideology of Control?'. *Corporate Governance*, 5(2): 22–33.

Ashman, I. and D. Winstanley. (2007) 'For or Against Corporate Identity? Personification and the Problem of Moral Agency'. *Journal of Business Ethics*, 76(1): 83–95.

Balmer, J. M. T., K. Fukukawa and E. A. Gray. (2007) 'The Nature and Management of Ethical Corporate Identity: A Commentary on Corporate Identity, Corporate Social Responsibility and Ethics'. *Journal of Business Ethics*, 76(1): 7–15.

Bowen, H. R. (1953) *Social Responsibilities of the Businessman*. New York: Harper & Row.

Buchholz, R.A. and S. B. Rosenthal. (2005) 'Toward a Contemporary Conceptual Framework for Stakeholder Theory'. *Journal of Business Ethics*, 58: 137–48.

Carroll, A. B. (1979) 'A Three-Dimensional Conceptual Model of Corporate Performance'. *Academy of Management Review*, 4(4): 497–505.

Chapple, W. and J. Moon. (2007) 'Introduction: CRS Agendas for Asia'. *Corporate Social Responsibility and Environmental Management*, 14: 183–88.

Frost, S. (2006) 'CSR Asia News Review: April-June'. *Corporate Social Responsibility and Environmental Management*, 13: 238–44.

Fukukawa, K. and J. Moon. (2004) 'A Japanese Model of Corporate Social Responsibility?: A Study of Website Reporting'. *Journal of Corporate Citizenship*, 14: 45–59.

Fukukawa, K. and Y. Teramoto. (2009) 'Understanding Japanese CSR: The Reflections of Managers in the Field of Global Operations'. *Journal of Business Ethics*, 85(1): 133–46.

Fukuyama, F. (1989) 'The End of History?'. *The National Interest*, 16(summer): 3–18.

—— (1992) *The End of History and the Last Man*. London: Penguin.

Gould, S. J. (1997) *Life's Grandeur: The Spread of Excellence from Plato to Darwin*. London: Vintage.

Khurana, R. and N, Nohria. (2008) 'It's Time to Make Management a True Profession'. *Harvard Business Review*, October: 70–77.

Klein, S. (2003) 'The Natural Roots of Capitalism and Its Virtues and Values'. *Journal of Business Ethics*, 45: 387–401.

Lockett, A., J. Moonand W. Visser. (2006) 'Corporate Social Responsibility in Management Research: Focus, Nature, Salience and Sources of Influence'. *Journal of Management Studies*, 43(1): 115–36.

Maignan, I. and O.C. Ferrell. (2004) 'Corporate Social Responsibility and Marketing: An Integrative Framework'. *Journal of the Academy of Marketing Science*, (1): 3–19.

Manghani, S. (2008) *Image Critique & The Fall of The Berlin Wall*. Bristol: Intellect Books.

Marta, J. K. M. and A. Singhapakdi. (2005) 'Comparing Thai and US Businesspeople: Perceived Intensity of Unethical Marketing Practices, Corporate Ethical Values, and Perceived Importance of Ethics'. *International Marketing Review*, 22(5): 562–77.

Marx, K. and F. Engels. (1967) *The Communist Manifesto*. London: Penguin Books.

McIntosh, M. (2008) 'Time for Rapid Adaptation: From CSR to Sustainable Enterprise in the UK' in *Philanthropic Activities by Japanese Companies in Europe*. Tokyo: Japan Foundation: 8–18.

Michalos, A. C. (1995) *A Pragmatic Approach to Business Ethics*. Thousand Oaks: SAGE Publications.

—— (2008) 'The Monster of Supercapitalism'. Keynote speech at the Second World Business Ethics Forum, Hong Kong Baptist University, Hong Kong, 11 December 2008.

Miles, L. (2006) 'The Application of Anglo-American Corporate Practices in Societies influenced by Confucian Values'. *Business and Society Review*, 111(3): 305–21.

Nakano, C. (2007) 'The Significance and Limitations of Corporate Governance from the perspective of Business Ethics: Towards the Creation of an Ethical Organizational Culture'. *Asian Business & Management*, 6: 163–78.

Reich, R. B. (2007) *Supercapitalism: The Transformation of Business, Democracy, and Everyday Life*. New York: Alfred A. Knopf.

Rupp, D. E., J. Ganapathi, R. V. Agulilera and C.A. Williams. (2006) 'Employee Reactions to Corporate Social Responsibility: An Organizational Justice Framework'. *Journal of Organizational Behaviour*, 27: 537–43,

Walters, P. G. P. (2001) 'Viewpoint: Research at the "Margin": Challenges for Scholars Working Outside the "American-European" Domain'. *International Marketing Review*, 18(5): 468–73.

Welford, R. (2007) 'Corporate Governance and Corporate Social Responsibility: Issues for Asia'. *Corporate Social Responsibility and Environmental Management*, 14: 42–51.

Wicks, A. C., D. R. Gilbert and R.H. Freeman. (1994) 'A Feminist Reinterpretation of the Stakeholder Concept'. *Business Ethics Quarterly*, 4(4): 475–97.

Williams, R. (1965) *The Long Revolution*. Harmondsworth: Penguin Books.

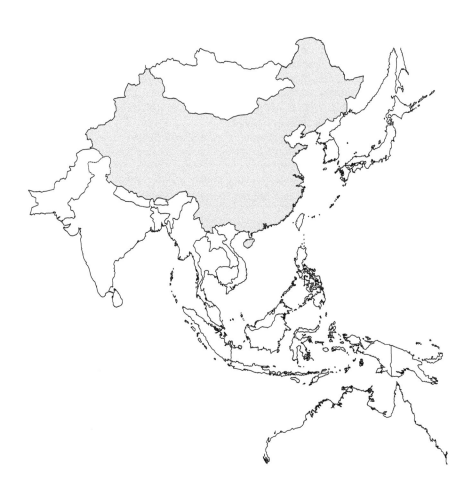

1 Social paradigms in China and the West

William E. Shafer

Introduction

Recent research has found that the extent to which individuals subscribe to the dominant social paradigm (DSP) of Western societies is a critical determinant of their attitudes toward social and environmental issues (Shafer 2006; Kilbourne, Beckman and Thelen 2002; Kilbourne, Beckmann, Lewis and Van Dam 2001). The DSP concept, initially developed by social psychologists (Milbrath 1984; Dunlap and Van Liere 1984; Pirages 1977), is generally recognized to include economic, political and technological dimensions. The economic dimension includes attitudes such as support for free market capitalism and belief in the possibility and desirability of unlimited economic growth. The political dimension is usually theorized to include support for limited or no government regulation, private property rights and individual freedom. The technological dimension includes such tenets as belief in the ability of science and technology to solve mankind's challenges and a concomitant faith in future material abundance and prosperity.

The world view encapsulated in the DSP appears tailor-made to support the neoliberal agenda of unfettered capitalism, and indeed many would suggest this system of beliefs has been socially constructed and propagated by economic elites for this very reason (cf. Shafer 2006). Although the DSP concept was developed to describe the dominant world view supporting late twentieth century Western capitalism, the current environment of globalization has obviously encouraged the adoption of similar beliefs worldwide. Indeed, the long-standing backlash against globalization is a testament to resistance against the forced imposition of the world views of Western capitalism. Given that the DSP supports a system that is arguably allowing corporations to inflict serious harm to the biosphere (Bakan 2004; Kelly 2001; Korten 1999, 1995), it is important to understand the extent to which this perspective is being adopted worldwide.

There are particular reasons to be concerned about the influence of the DSP in the People's Republic of China. It has been well documented for years that China's economic development and expansion have come at a tremendous cost to the environment and, consequently, public health (Economy 2004; Edmunds 1998). Although the Chinese government has recently attempted to rein in environmental degradation, the problems have continued to mount, and accounts of China's environmental crises regularly appear in the media (Leslie 2008; Ziegler 2007; Economy 2007; Engardio, Roberts, Balfour and Einhorn 2007; Kahn and Yardley 2007; Yardley 2007a, 2007b, 2007c). As observed by Harris (2006: 5),

> 'One would be hard pressed to find a more explicit and profound example of how human behavior can adversely affect the ecological environment than the ongoing experience of China. A huge population and rapid economic growth have conspired to create an expanding environmental catastrophe.'

Harris (2006: 6) goes on to suggest the root causes of most of China's environmental problems are 'the behaviors and underlying attitudes of the Chinese people. How they perceive and value the environment will largely determine how they behave in relation to it.'

A central premise of this chapter is that one should look deeper than the manifest attitudes and behaviors of the citizenry and question the systemic factors that produce and replicate such attitudes and behavior. For instance, the concept of the DSP highlights the role of economic and political elites in promoting ideologies that may profoundly influence individuals' world views. Thus, obtaining a greater understanding of the role and influence of social paradigms in contemporary China seems to be part of a much-needed examination of the underlying conditions contributing to the country's social and environmental problems.

Social paradigms and corporate social responsibility

Before discussing the relationship between social paradigms and corporate social responsibility, it is helpful to examine more closely the concept of the dominant social paradigm, and the alternative perspective commonly referred to as the new ecological paradigm. The basic concept of the DSP is similar to Kuhn's (1962) notion of scientific paradigms, which define accepted ways of thinking about particular issues and tend to be quite resistant to change. Although there have been many conceptualizations of the DSP in varying degrees of detail, Figure 1.1 illustrates the similarities between the DSP elements theorized in two influential papers, those of Dunlap and Van Liere (1984) and Kilbourne *et al.* (2002). As shown in the Figure, both conceptualizations include support for 'free enterprise' or 'free markets' and belief in the feasibility of essentially unlimited economic growth, ideas collectively described by Kilbourne *et al.* (2002) as the economic dimension of the DSP. They also share three key political elements: a commitment to limited government regulation, an emphasis on private property rights and a focus on individualism or individual 'freedoms'. Dunlap and Van Liere propose two closely related ideas combined by Kilbourne *et al.* as 'belief in the techno fix': faith in the ability of science and technology to solve environmental problems, and a resulting confidence in future material abundance and prosperity. Dunlap and Van Liere also include support for the status quo as an element of the DSP; however, as argued by Shafer (2006), support for the status quo can be thought of as a characteristic of paradigms in general rather than a component of any particular world view.

Dunlap and Van Liere (1984)	Kilbourne *et al.* (2002)
Economic dimension:	
1. Support for free enterprise	1. Support for free markets
2. Belief in unlimited economic growth	2. Belief in unlimited economic growth
Political dimension:	
3. Commitment to limited government	3. Limited government regulation
4. Devotion to private property rights	4. Focus on private property
5. Emphasis on individualism	5. Focus on the free individual
Technological dimension:	
6. Faith in science and technology	6. Faith in the 'techno fix'
7. Faith in future material abundance and prosperity	
8. Support for the status quo	

Figure 1.1 Dominant social paradigm (DSP) components.

The concept of a dominant social paradigm is consistent with Gramsci's (1971) theory of hegemony, which recognizes that social and political elites attempt to maintain their power by promoting certain preferred ideologies or ways of thinking (Bates 1975). The concept is also broadly consistent with many classic works of political theory that question the possibility of true democracy in modern nation-states, assuming that societies are controlled by 'power elites' that use various mechanisms (such as media control) to mould and subvert the will of the masses (Dahl 1961; Mills 1956; Schumpeter 1947; Mosca 1939). If public opinion cannot be controlled through such 'soft' mechanisms, the ruling elites may be forced to resort to state-sanctioned (i.e. military) violence to maintain their position of power and control.

It has been argued for years that the DSP is being supplanted by a more enlightened world view referred to as the new environmental paradigm or new ecological paradigm (NEP) (Cotgrove 1982; Dunlap and Van Liere 1978; Dunlap, Van Liere, Mertig and Jones 2000). The NEP generally reflects a variety of common environmentalist perspectives, such as limits to growth in a finite ecological system, the belief that we are facing a man-made ecological crisis and a lack of faith in the ability of science and technology to rectify ecological challenges. Given the obvious contrast between this perspective and key elements of the traditional DSP, it is not surprising that several studies have found strong negative correlations between these alternative perspectives (Shafer 2006; Kilbourne *et al.* 2001; Kilbourne *et al.* 2002).

Reflection on these competing world views clearly suggests that belief in the

DSP should be negatively associated with support for corporate social responsibility, while support for the NEP should be positively associated. The DSP emphasis on 'free' or self-regulating markets and limited government regulation are consistent with the classic neoliberal arguments that any form of regulation or constraint of market behavior is unnecessary and counterproductive, and that the only 'social responsibility' of business in a capitalist system is to maximize profits within legal constraints (Friedman 1962). Belief in the feasibility of unlimited economic growth and in the ability of science and technology to solve environmental problems should reinforce opposition to social restraints on corporate behavior by reducing the perceived moral intensity of threats to the natural environment.[1] In contrast, the world view encapsulated in the NEP should greatly increase the perceived moral intensity of environmentally harmful corporate behavior, leading to demands for the enforcement of standards of corporate social responsibility. This line of reasoning suggests the DSP may be a significant impediment to substantive advances in corporate social responsibility.

Political, economic and social context in China

It seems apparent that since embarking on the transition from a state-controlled to a market-based economy, China's leaders have been searching for an identity and an ideology that will justify and rationalize the country's economic, political and social order. The aggressive pursuit of market reforms directly clashes with the socialist ideology of Marx and Mao that provided the unifying framework for the country after 1949. How to rationalize the transition to capitalism yet justify the retention of an authoritarian political regime designed for a state-controlled economy became a central problem for Chinese leaders (Bell 2007; Knight 2003; Wang 2003; Burton 1987). The need to maintain the legitimacy of the ruling communist party led the central government to insist that the country was transitioning to a 'socialist market system' or a system of 'socialism with Chinese characteristics' (Chai 2003; Burton 1987). Socialism remains the official ideology of the Chinese Communist Party (CCP), and the stance of the CCP is that 'the current system is the "primary stage of socialism", meaning that it's a transitional phase to a higher and superior form of socialism …' (Bell 2007: 1).[2]

It is well known that many intellectuals have been highly critical of such arguments over the past two decades, as the fundamental conflict between the official ideology of socialism and actual economic practices widened (Wang 2003; Chen 1995; Kwong 1994; Burton 1987). The CCP leadership has long been criticized for failing to even provide basic definitions for catchphrases such as 'socialism with Chinese characteristics'. Reviewing early criticisms of the disconnect between socialist ideology and market reforms, Burton (1987: 437) suggested the most striking characteristic of the party's attempt to redefine its role in society was a 'complete lack of reliance on any *theoretical* rationalization for the change'. Influential Chinese scholar Wang Hui (2003) argues that the economic and social policies pursued by the Chinese government since the mid-1980s reflect an underlying neoliberal ideology, with its emphasis on unregulated free markets and assimilation into the system of global capitalism.[3] Beginning with Deng Xiaoping's famous invocation in the late 1970s, 'To get rich is glorious', there has been a general obsession in China with wealth creation and economic growth (Yan 2006; Harris 2005; Smil 1996). Wang (2003) argues that in contemporary China the single-minded pursuit of growth and development has trumped all other concerns, including social justice and democracy.

The Chinese government has, implicitly or explicitly, endorsed many of the characteristics of neoliberalism while at the same time refusing to abandon its official mantra of socialism. China's neoliberalism

> ... sought to radicalize the devolution of economic and political power in a stable manner, to employ authority to guarantee the process of marketization in turbulent times, and to seek the complete withdrawal of the state in the midst of the tide of globalization.
>
> (Wang 2003: 81)

The pursuit of this radical free-market agenda led to numerous social problems as the wealth and income gaps between the new capitalists and the majority of China's population widened, creating tension between the official ideology and economic realities. Deng Xiaoping modified China's

> pristine socialist ideology into a variant form of reform socialism ... the Chinese leader denounced egalitarianism for retarding progress and tolerated and advocated measures that increased income polarization ... They ignored the contradictions. Instead they emphasized the pragmatic benefits and called themselves socialists.
>
> (Kwong 1994: 249)

By the time of the initial publication of his essay on China's 'neoliberalism' in 1997, Wang's frustration with the situation was evident:

> ... the Chinese government's persevering support for socialism does not pose an obstacle to the following conclusion: in all of its behaviors, including economic, political, and cultural – even in governmental behavior – China has completely conformed with the dictates of capital and the activities of the market.
>
> (Wang 2003: 141)

Thus, many intellectuals have long dismissed any residual pretensions of the Chinese government to 'socialism'. But what has perhaps been most troubling about China's 'transition' to a market economy has been the perception of systemic corruption in the devolution of economic and political power, in particular, the common belief that public assets were being transferred to party elites (Wang 2003; Dickson 2001, 1999; Kwong 1994). This perception, combined with the government's insistence on adhering to socialist ideology at a time of growing wealth and income inequality, created the crisis of state legitimacy that led to the 1989 social movement (Wang 2003). The basic demands of this movement included

> '... opposition to official corruption and peculation, opposition to the "princely party" ..., demands for social security and fairness, as well as a general request for democratic means to supervise the fairness of the reform process and the reorganization of social benefits'
>
> (Wang 2003: 57)

However, there was a fundamental conflict between these popular demands and the interests of ruling elites in a system of radical privatization, and 'collusive links' between these elites and the 'world forces of neoliberalism' (Wang 2003: 62). What took place under the guise of 'free markets' and 'privatization' in China '... was the creation of interest groups that colluded to use their power to divide up state resources, used monopoly power to earn super profits, and worked in concert with transnational or indigenous capital to seize market resources' (Wang 2003: 101).

Wang (2003) sees no inherent conflict between the authoritarian Chinese state and neoliberalism, arguing that neoliberalism often relies on state power for its enforcement. He is highly critical of the common assumption that the process of market reforms in China will inevitably lead to political democracy, arguing that the proponents of this assumption have failed to analyze in any meaningful detail the mechanisms through which this transformation would occur.[4] Indeed, Wang (2003: 122) emphasizes that modern capitalism (as opposed to truly 'free markets') is a system that relies on and tends towards monopoly power, and since the failure of the 1989 social movement in China it has depended critically on the power of the central government for its development. Wang (2003: 66–67) argues that:

> The failure of the 1989 social movement simultaneously marked the failure of state ideology, and the ... policy put into effect after that time became, in fact a combination of dictatorial methods – relative to prior ideological mechanisms – and economic reform, demonstrating the basic loss of efficacy of the old state ideology. It was precisely under such conditions that neoliberalism could replace it as the new hegemonic ideology and provide direction and a rationale for national policy, international relations and a value-orientation for the media.

This argument closely mirrors Gramsci's (1971) theory of hegemony, recognizing that if the populace cannot be controlled through ideological means, the state will ultimately resort to more coercive methods to impose its will. However, it appears that the government's imposition of a market society in China not only failed to rectify the conditions that motivated the 1989 social movement, but has only exacerbated them by leading to greater inequality and more widespread corruption and abuses. Wang (2003: 186) argues that corruption has '... seeped into every aspect of the political, economic, and moral spheres' in contemporary Chinese society.

A great deal of research in the business literature supports this contention, suggesting that corruption, unethical practices and a general disregard of social responsibility are widespread in the Chinese business community (Wright, Szeto and Lee 2003; Snell and Tseng 2002; Tam 2002; Young 2002). The rampant business corruption is often attributed to the fact that China lacks the social, political and legal infrastructures necessary to constrain market behavior (Tam 2002). Consistent with this assertion, Snell and Tseng (2002: 449) characterize the contemporary Chinese business environment as possessing a '... weak legal system, weak civic accountability, market distortions, public cynicism, and workforces lacking moral self-efficacy'. Thus, the economic system in China appears to be effectively unregulated – an environment consistent with neoliberal ideology and the Western DSP, with their emphasis on 'free market' capitalism and disdain for social restraints on business.

China and the Western DSP

It is apparent from the foregoing discussion that China's ruling elites have embraced key tenets of the Western capitalist world view during the country's long period of 'transition' to a 'socialist market economy', such as the emphasis on economic growth and support for free-market capitalism. The argument to be made is that the confluence of many factors has made China particularly susceptible to the influence of the Western dominant social paradigm, but the paradigm is producing disastrous results in China due to the inability of the current sociopolitical system to control the negative effects of a free market economy.

Susceptibility to the DSP in China

Their history of relative economic deprivation predisposes contemporary Chinese citizens to value economic growth and the accumulation of private property,[5] thus rendering them vulnerable to the influence of the Western DSP. Contemporary research supports this assertion, indicating that the top priorities of the Chinese are poverty alleviation, economic development and wealth creation (Harris 2006). Today's Chinese, particularly the generation who grew up in the post-Mao period, have an 'admiration for all things foreign' and aspire to adopt Western consumerist lifestyles, as reflected in the rapid growth of markets for luxury goods (Harris 2006, 2005; Weber 2002; Kwong 1994). China's '80ers generation' are highly individualistic, materialistic and obsessed with money and power; they are also politically apathetic and show little concern for participation in the public sphere (Yan 2006). Such characteristics reflect and reinforce the growing influence of Western consumerism and economic individualism.

Despite China's traditional reliance on top-down government regulation, as previously discussed, the market system in China appears to be largely unregulated, and the behavior of market participants shows little evidence of concern for socialist values. On the contrary, the widespread documentation of unethical business dealings and systemic corruption in contemporary Chinese society indicate that the general mood has gone far beyond a lack of concern for 'socialism', to a lack of respect for the rule of law and any form of regulation or restraint of business. What we are witnessing in contemporary Chinese society is the old capitalist mentality of 'getting rich quick', often at the expense of consumers and society at large. This reflects a general contempt or disrespect for any form of regulation or restraint on market behavior – another key element of the Western DSP. A number of factors have made the Chinese susceptible to this mentality. Their recent history of material deprivation is, again, clearly a contributing factor. Other factors include the often discussed 'moral vacuum' or 'ideological crisis' that has befallen the country since the advent of market reforms,[6] and a general distrust of the government. Kwong (1994) suggests the contradictions between the official socialist ideology and the economic realities in China introduced tensions and led to perceptions of government hypocrisy. Add to this a widespread recognition of systemic corruption among government officials, and it is easy to understand why the Chinese developed a general disregard for government regulations or restraints on the free-market system.

> 'The populace realized that the real official culture was a far cry from the idealistic socialism of its utopian hegemonic ideology … Becoming rich was not necessarily achieved through fair means. They too emulated the communist officials and tried to benefit themselves in every way'.
>
> (Kwong 1994: 251)

A cavalier attitude toward the natural environment is also consistent with the DSP, whose proponents tend to dismiss environmental concerns. It is well documented that China has a centuries-old tradition of environmental destruction and lack of respect for the natural environment (Elvin 2004, 1993; Economy 2004; Elvin and Liu 1998; Smil 1996).[7] Contemporary research also indicates that the Chinese view the environment in a very instrumental way. As noted by Harris (2006: 8), 'The aesthetic and ethical valuation of the environment and nature are very low among most Chinese; nature is commonly viewed as being alien and worthy of improvement by human manipulation.' Such attitudes are clearly consistent with the DSP's emphasis on the ability of science and technology to solve environmental problems through manipulation or 'climate engineering'. And indeed, the Chinese have demonstrated a tendency throughout their history to attempt to manipulate the natural environment to serve human needs (Elvin 2004, 1993).

In modern times this tendency has often translated into disastrous results, such as Mao's 'war against nature' (Shapiro 2001). Maoist policies showed little respect for the environment, and viewed it as something to be tamed or conquered in the interest of economic development (Harris 2005; Kobayashi 2004; Shapiro 2001; Gardner and Stern 1996). Beginning in the 1950s, the officially sanctioned view was that humans could 'exploit resources and conquer nature if armed with Mao Zedong thought and "science"' (Edmonds 1999: 640). Harris (2005: 127) suggests 'Mao's world view was so powerful that it remains pervasive, often shaping the way government officials think and leaving a vestige of low public awareness of the environment, especially in the countryside.' The enduring legacy of this world view is clearly evident today in the form of massive environmental engineering projects such as the Three Gorges Dam and the 'South-to-North Water Transfer Project', which have been widely denounced by environmentalists (Yardley 2007a, 2007b).

It is also well known that the Chinese government has shown relatively little genuine concern for environmental issues throughout the recent period of growth and development. The central government began to concede some awareness of environmental problems during the 1970s, but like other developing countries China defended its right to pollute the environment without international interference, claiming that the primary responsibility for pollution control at the international level should lie with more developed nations, and that economic growth must take precedence over the environment (Harris 2005, 2002; Kobayashi 2004; Tseng 1999; Ross 1999; Edmonds 1999; Economy 1998; Weller and Bol 1998; Jahiel 1998). The domestic environmental problems in China have become so severe and widely publicized, however, that concern over external perceptions has periodically compelled the government to undertake initiatives such as the 'Agenda 21' policies adopted at the 1992 United Nations Conference on Environment and Development (Harris and Udagawa 2004; Edmonds 1999). The most recent example is the extensive effort to reduce air pollution prior to the 2008 Beijing Olympic Games, which clearly illustrated the central government's concern with China's image in the eyes of the world. However, most observers assumed that Beijing's notorious pollution would return to unhealthy levels soon after the Olympic spotlight faded (Yardley 2007c, 2008c).

Even when the central government has attempted to improve ecological conditions, such efforts have often been undermined by the fact that much of the authority for enforcement of environmental regulations has been delegated to local government officials. Local officials are often compensated based on production and economic growth; thus, given the pervasive corruption, weak legal system and general lack of accountability in Chinese society, it should come as no surprise that many provincial authorities have continued to allow local industries to pollute at will (Kahn and Yardley 2007; Harris 2005; Harris and Udagawa 2004). In addition to a lack of concern for the environment, again we see apparent contempt for government authority to regulate market activities.

The predisposition for a lack of environmental concern is further reinforced in contemporary Chinese society by a general lack of knowledge or education on developing environmental issues. Based on reviews of surveys of Chinese environmental perspectives and behavior, Harris (2006, 2005) concludes that with the exception of the small minority of well-educated urban residents, environmental knowledge among Chinese is extremely limited. This is particularly true with respect to global challenges such as ozone depletion and climate change – most Chinese are primarily concerned with more immediate issues such as sanitation and local air and water pollution. Such findings clearly imply that only a small minority of Chinese has adopted the type of world view encapsulated in the NEP. Many scholars have also concluded over the last several years that Chinese citizens, reflecting the stance of the central government, subordinate environmental concerns to their desire for economic prosperity (Lo and Leung 2000; Tseng 1999; Weller and Bol 1998). As noted by Smil (1996: 184), 'this frenzied rush [for wealth and prosperity] is the understandable reaction to decades of Maoist deprivation'.

It is evident from the foregoing discussion that many factors, historical and contemporary, have contributed to the current environmental catastrophe in China: a long tradition of environmental abuse and propensity to view the environment instrumentally, systemic corruption among business and government officials, relatively low levels of environmental knowledge and a general obsession with wealth creation resulting from a history of material deprivation. As a result, the Chinese again appear to be very susceptible to the influence of the Western DSP, with its emphasis on economic growth and dismissal of environmental concerns. The DSP offers a convenient rationalization for the pursuit of Western consumerist lifestyles, and thus its influence in Chinese society seems likely to grow in the near future.

The remaining component of Kilbourne *et al.*'s (2002) conceptualization of the DSP is the focus on individualism or the 'free individual'. Liberal democracy is the prevailing mode of political organization within the Western DSP (Kilbourne *et al.* 2002). However, the DSP concept assumes that a 'power elite' largely controls society, shaping the will of the populace through the promotion of its preferred ideologies (cf. Shafer 2006). As previously discussed, this assumption is consistent with many political theories, which question the extent to which true 'democracy', or rule according to the will of the people, exists under conditions of modernity. Although scholars of the DSP acknowledge it exists within a liberal democratic framework, they emphasize that individual 'freedoms' or rights in modern Western democracies have often 'been reduced to freedom to participate in the market' (Kilbourne *et al.* 2002: 197), or what is commonly referred to as 'economic individualism'. Thus, the emphasis of the DSP tends to be on 'mere liberty' (Ophuls 1996), or the freedom to pursue self-interest, consumption and materialism within certain legal constraints, such as not causing undue harm to others. Obviously, the rule of law is critical to the effective functioning of such a system; otherwise, the unrestrained pursuit of hedonistic values can lead to social chaos.

In China, we see an extreme case of a society controlled by a 'power elite'. If the ruling elites who control the central government feel it is in their best interests to promote the type of economic individualism implicit in the Western DSP, they certainly have the necessary resources at their disposal. Although commercialization and the growth of alternative outlets over the last two decades has made it more difficult for the central government to maintain ideological control over all media content (Liu 1998), China is far from having a free press. Indeed, the Chinese government has adopted official policies regarding the 'correct' way to 'guide public opinion' through official media (Chan 2007). Their relative lack of access to objective information sources makes the Chinese particularly vulnerable to the influence of social paradigms propagated by ruling authorities. It has been suggested for years that the Chinese government has been endorsing economic individualism. As discussed by Kwong (1994) and Weber (2002), in the 1980s the government began heavily promoting an 'official advertised ideology' to Chinese youth that emphasized individual freedoms, entrepreneurship and wealth creation. Some members of the younger generation were emboldened by the message of freedom and assumed they could challenge the government's authority, but as the Tiananmen Square incident dramatically demonstrated, individual freedoms in China are limited to freedom to participate in the capitalist market, or economic individualism. Promoting economic individualism, the 'freedom' to participate in a capitalist society or the 'glory' of getting rich may be seen as part of the Chinese government's attempt to maintain 'social stability', currently acknowledged as one of the government's most important goals (Harris 2005). But this ideology is once again clearly consistent with the Western DSP. If the masses can be placated with material success, they will pose less of a threat to the power of the ruling regime.

Why the DSP is failing in China

It is apparent that China is passing through a phase that most economies go through during the early development of capitalism, before adequate legal and regulatory measures have been implemented to constrain abuses of the system (Tam 2002; Snell and Tseng 2002). As noted previously, markets in China are effectively unregulated at present, and the excesses of capitalism are vividly on display – the great disparity between the wealth of the owners of capital and the average worker, few worker protections or rights and a general disregard for the natural environment. This is the brand of capitalism practiced in the nineteenth century in the US, the age of the infamous capitalist 'robber barons' (Mihm 2007; Hofstadter 1955). In the US and most other Western countries, the forces of capitalism have been gradually tempered and constrained through decades of struggle to secure basic worker protections and environmental regulations (Zinn 2001; Hofstadter 1955).

In Western democracies, civil society organizations have historically played an essential role in fighting against the excesses of unfettered capitalism, helping to secure key advances in workers' rights, such as the right to unionize, minimum wage laws and the improvements in occupational safety (Zinn 2001). It is commonly recognized that pressure from environmental groups in modern industrial nations is a critical determinant of not only the effectiveness of domestic environmental policies, but also participation in international environmental accords (Haas, Keohane and Levy 1993). The enforcement of environmental regulations routinely requires litigation against corporations that often blatantly flaunt the law in the interest of profits (see Kennedy 2004). Without the right to force redress through an independent judiciary, there is little hope of effective environmental regulation in a capitalist economy. And of course, a free press is essential to the functioning of the Western system, providing the ability to expose wrongdoing and challenge 'official ideology'. The absence of these restraints on power has contributed to the dysfunctional state of contemporary Chinese society.

Historically, China has lacked effective civil society organizations (Harris 2005; Brettell 2000; Lo and Leung 2000), and it is often recognized that low income levels and limits on political participation have severely limited the potential for domestic environmental pressure (Ross 1999; Edmonds 1999). The central government granted legal status to citizens' groups in 1994, which ostensibly encouraged the growth of social movements such as environmentalism. However, environmental 'non-governmental organizations' in China are often closely related to and dependent on the government and thus have largely avoided participation in contentious politics, a classic case of a civil society movement being co-opted by the government (Brettell 2000). Given the lack of citizens' rights in China, it remains dangerous to challenge government policies. Indeed, reports of Chinese social activists being imprisoned or punished remain quite common (Yardley 2008a, 2008b, 2007b; Kahn 2007b). Such restrictions on freedom, combined with susceptibility to other elements of the DSP, create a particularly destructive variety of capitalism.

Discussion and future agendas

China's ongoing transitions and the accompanying social, political, economic and environmental issues have attracted a tremendous amount of attention from both academics and journalists, and it appears China's internal problems (particularly environmental issues) are becoming more acute. The current paper represents an initial attempt to consider these issues from the perspective of the DSP in Western societies and to understand the role and influence of this world view in contemporary Chinese society. At this stage only some tentative conclusions may be offered. It appears that the economic, political and technological perspectives associated with the Western DSP are also quite influential in China. Some of these views, such as faith in human ability to control and manipulate nature and the associated dismissal of environmental concerns, seem firmly rooted in the historical world views of the Chinese. Others, such as the belief in the desirability of unregulated free markets and private property rights, have been endorsed by China's ruling elites since embarking on the market reforms in 1978, and apparently eagerly accepted by a materially deprived populace. But it seems that the DSP is producing near-catastrophic results in China due to the lack of the proper social/political/legal mechanisms necessary to control the destructive tendencies of the free-market system.

Some journalists have recently noted that the balance of power in Beijing is subtly shifting leftward (Leonard 2008; Kahn 2007a), and debates are raging among intellectuals regarding China's future socio-economic direction. Arguably, the leaders of the 'new left', such as Wang Hui, have contributed to this shift through their challenges to the radical free-market agenda that has dominated since the 1990s (Leonard 2008). The leftward shift was evident in the most recent five-year plan published by the Chinese government at the end of 2005, which called for a 'harmonious society' and provided for substantial increases in state funding of pensions, unemployment benefits, health care and education. For the first time since 1978, economic growth was not the dominant goal (Leonard 2008). However, even China's new left, like the 'leftist' parties in most Western democracies, generally supports the overarching framework of free-market capitalism and is primarily advocating social equality and democratic reforms (Wang 2003).

As argued by Kilbourne *et al.* (2002), the political left in most Western democracies remains firmly rooted within the confines of the DSP, particularly with respect to belief in the desirability of continual economic growth and inadequate attention to environmental issues. Thus, reformist politics within the DSP will probably be inadequate to address the environmental challenges facing modern societies; rather, a more radical 'green' political movement is needed.

Clearly, more radical changes than those currently being undertaken are urgently needed in China to mitigate both social inequities and ongoing environmental destruction. Much additional research is needed to gain a better understanding of the influence of the DSP in contemporary Chinese society. Data are needed to assess the extent of endorsement of the DSP among various sections of the Chinese population, and its influence on attitudes and behavior. With respect to this issue, comparative studies of world views between China and Western societies may provide useful insights. It is commonly recognized that the media play an active role in the construction of attitudes toward social and environmental issues (Dispensa and Brulle 2003; Hannigan 1995); thus, media studies should also be conducted on an ongoing basis to assess the extent to which the Chinese leadership is promoting or endorsing the views associated with the Western DSP. Because many people implicitly accept prevailing world views with little thought or reflection (Kilbourne *et al.* 2002), the dissemination of research on the influence of the DSP could promote dialogue and increase awareness of the destructive potential of this ideology.[8]

As discussed by Harris (2006), more efforts are also needed to educate Chinese citizens regarding environmental issues and encourage pro-environmental attitudes, values and behavior. Harris (2006) suggests efforts to educate the general population on environmental issues could perhaps be funded by foreign governments and aid agencies. Consistent with theories of environmental politics (Dunlap 1995), such suggestions assume that despite the power exercised by social and political elites, public opinion ultimately will influence policy. Such an assumption might be questioned in the case of an authoritarian society such as China, but the Chinese government's apparent obsession with controlling or 'guiding' public opinion attests to the fact that even the CCP realizes the Chinese citizenry may pose a challenge to its power.

Harris (2006) also suggests educational efforts will be most effective if they focus on China's young elites, such as university students, who will play an influential role in shaping Chinese society in the future. Thus, academics teaching at universities in China (and indeed around the world, since many of China's young elites are seeking an education outside of China) may be able to play a positive role by challenging conventional wisdom on environmental issues and encouraging a shift in world views towards the NEP. As previously argued, support for the DSP is likely to reduce the perceived moral imperative of corporate social responsibility, and recent research (Shafer 2006) has found a negative relationship between endorsement of the DSP and support for legally mandated corporate environmental reporting. Thus, academics teaching courses on business ethics/corporate social responsibility at universities in China and elsewhere may be able to enhance

support for social and environmental responsibility by increasing students' awareness of the DSP and its potential negative effects, and encouraging the adoption of
a more enlightened world view.

Suggested further reading

Chan, A. (2001) *China's Workers Under Assault: The Exploitation of Labor in a Globalizing Economy*. Armonk, NY: M. E. Sharpe.

Dali, Y. (2006) 'Economic Transformation and its Political Discontents in China: Authoritarianism, Unequal Growth, and the Dilemmas of Political Development'. *Annual Review of Political Science*, 9: 143–64.

Gries, P. H. and R. Stanley (eds) (2004) *State and Society in 21st Century China: Crisis, Contention, and Legitimation*. New York: Routledge.

Guthrie, D. (1999) *Dragon in a Three-Piece Suit: the Emergence of Capitalism in China*. Princeton, NJ: Princeton University Press.

Misra, K. (1998) *From Post-Maoism to Post-Marxism: The Erosion of Official Ideology in Deng's China*. New York and London: Routledge.

O' Brien, K. J. and L. J. Li. (2006) *Rightful Resistance in Rural China*. New York: Cambridge University Press.

Peerenboom, R. (2002) *China's Long March Toward Rule of Law*. New York: Cambridge University Press.

Santoro, M. A. (2000) *Profits and Principles: Global Capitalism and Human Rights in China*. Ithaca, NY: Cornell University Press.

Sun, Y. (2004) *Corruption and Market in Contemporary China*. Ithaca, NY: Cornell University Press.

Notes

1   In his widely cited paper, Jones (1991) argues that attitudes toward ethical issues will be strongly influenced by the perceived 'moral intensity' or moral imperative associated with the issue. The components of moral intensity are defined as the magnitude of consequences, the probability of consequences occurring, the temporal immediacy of the consequences, the proximity between the moral agent and the victims of the consequences, the concentration of the effects and the degree of social consensus that the actions in question are ethical or unethical. It seems apparent that if one subscribes to the environmentally optimistic view inherent in the DSP, with its belief in the feasibility and desirability of unlimited economic growth and the ability of science and technology to mitigate environmental damage and ensure future material abundance, the perceived moral intensity of actions with environmental consequences will be greatly reduced.

2   The 'guiding ideology' of the CCP includes Marxism, Leninism, Mao Zedong Thought, Deng Xiaoping Theory and the 'Three Represents' theory of Jiang Zemin (Chai 2003). Deng Xiaoping Theory was officially enshrined in the Chinese constitution at the Fifteenth Party Congress in 1997, and emphasizes building 'socialism with Chinese characteristics'. To justify Deng's theory, China's leaders began arguing in the 1980s that China could not achieve the goal of socialism without first going through a stage of capitalist development. The 'Three Represents' theory, also introduced at the Fifteenth Party Congress and added to the constitution in 2002, maintains that the Chinese Communist Party represents 'China's progressive forces' (e.g. capitalism), 'China's advanced culture' and 'the overwhelming majority of the Chinese people'. This theory, which was denounced for its hypocrisy in claiming to represent both 'progressive

forces' and the mass of Chinese citizens, helped provide the rationalization for inviting capitalists to join the CCP (Chai 2003).

3 Similar observations are common. For instance, Knight (2003: 320) suggests the CCP's 'obvious policy implication [is] to integrate China deeply in a global economy dominated by capitalism'.

4 There remains much uncertainty and speculation regarding China's political future (Wang 2008; Tsai 2007; Bell 2006; Pei 2006; Tang 2005; Gilley 2004). However, given that the vast majority of the country remains at relatively low income and education levels, it seems implausible that drastic political changes will occur in the near future. Bell (2007: 8) suggests even most Chinese intellectuals are opposed to nationwide democracy during the next decade, which would amount to 'turning over the levers of the state to eight hundred million farmers with primary school education'. Schubert (2008) argues that, contrary to conventional wisdom, the current political regime in China has been able to maintain a substantial amount of legitimacy through gradualist reforms, such as enhanced accountability of party cadres and the introduction of direct elections at the local level. In addition, most Chinese citizens prefer to see the party remain in power to ensure political stability (Schubert 2008). Based on her extensive study of private entrepreneurs in China, Tsai (2007: 201) concludes that

'... economic growth has not created a prodemocratic capitalist class. Only a handful of intellectuals, dissidents, and foreigners have openly called for political reforms that would result in multiparty competition, competitive, direct elections at the national and local levels, and guarantees for political and civil liberties.'

It appears likely, therefore, that in the foreseeable future China will retain an authoritarian government that places significant restrictions on individual rights.

5 The growing emphasis on private property is illustrated by the recent passage of a law enhancing property rights in China. The fact that this law was delayed in 2006 and finally passed over the opposition of left-leaning members of the Communist Party in 2007 (Kahn 2007a) illustrates there are still some adherents to socialist ideology in the CCP. Despite the opposition, the passage of the law may be viewed as a further indication of China's transition towards compliance with the Western DSP, which sanctifies private property.

6 China's search for a moral or spiritual compass is illustrated by recent reports of a resurgence of Confucianism, which was the dominant philosophy in China for over 2,500 years, but fell out of favour after the May Fourth Movement of 1919 and was vanquished by the Communist Party. Mooney (2007) and Bell (2007) attribute the renewed popularity of Confucianism to the ideological vacuum left in the wake of China's quick transition from Communism to free-market capitalism. There have also been frequent discussions of 'ideological crisis' among young people in China, resulting from the country's sudden move away from Maoist ideology to a system that encouraged economic individualism but retained tight government control over most other aspects of life (Weber 2002; Kwong 1994).

7 Given the history of environmental destruction in China and other Asian countries, it seems somewhat ironic that Asian intellectual and spiritual traditions such as Buddhism, Taoism and Hinduism are often counted among the most influential forces shaping the environmental movements in North America and Europe (Peterson 2001). Many scholars of environmental attitudes have noted this apparent paradox and explained it in various ways. Some argue these ancient spiritual traditions are simply irrelevant to the beliefs and attitudes of people in modern industrial societies (Peterson 2001; Kellert 1995). Others note these intellectual traditions never resulted in the establishment of sound environmental policies or practices in China. Citing Gardner and Stern (1996), Harris (2005: 126) argues that 'Regardless of their valuing of the environment, in pre-revolutionary China traditional values were overwhelmed or co-opted by powerful

political and economic actors, and were too weak relative to "pressures of poverty, tyranny, and competition for scarce resources"'. Thus, despite the fact that Asian traditions have influenced Western environmentalists, it seems these traditions have little relevance for the study of environmental attitudes and behavior in contemporary China.

8 It must be acknowledged that dissemination of viewpoints that challenge the agenda of the CCP may pose challenges and risks, but the ongoing debates among intellectuals regarding the future course of Chinese society suggest there is at least some opportunity to challenge the status quo in academic discourse.

References

Bakan, J. (2004) *The Corporation: The Pathological Pursuit of Profit and Power*. New York: Free Press.

Bates, T. R. (1975) 'Gramsci and the Theory of Hegemony'. *Journal of the History of Ideas*, 36: 351–66.

Bell, D. A. (2006) *Beyond Liberal Democracy: Political Thinking for an East Asian Context*. Princeton, NJ: Princeton University Press.

—— (2007) 'From Marx to Confucius: Changing Discourses on China's Political Future'. *Dissent* (Spring). <http://www.dissentmagazine.org/article/?article = 767> (accessed 3 March 2008).

Brettell, A. (2000) 'Environmental Non-Governmental Organizations in the People's Republic of China: Innocents in a Co-opted Environmental Movement?'. *The Journal of Pacific Asia*, 6: 27–56.

Burton, C. (1987) 'China's Post-Mao Transition: The Role of the Party and Ideology in the "New Period"'. *Pacific Affairs*, 60: 341–446.

Chai, W. (2003) 'The Ideological Paradigm Shifts of China's World Views: From Marxism-Leninism-Maoism to the Pragmatism-Multilateralism of the Deng-Jiang-Hu Era'. *Asian Affairs, an American Review*, 30: 163–75.

Chan, A. (2007) 'Guiding Public Opinion Through Social Agenda-Setting: China's Media Policy Since the 1990s'. *Journal of Contemporary China*, 16: 547–59.

Chen, F. (1995) *Economic Transition and Political Legitimacy in Post-Mao China: Ideology and Reform*. Albany, NY: State University of New York Press.

Cotgrove, S. (1982) *Catastrophe or Cornucopia: The Environment, Politics and the Future*. New York: John Wiley & Sons.

Dahl, R. A. (1961) *Who Governs?* New Haven, CT: Yale University Press.

Dickson, B. J. (1999) 'Who Gets What, How? When Chinese State-Owned Enterprises Become Shareholding Companies'. *Problems of Post-Communism*, 46: 32–41.

—— (2001) 'The Illicit Asset Stripping of Chinese State Firms'. *China Journal*, 43: 1–28.

Dispensa, J. M. and R. J. Brulle. (2003), 'Media's Social Construction of Environmental Issues: Focus on Global Warming – a Comparative Study'. *International Journal of Sociology and Social Policy*, 23: 74–105.

Dunlap, R. E. (1995) 'Public Opinion and Environmental Policy', in J. P. Lester (ed.) *Environmental Politics and Policy*, 2nd edn, Durham, NC: Duke University Press.

Dunlap, R. E. and K. D. Van Liere. (1978) 'The "New Environmental Paradigm": A Proposed Measuring Instrument and Preliminary Results'. *Journal of Environmental Education*, 9: 10–19.

—— (1984) 'Commitment to the Dominant Social Paradigm and Concern for Environmental Quality'. *Social Science Quarterly*, 65: 1013–28.

Dunlap, R. E., K. D. Van Liere, A. G. Mertig and R. E. Jones. (2000) 'Measuring Endorsement of the New Ecological Paradigm: A Revised NEP Scale'. *Journal of Social Issues*, 56: 425–42.

Economy, E. (2007) 'China vs. Earth'. *The Nation* (7 May)., <http://www.thenation.com/doc/20070507/economy> (accessed 24 April 2007).

Economy, E. C. (2004) *The River Runs Black: The Environmental Challenge to China's Future.* Ithaca, NY: Cornell University Press.

—— (1998) 'China's Environmental Diplomacy', in S. S. Kim (ed) *China and the World: Chinese Foreign Policy Facing the New Millennium.* Boulder, CO: Westview Press.

Edmonds, R. L. (1999) 'The Environment in the People's Republic of China 50 Years on'. *The China Quarterly*, 159: 640–49.

—— (1998) *Managing China's Environment.* New York: Oxford University Press.

Elvin, M. (2004) *The Retreat of the Elephants: An Environmental History of China.* New Haven, CT: Yale University Press.

—— (1993) 'Three Thousand Years of Unsustainable Growth: China's Environment from Archaic Times to the Present'. *East Asian History*, 6: 7–46.

Elvin, M. and T. Liu. (1998) *Sediments of Time: Environment and Society in Chinese History.* Cambridge: Cambridge University Press.

Engardio, P., D. Roberts, F. Balfour and B. Einhorn. (2007) 'Broken China'. *Business Week* (July 23): 39–45.

Friedman, M. (1962) *Capitalism and Freedom.* Chicago: University of Chicago Press.

Gardner, G. T. and P.C. Stern. (1996) *Environmental Problems and Human Behaviour.* Boston: Allyn & Bacon.

Gilley, B. (2004) *China's Democratic Future.* New York: Columbia University Press.

Gramsci, A. (1971) *Selections from the Prison Notebooks.* New York: International Publishers.

Haas, P. M., R. O. Keohane and M. A. Levy. (1993) *Institutions for the Earth: Sources of Effective International Environmental Protection.* Boston: MIT Press.

Hannigan, J. A. (1995) *Environmental Sociology: A Social Constructionist Perspective.* London: Routledge.

Harris, P. G. (2006) 'Environmental Perspectives and Behavior in China: Synopsis and Bibliography'. *Environment and Behavior*, 38: 5–21.

—— (2005) 'Environmental Values in a Globalizing World: The Case of China'. in J. Paavola and I. Lowe (eds) *Environmental Values in a Globalizing World: Nature, Justice and Governance.* New York: Routledge.

Harris, P. G. (ed.) (2002) *International Environmental Cooperation: Politics and Diplomacy in Pacific Asia.* Boulder, CO: University Press of Colorado.

Harris, P. G. and C. Udagawa. (2004) 'Defusing the Bombshell? Agenda 21 and Economic Development in China'. *Review of International Political Economy*, 11: 618–40.

Hofstadter, R. (1955) *The Age of Reform.* New York: Knopf.

Jahiel, A. R. (1998) 'The Organization of Environmental Protection in China'. *China Quarterly*, 156: 757–87.

Jones, T. M. (1991) 'Ethical Decision Making by Individuals in Organizations: An Issue-Contingent Model'. *Academy of Management Review*, 16: 366–95.

Kahn, J. (2007a) 'China Backs Property Law, Buoying Middle Class'. *New York Times.* <http://www.nytimes.com/2007/03/16/world/asia/16china.html?scp = 8&sq = Joseph+Kahn&st = nyt> (accessed 20 March 2007).

—— (2007b) 'In China, a Lake's Champion Imperils Himself'. *New York Times*. <http://www.nytimes.com/2007/10/14/world/asia/14china.html?scp = 14&sq = Joseph+Kahn&st = nyt> (accessed 22 October 2007).

Kahn, J. and J. Yardley. (2007) 'As China Roars, Pollution Reaches Deadly Extremes'. *New York Times*. <http://www.nytimes.com/2007/08/26/world/asia/26china.html?scp = 55&sq = Jim+Yardley&st = nyt> (accessed 25 September 2007).

Kellert, S. R. (1995) 'Concepts of Nature East and West', in M. E. Soulé and G. Lease (eds) *Reinventing Nature? Responses to Postmodern Deconstruction*. Washington, DC: Island Press.

Kelly, M. (2001) *The Divine Right of Capital: Dethroning the Corporate Aristocracy*. San Francisco: Berrett-Koehler Publishers.

Kennedy, R. F. Jr. (2004) *Crimes Against Nature*. New York: HarperCollins Publishers.

Kilbourne, W. E., S. C. Beckmann, A. Lewis and Y. Van Dam. (2001) 'A Multinational Examination of the Role of the Dominant Social Paradigm in Environmental Attitudes of University Students'. *Environment and Behavior*, 33: 209–28.

Kilbourne, W.E., S. C. Beckmann and E. Thelen. (2002) 'The Role of the Dominant Social Paradigm in Environmental Attitudes: A Multinational Examination'. *Journal of Business Research*, 55: 193–204.

Knight, N. (2003) 'Imagining Globalization: The World and Nation in Chinese Communist Party Ideology'. *Journal of Contemporary Asia*, 33: 318–37.

Kobayashi, Y. (2004) 'The "Troubled Modernizer": Three Decades of Chinese Environmental Policy and Diplomacy', in P. G. Harris (ed.) *Confronting Environmental Change in East & Southeast Asia: Eco-Politics, Foreign Policy, and Sustainable Development*. London: Earchscan.

Korten, D. C. (1995) *When Corporations Rule the World*. West Hartford, CT and San Francisco: Kumarian Press and Berrett-Koehler Publishers.

—— (1999) *The Post-Corporate World: Life After Capitalism*. West Hartford, CT and San Francisco: Kumarian Press and Berrett-Koehler Publishers.

Kuhn, T. S. (1962) *The Structure of Scientific Revolutions*. Chicago: University of Chicago Press.

Kwong, J. (1994) 'Ideological Crisis Among China's Youth: Values and Official Ideology'. *British Journal of Sociology*, 45: 247–64.

Leonard, M. (2008) 'China's New Intelligentsia'. *Prospect Magazine* 144. <http://www.prospect-magazine.co.uk/article_details.php?id = 10078> (accessed 28 April 2008).

Leslie, J. (2008) 'The Last Empire: Can the World Survive China's Headlong Rush to Emulate the American Way of Life?' *Mother Jones*, (February): 28–39, 83–85.

Liu, H. (1998) 'Profit or Ideology? Tthe Chinese Press Between Party and Market'. *Media, Culture & Society*, 20: 31–41.

Lo, C. W. H. and W. W. Leung. (2000) 'Environmental Agency and Public Opinion in Guangzhou: The Limits of a Popular Approach to Environmental Governance'. *China Quarterly*, 163: 677–704.

Mihm, S. (2007) *A Nation of Counterfeiters*. Boston: Harvard University Press.

Milbrath, L. W. (1984) *Environmentalists: Vanguard for a New Society*. Albany, NY: State University of New York Press.

Mills, C. W. (1956) *The Power Elite*. New York: Oxford University Press.

Mooney, P. (2007) 'Confucius Comes Back'. *Chronicle of Higher Education*. <http://chronicle.com/weekly/v53/i33/33a04601.htm> (accessed 20 April 2007).

Mosca, G. (1939) *The Ruling Class*. New York: McGraw-Hill.

Olsen, M. E., D. G. Lodwick. and R. E. Dunlap. (1992) *Viewing the World Ecologically*. Boulder, CO: Westview.

Pei, M. (2006) *China's Trapped Transition: The Limits of Developmental Autocracy*. Cambridge, MA: Harvard University Press.

Peterson, A. L. (2001) *Being Human: Ethics, Environment, and Our Place in the World*. Berkeley, CA: University of California Press.

Pirages, D. C. (1977) 'Introduction: A Social Design for Sustainable Growth', in D. C. Pirages (ed.) *The Sustainable Society: Implications for Growth*. New York: Praeger Publishers.

Ross, L. (1999) 'China and Environmental Protection', in E. Economy and M. Oksenberg (eds) *China Joins the World: Progress and Prospects*. New York: Council on Foreign Relations Press.

Schubert, G. (2008) 'One-Party Rule and the Question of Legitimacy in Contemporary China: Preliminary Thoughts on Setting Up a New Research Agenda'. *Journal of Contemporary China*, 17: 191–204.

Schumpeter, J. (1947) *Capitalism, Socialism, and Democracy*. New York: Harper.

Shafer, W. E. (2006) 'Social Paradigms and Attitudes Toward Environmental Accountability'. *Journal of Business Ethics*, 65: 121–47.

Shapiro, J. (2001) *Mao's War Against Nature: Politics and the Environment in Revolutionary China*. Cambridge: Cambridge University Press.

Smil, V. (1996) 'Barriers to a Sustainable China', in D. C. Pirages (ed.) *Building Sustainable Societies: A Blueprint for a Post-Industrial World*. Armonk, NY: M. E. Sharpe.

Snell, R. and C. S. Tseng. (2002) 'Moral Atmosphere and Moral Influence Under China's Network Capitalism'. *Organization Studies*, 23: 449–78.

Tam. O. K. (2002) 'Ethical Issues in the Evolution of Corporate Governance in China'. *Journal of Business Ethics*, 37: 303–20.

Tang, W. (2005) *Public Opinion and Political Change in China*. Palo Alto, CA: Stanford University Press.

Tsai, K. S. (2007) *Capitalism Without Democracy: The Private Sector in Contemporary China*. Ithaca, NY: Cornell University Press.

Tseng, E. C. Y. (1999) 'The Environment and the People's Republic of China', in D. L. Soden and B. S. Steel (eds) *Handbook of Global Environmental Policy and Administration*. Basel: Marcel Dekker.

Wang, H. (2003) *China's New Order: Society, Politics, and Economy in Transition*, T. Huters (ed.). Cambridge, MA: Harvard University Press.

Wang, X. (2008) 'Divergent Identities, Convergent Interests: The Rising Middle Income Stratum in China and its Civic Awareness'. *Journal of Contemporary China*, 17: 53–69.

Weber, I. (2002) 'Shanghai Baby: Negotiating Youth Self-Identity in Urban China'. *Social Identities*, 8: 347–68.

Weller, R. P. and P. Bol. (1998) 'From Heaven-and-Earth to Nature: Chinese Concepts of the Environment and Their Influence on Policy Implementation', in M. B. McElroy, C. P. Nielson, and P. Lydon (eds) *Energizing China: Reconciling Environmental Protection and Economic Growth*. Cambridge, MA: Harvard University Press.

Wright, P. C., W. F. Szeto and S. K. Lee. (2003) 'Ethical Perceptions in China: The Reality of Business Ethics in an International Context'. *Management Decision*, 41: 180–89.

Yan, Y. (2006) 'Little Emperors or Frail Pragmatists? China's "80ers Generation"'. *Current History* (September): 255–62.

Yardley, J. (2007a) 'Beneath Booming Cities, China's Future Is Drying Up'. *New York*

Times. <http://www.nytimes.com/2007/09/28/world/asia/28water.html?scp = 56&sq = Jim+Yardley&st = nyt> (accessed 22 October, 2007).

—— (2007b) 'Chinese Dam Projects Criticized for Their Human Costs'. *New York Times*. Online. <http://www.nytimes.com/2007/11/19/world/asia/19dam.html?scp = 1&sq = chinese+dam+projects+criticized&st = nyt> (accessed 21 November 2007).

—— (2007c) 'Beijing's Olympic Quest: Turn Smoggy Sky Blue'. *New York Times*. <http://www.nytimes.com/2007/12/29/world/asia/29china.html?scp = 1&sq = Beijing%27s+olympic+quest&st = nyt> (accessed 21 January 2008).

—— (2008a) 'Chinese Lawyer Says He Was Detained and Warned on Activism'. *New York Times*. <http://www.nytimes.com/2008/03/09/world/asia/09china.html?scp = 35&sq = Jim+Yardley&st = nyt> (accessed 28 April 2008).

—— (2008b) 'Chinese Rights Advocate Is Jailed'. *New York Times*. <http://www.nytimes.com/2008/04/04/world/asia/04china.html?scp = 21&sq = Jim+Yardley&st = nyt> (accessed 28 April 2008).

—— (2008c) 'After Glow of Games, What Next for China?'. *New York Times*. <http://www.nytimes.com/2008/08/25/sports/olympics/25china.html?ref = olympics&pagewanted = all> (accessed 5 January 2009).

Young, N. (2002) 'Three "C"s: Civil Society, Corporate Social Responsibility, and China'. *China Business Review*, 29: 34–38.

Ziegler, D. (2007) 'Grim Tales: The More Growth, the More Damage to the Environment'. *The Economist*, (March 31): 10–11.

Zinn, H. (2001) *A People's History of the United States*. New York: HarperCollins.

2 Structural change in corporate society and CSR in Japan

Kanji Tanimoto

Introduction

This chapter focuses on analyzing the structure of corporate society and the current discussions on CSR in Japan. CSR has boomed in Japanese business since around 2003. Management organizations and consulting companies have led and been involved in this boom. They have introduced a global business trend and focused their discussion on a practical level.[1] It has become increasingly important to incorporate CSR into the management process, and to discuss how to incorporate CSR management into the Japanese context. However, it is important to analyze CSR not only from a managerial viewpoint, but also from a social movement viewpoint. Considering how to respond to environmental changes only from a managerial viewpoint cannot explain the backgrounds of such changes, nor go much beyond risk management or corporate brand management. On the other hand, criticizing business activities only from a social movement viewpoint cannot explain what problems corporations have in the managerial process, nor suggest a sustainable business model to top management.[2]

It is necessary to analyze CSR from the viewpoint of a mutual relationship between business and society/stakeholders. This chapter begins by first analyzing the transitions in the meaning and adoption of the concept of CSR, before examining the current debates around CSR and the perceived future task of embedding CSR in Japanese market society.[3] Since around 2000, a number of structural issues in corporate society have been discussed as well as CSR issues in Japan: (1) changing structures of ownership and emphasis upon stakeholder relationships; (2) growing consumer criticism over corporate scandals; and (3) growing global pressure for CSR by NGOs and international organizations.

The question of 'who *owns* corporations' is both an old problem and one that remains relevant today, which continues to be discussed actively. Between 2005 and 2006, there were two main reasons for such active discussion. First, the rise of hostile mergers and acquisitions, which have been rarely seen before in Japan, but were now initiated by new IT ventures such as Livedoor Co. Ltd. and M&A Consulting, Inc. Secondly, increasingly strong calls were made for shareholder-ism from overseas investment funds. Friedman's (1962) work is a classical example of shareholder-ism, with the premise of an economic market model based on traditional economics. He insisted that corporations should not take social responsibility, because corporations should concentrate on economic activities to maximize their profit, and should not be engaged in social and political activities. The following three changes, however, seen in the real market as opposed to the market models in Friedman's discussion, are what we should bear in mind when discussing CSR: (1) changes in the values and norms at the foundation of the marketplace; (2) changes in the relationship between corporations and stakeholders; and (3) changes in the roles and expectations of corporations and the market.

Iwai (2002, 2005) considers the question 'Who owns corporations?' and with respect to CSR suggests a company approved as a juridical personality from society has a duty to pursue social responsibility beyond issues of profit-making or the mere fulfilment of legal obligations. In other words, to pursue CSR even if less profit is to be made. This kind of understanding on CSR can be seen in the 1970s, namely an approach that considered CSR from the conventional framework of corporation theory. This approach, however, provides no explanation as to why CSR is being demanded now, nor can it elucidate the relationship between corporations and contemporary society. The answer to the question of 'Who owns corporations?' will depend, then, on the observer's concern or academic perspective on corporations. In terms of property rights, a corporation belongs to the stockholders; but in looking from the perspective of an organization, a corporation can be said to belong to its employees. And with regards to the discourse of 'Business in Society', it is important to examine corporations in terms of their relations with various stakeholders.

Society has unleashed severe criticism towards corporate scandals, which in recent years have occurred not infrequently. Health and safety problems have frequently occurred in food-related industries and accidents have repeatedly occurred in nuclear power plants, as well as incidents involving the deliberate alteration of dates in documentation, irresponsible inspections and poor risk management systems in the electric power industry. Concerns have been raised over bid-rigging problems in the construction industry and regarding techniques designed to conform to legal requirements on earthquake-proofing while in actuality not doing so, and cases have occurred regarding the non-payment of claims in the insurance industry. One particular feature of corporate crime in Japan is it may well be committed collectively for the benefit of the company, rather than for personal gain. We will examine this phenomenon more closely later.

There is growing expectation for corporations to be socially responsible and reliable. In order to provide better protection for consumers, supervisory agencies such as the Japan Fair Trade Commission and Financial Services Agency have strengthened the exposure of companies with respect to violations of the law in recent years. Market criticism, both consumer and investor, of such companies is severe, and once a company's reputation is lost, stock prices will decline sharply and consumer trust will not be regained easily. In fact, the stock prices of 50 companies involved in various corporate scandals declined by an average of 11 per cent in the five days after the first press coverage of a corporate scandal/crime, with four of them declining sharply, by more than 35 per cent (*Asahi Shinbun* 3 February 2008). Some companies that have been subjected to harsh criticism from consumers have found it difficult to rebuild business. For example, the confectionery company Fujiya Co. Ltd. was severely criticized for their lack of health and safety management in 2007. Following which, the leading bakery company Yamazaki Baking Co. Ltd. bought a 35 per cent share of Fujiya and provided managerial and technical support. Other companies have found themselves unlisted by the stock exchange, for example, IT company Livedoor Co. Ltd., which was found to have broken the stock trading laws in 2006.

Discussions on CSR have been growing in Japan for the past five years due to global pressures and competition. In Japan, however, the civil society movement and the power of NGOs have been relatively weak. In Europe and the US, global business is now unable to disregard CSR, following the demands of NGOs and the discussions on environmental and social issues that have emerged in global society since the 1990s. Many Japanese companies have received questionnaires from European and American socially responsible investment (SRI) rating organizations, and also find themselves affected by various international codes of conduct and standards issued by international institutions and NGOs. The development of guidance through the ISO/SR (Social Responsibility) is expected to have a significant influence on Japanese corporations, which have thus far been sensitive in responding to the ISO 14001 standard, the environmental management standard.[4] At the time of writing, the ISO/SR guidance standards are being developed by a working group, and a working draft is scheduled to be sent to committee and the ISO national member bodies for comments and voting in late 2009.[5] Following approval as a final draft International Standard, these guidance standards for social responsibilities will be published in 2010 as ISO 26000. The working group consists of experts from developed and developing countries and from five key stakeholders: government, industry, labour, NGOs and consumers. It manages the discussion process through the principle of unanimous decision. It is expected that the ISO 26000, compiled in such an unprecedented style, will come to have a big impact on the global market society after it is issued.

Incidentally, the Japanese government is less than active in its policies regarding CSR. They have not taken a proactive stance in supporting CSR activities across its offices and ministries because it has traditionally understood CSR issues as belonging to corporate management itself. On the other hand, demands for CSR management in, and communication throughout, the business world have been growing in response to global movements. Businesses providing CSR support, such as consulting companies, audit companies, PR agencies and companies that can assist in the drawing up of CSR reports, have rapidly developed in the past five to six years. Many publications have appeared, such as diverse business guidelines and guidebooks on CSR. Consultants and think tank researchers are working actively to meet the business needs of this CSR boom. Interestingly, however, there have been few academic studies or books, just as policy proposals have been scant. Academic research has been less than dynamic in this field, and the number of researchers is limited.

The concept of CSR

The diverse nature of CSR makes it difficult to be clearly and specifically defined. It is a fact that how far one considers the scope of CSR to spread depends on region and time. The essence, however, of CSR activities is about the nature of management itself and its business process. In papers by the European Commission, the essence of CSR is defined as follows: 'to integrate social and environmental concerns in their business operations and in their interaction with their stakeholders on a voluntary basis' (EC 2001: 8). Moreover,

> 'CSR is behavior by business over and above legal requirements, voluntarily adopted. Business need to integrate the economic, social and environmental impact in their operations. CSR is not an optional "add-on" to business core activities, but about the way in which businesses are managed'.
>
> (EC 2002: 5)

Furthermore, the International Labor Organization (2007: 125) regards CSR to be incorporated and integrated into business processes.

The concept of CSR from a holistic viewpoint, regarding the relationship between business and society, is shown in Table 2.1 (Tanimoto 1999, 2002, 2006). In itself, CSR in a narrow sense can be defined as incorporating social fairness, ethics and considerations for environment, human rights, and so on, into the process of corporate activity, and taking into account all stakeholders such as shareholders, employees, consumers/customers, environment and the community. In a broader sense, it also includes philanthropic activities and social businesses addressing social issues to create new comprehensive business.

Most business people in Japan have come to understand that the essence of CSR is based on the nature of management, and practical activities towards its implementation have been pushed forward in recent years (Fukukawa and Teramoto 2009). However, there are significant differences in how CSR is understood in each industry and also in each company. Some companies see CSR as being almost equivalent to philanthropic activity, and others take the view that its core business activity itself can be some help in society, so there is no need to do more CSR activity. Ito (2004) holds that CSR activity is connected directly to the promotion of the corporate brand.

Some examples of the misunderstanding of CSR can be drawn from the construction and financial industries in Japan, which are both considered to have been slow in tackling CSR issues. Research conducted by both the Construction Industry Information Center and the Research Institute of Construction and Economy on understanding of CSR in the Japanese construction industry (October 2006) showed the following results.[6] The majority, 65.7 per cent of the answers, chose 'a good quality of construction' as the option best describing the most important element of CSR within their industry. Another 8.9 per cent chose tax payment, 6.5 per cent chose community contribution and 4.3 per cent the creation and retention of employment. In response to a question on their commitment to CSR, the number

Table 2.1 The three dimensions of CSR

■ *CSR=Corporate management itself*	
(1) Nature of management	Incorporating social fairness, ethics and environmental and human rights considerations into management practices
	→<Approach to compliance and risk management> – <Approach to the creation of corporate values> (=innovative approach)
	Environmentalism, fairness of employment and promotion, human rights, quality and safeness of products, work conditions and human rights in developing countries, information disclosure and so on.
■ *Approach to social issues: social business*	
(2) Social business	Social goods and services, and development of social business → <Approach to new social issues> (=create social innovations)
	R&D of environmentally friendly products, development of products and services for the handicapped and the elderly, eco-tours, fair trade and community development projects
(3) Philanthropy	Community support utilizing management resources → <Approach to strategic philanthropy>
	Social contributions (1) through donations, (2) through the utilization of business' own facilities and employees, (3) through core business activities

of companies answering 'we have already tackled it' reached 62.4 per cent. A total of 66.1 per cent also said their most important stakeholder was the 'outsourcer and customer'. Asked their reasons for tackling CSR issues, 85 per cent responded that it 'is a duty for a company'. This shows the construction industry understands CSR as being equivalent to core business itself. This, in turn, reveals that the industry has not come to recognize what is being questioned in terms of CSR now, such as the process in which buildings are constructed, and how management is held accountable.

For financial institutions, the 'CSR survey of Japanese financial institution' carried out by Kinyû-cho (Financial Services Agency of the Japanese Government) (March 2006) provides us with some useful insight.[7] In depositary financial institutions, 78.1 per cent of the total number of respondents answered they were implementing CSR as an important issue. In terms of the concrete areas on which their measures focused, the ranking was as follows (with percentages given in parenthesis for the categories of major and local banks respectively): (1) community contribution, 32.7 per cent (major, 9.4 per cent; local, 34.6 per cent); (2) social contribution, 27.9 per cent (major, 33.9 per cent; local, 25.4 per cent); and (3) environmental preservation, 15.1 per cent (major, 22 per cent; local; 21.4 per cent). In terms of the reasons behind their decisions to implement CSR management, answers citing the coexistence and co-prosperity with community took first place at 80.1 per cent (major, 27.1 per cent; local, 90.8 per cent), with only 7.1 per cent (major, 18.8 per cent; local, 2.8 per cent) referring to the public nature of their business activities. For depositary financial institutions, then, it appears that CSR is regarded as a philanthropic activity and assistance to environmental preservation, and is not regarded as being a management issue.

It is worth noting, the present discussion on the concepts of CSR differs from those formerly demanded from Japanese corporations in the 1960s–80s. The 'social responsibility' to which a corporation would have been held previously was, fundamentally, to maintain its employment and to distribute its business results as fairly as it could to its core stakeholders. The next section examines why CSR used to be understood in this way.

Economic, political and social contexts

Having considered the understanding of CSR in Japan thus far, questions can be raised regarding how corporations have been positioned in society, and what kind of roles are they expected to fulfil. In order to answer these questions, there is a need to consider the relationship between a corporation and its stakeholders. Figure 2.1 is a diagram typically seen in standard textbooks used at US universities (Steiner *et al.* 2000, Lawrence *et al.* 2005). Here, corporation is positioned at

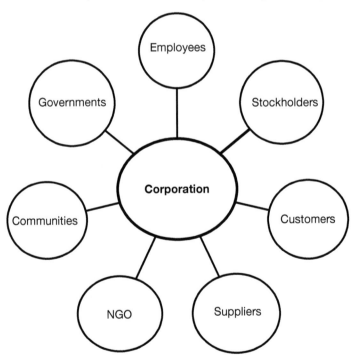

Figure 2.1 Relationship of corporation and stakeholders.

the center, surrounded by independent stakeholders. It suggests the corporation and each stakeholder are in a power relationship built upon a check-and-balance system. However, can the same picture be applied to describe the relationship between corporations and stakeholders in Japan?

There are some opinions calling for business models to be divided into an Anglo-Saxon and a Japanese style (Thurow 1993, Dore 2000, Aoki 2001), arguing that in the Anglo-Saxon corporate model the stockholder is strongly emphasized, but in the Japanese corporate model it is stakeholders such as the employees who take up a role of central importance. There are also those who argue that performance is better in those corporations that are based on a model that ensures there is a balance between each stakeholder's interest (Dore 2000, Collins and Porras 1994). A company aiming for the maximization of the financial values enjoyed by shareholders will not necessarily achieve a good performance or engender a good reputation in the market society. For example, when Collins and Porras (1994) compared companies aiming at the maximization of shareholder value with more visionary companies, the results of their comparison led them to insist that the latter companies had achieved shareholder value up to six times higher than the former firms. In a standard management textbook in Europe (Haberberg and Rieple 2007), the Japanese firm model has been seen as a stakeholder-oriented model. Japanese corporations, then, are frequently regarded as being based on a well-balanced model that considered the stakeholders' interests. In other words, they have placed emphasis on stakeholders' interests, rather than simply focusing on the maximization of stockholders' value, as well as making decisions based on a long-term perspective. Does this model describe the real picture, however? Under what kind of structures does the 'Japanese firm model' function? What was the social role and responsibilities required of corporations in the past?

In the 1970s, discussion on CSR experienced a boom for the first time in Japan. At that time CSR was a response to environmental pollution and corporate scandals and crime around the period of the oil shocks. The concept of CSR was imported from the US. In 1974, the Japan Society of Business Administration held their national conference, and chose 'Corporate Social Responsibility' as their main theme (JSBA 1975). Many books related to CSR were published in the fields of economics, management and law.[8] Most of the books introduced, interpreted or criticized discussions on CSR featured in US textbooks and papers, and re-examined the commonly accepted firm theories in each academic field from the viewpoint of CSR. Reports or proposals[9] were published by Keidanren (Japan Business Federation) and Keizai Dôyûkai (Japan Association of Corporate Executives). Keizai Dôyûkai issued a recommendation paper, 'For Establishing Mutual Trust between Business and Society', in March 1973. It pointed out that 'corporate social responsibility must be understood as having the same meaning of managerial social responsibility in corporate principles. Therefore, top management needs to make decisions not only for profit-seeking, but also to seek balance between social goals and corporate merit.' There were, however, only a few research papers that analyzed the structure of Japanese corporate society or addressed policy proposals to business management and/or the government.

With the second oil crisis, however, these arguments diminished rapidly both in the business and academic world. There are likely reasons for this outcome. First, discussions remained on an idealistic and impractical level, with CSR not being incorporated into actual management; and secondly, civil society organizations had not yet developed into maturity, and the social and environment issues related to business activity were not being broadly debated.

Later on in the 1980s and 1990s, from the period of low-growth rate to the period of bubble economy, there were almost no discussions on CSR in spite of a spate of consecutive corporate scandals. The interest of academia in CSR as a research field was negligible, and only a very few researchers were engaged in approaching issues related to 'business and society'. This came from the fact that corporate society itself had a low interest in CSR, and thus had equally low expectations for researchers to study CSR (Tanimoto 2002: 28). Generally speaking, those research fields in the social sciences of which little is expected or required from corporate society will make only slow progress. A parallel can be drawn with the natural sciences. Ravetz (1971) has pointed to how science is closely connected with the political interests of the state and the practical interests of companies. In effect, 'academic science' is transformed into 'industrialized science.'

Transitions in the relationship between the corporation and stakeholders

After the post-war period, throughout its high-growth period and up until the 1980s, the Japanese corporate system had territorialized its stakeholders, forming a 'closed network of corporate society'. The core members of a corporation's main stakeholders, especially corporate stockholders, core labourers and main suppliers, were internalized within the corporate system, and pursued common interests as members of a corporate society. They did not play any active role in monitoring corporate activity or management objectively from an independent position. This section will examine the relationship between the corporation and three main stakeholders: stockholders, employees and suppliers.

Stockholder relationships: In Japanese corporate society, corporations had built up structures of mutual ownership. That is, by holding shares mutually among two or more corporations, a relationship of 'mutual ownership – mutual control' was constructed (Okumura 2000). Closed networks were formed in which a corporation would reciprocally own a small fraction of the shares of other corporations, giving each other a share of control and approval rights. As the number of corporations within the network relationship increases, so each corporation needs fewer shares to build the mutual control system. Within this structure, corporations became stable shareholders with each other. This relationship was typically observed in corporate groups called '*kigyôshûdan*', many of which formed after the end of World War II. Inside these groups, cross-shareholding was made with a view to reinforcing corporate strength.

The highest ratio of cross-shareholding within this *kigyôshûdan* is owned by the Mitsubishi group, exceeding 30 per cent from the 1970s to 80s (peaking at

36.94 per cent in 1985) (Toyo Keizai 1972–2000). The average ratio of the six major *kigyôshûdan* was 23.78 per cent during this period. The ratio of mutual shareholding of all listed companies was 18.4 per cent at its peak in 1987, with the ratio of stable shareholding reaching 45.8 per cent. In major corporations, there were no individual investors, nor institutional investors, who had a powerful influence. In general, practical arguments were not aired at shareholder meetings, since blank proxies were simply exchanged between the group corporations. As a result, such meetings came to lose substance, becoming a mere façade: practical management control had been perfected within such a 'mutual ownership-mutual control system'. After the collapse of the bubble economy in the 1990s, corporations' alliance and reconstruction developed beyond the borders of these traditional groups, and the old corporate structure of such groups collapsed.

In response to the question of who should decide on the election of an incoming company president in the 1980s, a Nikkei Business study (1989) found that 69.9 per cent of respondents answered 'the present president', while only 3.7 per cent answered 'the stockholder'. Moreover, on the question of to whom the stakeholder manager should give priority to, another study (*Nihon Keizai Shimbun* 1986) found 63.2 per cent said the employees, with 11.5 per cent responding in favour of the stockholder. Demands for shareholder-oriented management were very weak, and the idea of a fair dividend distribution to shareholders was not popular either. Return on equity (ROE) was also as low as 7.8 per cent in 1988 (in the US, 16.1 per cent).[10] Such a structure allowed the management to carry out unrestricted decision-making with high levels of flexibility on a long-term basis, without having to give particular consideration to the stockholders. As Table 2.2 indicates, the medium- and long-term business strategies formulated within Japanese companies (in contrast to the US) placed more focus on capital investment or in the development of new products than on maintaining a good relationship with stockholders.

Employee relationships: A tacit long-term employment understanding, although not stipulated, has existed in Japan between corporations and employees, and this has meant they had mutually been committed either positively and/or passively with each other. That is, an 'internal labour market' has been formed since the end of World War II, whereby the company educates, redeploys and evaluates employees *within* the organization, adopting a medium and long-term perspective

Table 2.2 Strategically important business objectives (1988)

	Japan	US
Development of new products and new business	60.8%	11.0%
Maintain and increase market share	50.6%	53.4%
Maintain and increase return on investment	35.6%	78.1%
Maximized sales	27.9%	15.1%
Investor capital gain	2.7%	63.0%

Source: Keizai Dôyûkai, 'Company White Paper', 1988.

(Koike 1996, Kamii and Nomura 2004). Personnel were evaluated over the long term according to their merit and by the traditional seniority system. Employees hold certain tacit expectations as to how they will be treated appropriately in the long run if they work hard, show loyalty to the organization and commit to it voluntarily (Tanimoto 2002). Mid-career recruitment was not common, with the labour market underdeveloped. Fringe and welfare benefit programmes have developed within companies, with larger corporations having better programmes, and a so-called system of 'company familism' has been built. In contrast with short-term employment relationships, which show high mobility in the labour market, improvements in the quality of the labour force is expected through in-company education and support systems over longer periods of time, with behavior reflecting the long-term and mutual interests of labour and management. Moreover, labour unions basically consisted of core members of company's employees, and harmonious labour-management relations have been built. Such an intra-company union, however, did not have the power to check corporate governance. Core labour and management cooperated in their mutual objective of raising profits and distributing the results as fairly as possible. A labour-management consultation system was simply a platform for reporting what had already been decided; it did not develop into any labour disputes involving management rights.

Supplier relationship: In Japan, manufacturers had formed closed systems of affiliation with their main suppliers, thus internalizing the market since the end of World War II. This system is known as '*keiretsu*,' which can be imagined as a pyramid shape, connecting the first tier, second tier and third tier of suppliers, constituting a closed network. So, for example, within the automobile industry, no deals were done between Toyota's keiretsu and Nissan's keiretsu. Such a closed 'internal market', formed by specific members only, is contradictory to the basic definition of a market, which should be opened to all players. Major companies had built themselves 'rational' systems by saving on transaction costs by forming closed networks between suppliers (Asanuma and Kikuya 1997). The market was thus internalized, controlled by a parent company.

Based on this structure, the social responsibility demanded of corporations used to be understood as to create and retain employment, and to distribute profit to the core members as fairly as possible. Core stakeholders shared the idea that growth of the company was directly linked to the prosperity of general society. However, contrary to this ideal, peripheral stakeholders were not necessarily able to receive the fruits of the prosperity. Rather, they were utilized by the corporation in order to overcome the recession. As a result of high economic growth, however, Japan has been able to achieve the reality of an affluent society with comparative disparity in income. This was the main feature of corporate society in Japan until around the 1980s.

As Figure 2.2 indicates, the corporate system has been structured in order that the main stakeholders be internalized. The boundaries of the corporation have been extending towards the outside of its organization, while internalizing the core stakeholders.

Since 2000, as a result of the collapse of the bubble economy, the relationship

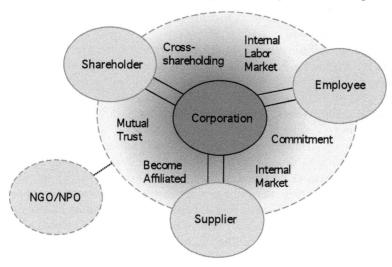

Figure 2.2 Relations between corporation and stakeholders (until the 1980s).

between corporations and stakeholders has been changing. The main factors in this change related to structural changes in stockholding, an increasingly globalized market and changes in civil society.

Structural changes occurred in stockholding, especially in terms of the cross-shareholding system. The ratio of cross-shareholding was 18.4 per cent of the total in 1987, falling to 7.4 per cent in 2002. The ratio of stable shareholders was 45.8 per cent in 1987 and 27.1 per cent in 2002 (Kuroki 2003: 4). The ratio of shareholding of foreign investors – institutional investors – was just 3.9 per cent of the total in 1989, increasing to 26.7 per cent in 2005. In 2005, over 100 Japanese corporations had more than 30 per cent of their shares held by foreign investors. Examples include the ORIX Corporation at 60.3 per cent, Canon Inc. at 52.0 per cent and Sony Corporation at 49.6 per cent. Moreover, institutional investors with a high shareholding ratio began to use proxy voting. This represents, in other words, the emergence of 'active voice shareholders'. Moreover, since 1999 Socially Responsible Investment (SRI) funds have been started up, which individual investors have begun to show increased interest in.

The extended globalization of the marketplace, not least relating to financial markets and production/sales markets, has meant many big businesses depend on foreign markets, especially when the ratio of sales in the foreign market exceeds the majority, as is the case in the automobile, electricity and machine industries. The top five companies that had a high ratio of sales in foreign markets in 2008 are: Honda Motors, 86.8 per cent; Makita Corporation, 84.8 per cent; Brother Industries, 82.7 per cent; TDK, 82.4 per cent; Mitsubishi Motors, 81.8 per cent (*Nihon Keizai Shimbun* 6 June 2008). An important management theme concerns which markets global corporations are selling their products to, as well as within which markets they raise funds. Added to which, it is no longer possible to disregard the environmental standards or the CSR criteria demanded by the markets they move into.

Changes in civil consciousness and the rise of civil society organizations have meant the relationship between corporate organization and employees has been changing since the 1990s. Subsequently, companies could not maintain conventional systems of long-term employment, and introduced merit-based wage systems instead of seniority-based wage systems. According to a survey on the sense of belonging to a company in 1995 (*Nihon Keizai Shimbun*, 20–25 November 1995, 28 December 2000–2006 January 2001), 35.2 per cent answered their loyalty to the company was as strong as before, but the number had decreased to 23.7 per cent in 2000. Also, the number of businessmen who felt less loyalty increased to 32.2 per cent in 2000, from 19.4 per cent in 1995. Furthermore, 23.7 per cent proclaimed themselves to have only a weak sense of belonging in 2000. It can be concluded that totally 55.9 per cent of businessmen were keeping a certain distance from their companies. The Great Hanshin earthquake in 1995 became a catalyst for many in developing an interest in volunteer activities. That year is generally regarded as the 'First Year of Volunteerism'. The law for promotion of activities of Non-Profit Organizations (NPO), which gives juridical status to civil society organizations, was enforced in 1998, and it was named as the 'First Year of NPOs'. People became interested in the social issues of the local and global communities, and tried to get involved in them and to support NPOs. People who want to contribute to society have been gradually increasing in Japan. According to the 'National Survey of Lifestyle Preferences' held by the Cabinet Office in 1983, 43.2 per cent of participants responded 'I would like to be helpful to society as a community member'. This number exceeded 50 per cent in 1987, was more than 60 per cent in 2000 and 62.6 per cent in 2007.

Current situation of CSR and its tasks

CSR has become popular in Japan in recent years due to global debates since the latter half of the 1990s, and due to changes in the structure of corporate society, including the relationship between corporations and stakeholders. According to the 'CSR Database 2007' (Toyo Keizai Shinposha), 63.2 per cent of 1071 major companies established a CSR section or department in 2009, compared to 25.6 per cent in 2006. Moreover, 58.8 per cent of respondents had appointed a director for CSR activities, compared to 35.2 per cent in 2006. The responsiveness of corporations to CSR issues, then, has been becoming increasing dynamic in the past few years. The number of companies publishing reports on CSR has also increased rapidly. In these reports, many companies try to disclose not only environmental issues but also social issues and issues of corporate governance. Underpinning this trend is the change in awareness of CSR among management executives. This trend is succinctly illustrated by the 'Managerial opinion poll about CSR' (March 2006) published by Keizai Dôyûkai. In response to the question 'what is the meaning of CSR in business management?', 69.1 per cent answered it was 'a core theme of management', compared to 50.7 per cent in 2002. Equally, the number of respondents selecting 'the redistribution of profits to society' as their answer totalled 9.4 per cent, down from 17.5 per cent in 2002; 55.4 per cent understood 'CSR as the cost which should be paid' (65.3 per cent in 2002). Furthermore, 25.9 per cent chose the response that described CSR 'as investment which produces future profits' (compared to 17.4 per cent in 2002). More than half of the companies surveyed still considered CSR as a necessary cost against risk, however, a quarter of the companies had come to recognize it as an investment.

The Japan Association of Corporate Executives, Keizai Dôyûkai (2007), says discussion on CSR has shifted to the next stage beyond compliance and CSR management should be considered more proactively and strategically. From this viewpoint, it is regarded that tackling legal and compliance issues is so-called 'passive CSR', and tackling social issues through core business and philanthropic activities is so-called 'active CSR'. This is not the same conception as with Frederick's (1994) 'from CSR1 to CSR2', which notes of a transition from the philosophical-ethical concept of CSR to a managerial concept of corporate social responsiveness to social pressure. The number of Japanese companies that understand active CSR as strategic social business, undertaken through core business schemes in order to improve corporate image and brand value, has been growing. Yet, there are certain problems in such an understanding, which need to be re-considered.

Let us consider the idea that CSR should be understood as something that goes beyond compliance, that is, a concept that is not limited to ensuring compliance with law and ethics. It is said that compliance is heteronymous and concerned with mandatory issues in the area of the law; but on the other hand, CSR is autonomous and concerned with voluntary issues in the area of management. As such, CSR needs to be driven by top initiatives and represent new, shared values throughout the organization (Okamoto and Umezu 2006). A compliance system, however, cannot be completed simply by an understanding of the law and by establishing a code of ethics. It is important to make an effort to re-examine both the organizational structure and the communication process, and to question the values shared in the organization. For example, when Japanese businessmen face dealing with an accident or an illegal trading activity, they tend to attempt to conceal it systematically. What should we conclude from this phenomenon? Systematic attempts to conceal trouble come from the strong desire of the employees to protect the company. This must mean there are certain values shared by the employees in the company. Although a person facing a certain compliance problem might judge that such an approach would not be appropriate from their own personal point of view, he or she might still seek to conceal or secretly deal with the problem in terms of his or her personal role within the organization. It can be said that this is a dysfunction of collective culture in Japanese corporate organization. In order to overcome such 'ethical dilemmas', many companies have been introducing an internal audit and reporting system. However, it is important that the inward-looking corporate culture should be examined. Corporate culture refers to generally shared values, ways of thinking (paradigms) and norms. It is corporate culture that determines the nature of communication and the nature of decision-making in the organization. In order, therefore, to strengthen compliance consciousness, executive managers should make efforts to change the inward-looking corporate culture through strong leadership. Employees should resolve problems through continuous peer discussion, as part of the process of organizational decision-making.

Some Japanese companies, which have received management improvement orders from supervisory agencies in government in response to violations of laws, have started to reconsider their management principles and to improve their management processes, as well as strengthen their external audit systems and re-examine their code of ethics. For example, Mitsui & Co. Ltd., or Sompo Japan Insurance Inc., have discussed such issues internally since 2006, and focused on the following:[11] (1) the purpose of their work, and whether or not the organization provides meaningful work (as discussed throughout the entire body of staff); (2) the evaluation of projects and personnel; and (3) attempts to complement the functions of the current system more efficiently by providing additional resources. Innovative management is required in order to implement these policies. These activities lead to the realization of the essence of CSR management.

Corporations cannot survive without support and trust from society. The roles and responsibilities of corporations, as expected by society, change throughout history. The meaning of a good company is changing and the definition is sought in the context of the contemporary age. What is important in terms of CSR today is basically to show transparent managerial accountability to stakeholders. Corporations that exist in society are always being asked whether or not they are indeed useful for society. These corporations need to recognize that the legitimacy of a corporation, or its 'license to operate' in the market, is awarded by society. The corporate reputation and its values also grow when those business activities are supported by and evaluated in the market society.

Future agendas

What tasks are needed now in order to embed CSR into Japanese market society? The Japanese business community, such as the Nippon Keidanren, has, until now, thought of CSR as something voluntary, consisting of spontaneous activities by individual companies, and not something to be regulated by the central government. It is said that since no legal framework would be able to control all of the aspects of CSR issues, voluntary activities are required in order for corporations to engender socially responsible business. If, however, individual companies address social and environment issues only discretely, will their efforts be automatically linked to the sustainable development of the whole socio-economic system? The voluntary approach can be criticized for the following reasons:

1 A system that relies only upon the spontaneity of companies will only result in those companies doing 'what they can' or 'what they want' on various CSR issues.
2 In order to develop a corporate brand, companies can tend to emphasize those philanthropic activities that have public appeal, rather than make efforts to enforce actual management discipline.

3 Despite the boom in CSR reporting, if each company individually sets their own standards on information disclosure, trustworthiness and transparency cannot be tracked easily, with no comparability between company data etc.
4 The so-called 'social dilemma' problem arises as a more fundamental issue. Here, social dilemma relates to the fact that rational activity by an individual does not necessarily heighten the rationality of society as a whole. So even if each company were to tackle CSR issues individually, such efforts do not guarantee a contribution to the sustainable development of society as a whole.

It is still important for each company to tackle CSR individually and spontaneously. At the same time, however, a certain degree of direction and ruling is needed to govern and enhance CSR activity. For example, voluntary rules issued by industrial associations, international organizations or NGOs have taken on some moderate roles in establishing such frameworks. Equally, public policy by the national government plays a significant, even indispensable, role in creating an overall framework through which companies can readily address CSR issues, and encourage the development of CSR in the marketplace. It is important to build new norms at the foundation of fair market competition. Policy tasks required to embed CSR in Japan can be examined at three levels: the micro, macro and intermediary levels (Tanimoto 2007; see Table 2.3).

Micro level (corporations): the implementation of CSR management practices spontaneously within each company. Each corporation needs to establish a CSR code of conduct based on its management principles and values, in order to incorporate CSR into mid-term management plans and to shape CSR strategy in each department. Companies can obtain improved trust and enhance corporate reputation in market society through the positive disclosure of non-financial data about environmental, social and corporate governance (ESG) issues. Reputation is an intangible asset in meeting the expectations of stakeholders. Fombrun (1996) indicates that customers expect reliability, investors and suppliers demand credibility, employees anticipate trustworthiness and communities expect responsibility.

Table 2.3 Three levels of policy iasks

1	Micro level	Individual corporation
	• CSR management (vision, strategy, P-D-C-A cycle)	
	• Promotion of social innovation	
2	Intermediate level	Business groups, industrial associations, labour unions, NGOs etc
	• Set a code of conduct, norms	
	• Support, coordination, collaboration	
3	Macro level	Government
	• Vision for sustainable development, its strategy	
	• Public policy to facilitate CSR activities	

'Reputation that constituents ascribe to a company is the aggregate of many personal judgments about a company's credibility, reliability, and trustworthiness' (72). Moreover, 'companies create value by investing in a wider range of activities that induce constituents to perceive them as reliable, credible, trustworthy, and responsible' (80). It is important for companies to re-examine their relationship with stakeholders, and to build a 'stakeholder engagement' system (AccountAbility 2005) to improve management through dialogue.

Macro level (government): the development of environments that will enhance CSR activity. The national government needs to construct a vision for building a sustainable socio-economic system in the future, and for the positioning of corporate roles and responsibilities within that vision; thus building a platform where multi-stakeholders can participate to discuss CSR.[12] The Cabinet Office and related ministries and government agencies need to hold cooperative discussions on how best to promote CSR within Japan, and include the practical subject of CSR in the foundation of national industrial policy.[13]

Fox, Ward and Howard (2002: 3–6) explain the following four key roles of public policy, in terms of it providing an 'enabling environment' for CSR: 1) Mandating: 'command and control' legislation, regulators and inspectorates, legal and fiscal penalties and rewards. 2) Facilitating: 'enabling' legislation, funding support, creating incentives, raising awareness, capacity building, stimulating markets. 3) Partnering: combining resources, stakeholder engagement and dialogue. 4) Endorsing: political support, publicity and praise. 'Endorsing' here means to support CSR in the market through policy documents. For example, setting standards for public procurement facilitates CSR in the market, and awards for CSR activities facilitate the enhancement of corporate reputation in this area. Since these activities are almost functionally the same as 'facilitating' and there are no clear lines between them, it is possible to classify fundamental public policies into three broad categories: regulation, encouragement and collaboration.

Regulation refers to the creation of a legal framework to control and enhance business operations. There are two basic mandating approaches, namely 'hard' regulations and 'soft' regulations. The former approach is not necessarily an appropriate way to enforce CSR in general. It is, however, an indispensable approach, in protecting consumers through, for example, the regulation of toxic substances. The latter approach is not intended so much to control business stringently, but rather to establish an appropriate framework to enable corporations to tackle CSR issues. For example, the incorporation of CSR into the criteria for public procurement practices, and introducing SRI methods into parts of public pension fund management[14] are examples of applicable approaches here. These represent an important way to create an appropriate socio-economic environment, as well as being significant in enabling the next category of encouragement, which refers to the creation of institutionalized incentives and guidance to enhance CSR. This approach is concerned with the establishment of fiscal frameworks, the granting of awards to socially responsible companies, the promotion of CSR awareness activities and the development of CSR research and CSR training. Another method is the promotion of voluntary benchmarking by setting standardized guidelines for CSR reports, social labelling and so on. Finally, collaborative relationships need to be created between government, business and NGOs. It is not possible for the government alone to mainstream CSR into market society. As such, collaboration with other sectors is important in the formulation of appropriate CSR policies, and to address development in the local and global communities. From a practical standpoint, national government may choose either a single proper public policy or a combination of them. For instance, it is feasible for a government to promote CSR reporting by using a combination of mandatory (enactment of legislation), encouraging (setting guidelines) and collaborative (engagement with stakeholders)[15] methods.

Intermediary level (intermediate organizations): Social issues on CSR should be dealt with not only by corporations but also by various organizations: industrial associations, labour unions, consumer groups, human rights groups, NGOs, universities and research institutions and so on. There are various important roles such organizations need to take on. Industrial organizations can provide information and support for members, and can set up codes of conduct and guidelines to address the specific problems of each industry. Financial institutions can promote CSR activities in non-financial industries through core finance business. When financial institutions undertake investment and financing, for example, CSR can be incorporated into its evaluation criteria, thus promoting the capability of the market to evaluate CSR – the United Nations has initiated the launch of the 'Principle of Responsible Investment' to provide a framework. Suppliers can incorporate CSR in their contract or procurement standards. It is important all corporations implement CSR procurement strategies and develop the supply chain management. Labour unions need to understand the meaning of CSR in a broad sense, supervise corporate management and strengthen the functions that check corporate governance. Collaboration with international industrial unions and NGOs is also vital. NGOs themselves can investigate and analyze corporate activity from an independent standpoint, as well as provide information to the public and make policy proposals to government and corporations. Moreover, companies and NGOs have also started to collaborate in tackling environmental and social issues in the local and international communities. Finally, universities/ and research institutions need to develop basic research on 'Business and Society' and 'CSR'. The development of educational programmes, management systems and policy recommendations from an independent standpoint is also important and to be expected.

To promote CSR concerns in society, then, the activities of corporations alone are not enough. The intermediary organizations also need to be active and involved. The creation of a workable framework for collaboration between government, business and NGOs is no easy task, but it is important to establish a platform through which these related parties can connect with each other. Growing public interest and the development of a social movement are the key factors in constructing a sustainable market society. It is important that each citizen, who is also a consumer, a labourer, an investor and a resident, begins to be concerned about social and environmental issues on CSR. Should large numbers of people get interested and involved in the evaluation of corporate activity from the social and environmental aspects of consumption, deposits, savings and investment, the resulting action can have a big impact on the market. Corporations will eventually come to recognize CSR as an essential managerial issue and start to tackle it strategically. This will happen when each stakeholder demands that the company be accountable, and when CSR elements come to be included in the standards of corporate evaluation prevalent in today's market.

Suggested Further Reading

Allouche, J. (ed.) (2006) *Corporate Social Responsibility*, Vol. 1 and Vol. 2. Hampshire: Palgrave.

ASrIA (ed.) (2003), *Foreign Versus Local: The Debate About SRI Priorities in Japan*. Hong Kong: Association for Sustainable & Responsible Investment in Asia.

Fukukawa, K. and J. Moon. (2004), 'A Japanese Model of Corporate Social Responsibility? A Study of Website Reporting'. *Journal of Corporate Citizenship*, 14: 45–59.

Fukukawa, K. and Y. Teramoto (2009) 'Understanding Japanese CSR: The Reflections of Managers in the Field of Global Operations'. *Journal of Business Ethics*, 85(1): 133–46.

Japan Association for the Comparative Studies of Management (ed.) (2007) *Business and Society, New Perspective for Comparative Studies of Management*. Kyoto: Bunrikaku.

Solomon, A, J. Solomon and M. Suto.(2004), 'Can the UK Experience Provide Lessons for the Evolution of SRI in Japan?'. *Corporate Governance: An International Review*, 12(4): 552–66.

Tanimoto, K. (2004) 'Changes in the Market Society and Corporate Social Responsibility'. *Asian Business & Management*, 3(2): 151–72.

Tsalikis, J. and B. Seaton.(2008), 'The International Business Ethics Index: Japan'. *Journal of Business Ethics*, 80(2): 379–85.

Welford, R. (2004), 'Corporate Social Responsibility in Europe and Asia: Critical Elements and Best Practice'. *Journal of Corporate Citizenship*, 13: 31–47.

Notes

1   The past five years have seen the publication of many management guidebooks written by consultants, and many magazines have also featured contents on CSR. Management seminars have been held frequently by consulting companies, business organizations and publishers. Almost all of these have focused mainly on introduction of current global management trends and how to address and manage issues of CSR.

2   Critical discussions of capitalist enterprises from a Marxist viewpoint were common in Japan throughout the 1970s and 1980s.

3   This paper defines the 'market society' as follows: in the actual market, economy, society, politics, culture, international relations interact, and a mutually restrictive relationship exists within the interplay. The market does not function in a 'vacuum' without restrictions. In this sense, a market is originally understood as a 'market society' (Tanimoto 2004: 152–53).

4   Japan is a leading country in terms of the number of certificates held on ISO 14001, at 23,466. The top three countries in the EU are Spain with 8,620, Italy with 7,080, and the UK at 6,050. The total number within the entire EU area is 44,714 (ISO Survey 2006).

5   http://iso.org/sr

6 http://www.rice.or.jp/j-home/publication1/20061130CSR.pdf
7 http://www.fsa.go.jp/status/csr/20060331/01.pdf
8 Typical of the CSR-related literature of that time are, for example, K. Takada, (1974) *Keieisha no Shakaiteki Sekinin [Managerial Social Responsibility]*, Chikura-shobo; A. Morita, (1978), *Gendaikigyô no Shakaiteki Sekinin [Corporate Social Responsibility]*, Shouji-houmu; T. Nakatani *et al.* (eds) (1979), *Keieirinen to kigyôsekinin) [Corporate Principle and Corporate Responsibility]*, Mineruva-shobo; K. Nakamura, (1980), *Kigyô no Shakaiteki Sekinin-Hougakuteki Kosatu [Corporate Social Responsibility – Juristic Consideration]*, Doubunkan.
9 Keizai Doyukai issued a recommendation paper, 'For Establishing Mutual Trust between Business and Society' in March 1973. It pointed out that 'corporate social responsibility must be understood as having the same meaning of managerial social responsibility in corporate principles. Therefore, top management needs to make decisions not only for profit-seeking, but also to seek balance between social goals and corporate merit.'
10 Research Report of the Life Insurance Association of Japan 2002. http://www.seiho.or.jp/date/news.
11 Mitsui & Co. Ltd., CSR Report 2007. http://www.mitsui.co.jp/en/csr/icsFiles/afieldfile/2008/03/13/csr2007e.pdf. Sompo Japan Insurance Inc., CSR Communication Report 2007 (in Japanese) http://www.sompo-japan.co.jp/about/environment/csr/report/download/re2007.pdf.
12 European Commission has set up and held a typical round of talks by multi-stakeholders, 'The European Multi-Stakeholders Forum on Corporate Social Responsibility', between 2002 and 2004.
13 The UK Government's policy on CSR is a useful example. See DTI (2002) *Business and Society: Corporate Social Responsibility Report*, DTI (2001) *Business and Society: Developing Corporate Social Responsibility in the UK*.
14 For instance, the UK 1995 Pension Act was partly revised to require that pension funds disclose whether or not they take social, environment and ethical issues into account, not to force them to adopt SRI operations. This move was not because they have been forced to operate SRI by the Pension Act, but simply because environmental and ethical issues have already come to be a major concern for UK people.
15 It is also apparent that some public sector activities, such as procurement, have multiple links with the contemporary CSR agenda. (Fox, Ward and Howard 2002: 3).

References

AccountAbility (2005) *AA1000 Stakeholder Engagement Standard. Exposure Draft.* London.

Aoki, M. (2001) *Information, Corporate Governance, and Institutional Diversity: Competitiveness in Japan, the USA, and the Transitional Economies.* Oxford: Oxford University Press.

Asanuma, B. and T. Kikuya. (1997) *Nihon no Kigyô Soshiki [Japanese Corporate Organization].* Tokyo: Toyo Keizai Shinposha.

Collins, J. C., and J. I. Porras. (1994) *Built to Last: Successful Habits of Visionary Companies.* New York: HarperCollins.

Dore, R. (2000) *Stock Market Capitalism: Welfare Capitalism: Japan and Germany versus the Anglo-Saxons.* Oxford: Oxford University Press.

EC (2001) 'Green Paper, Promoting a European Framework for Corporate Social Responsibility'. COM (2001) 366.

—— (2002) 'White Paper, Communication on Corporate Social Responsibility Business Contribution to Sustainable Development'. COM (2002) 347.

Fombrun, C. J.(1996) *Reputation: Realizing Value from the Corporate Image*. Boston: HBS Press.

Fox, T., H. Ward B. and Howard. (2002) *Public Sector Roles in Strengthening Corporate Social Responsibility: A Baseline Study*. The World Bank.

Frederick, W. C. (1994) 'From CSR1 to CSR2: The Maturing of Business-and-Society Thought'. *Business & Society*, 33(2):150–64.

Friedman, M. (1962) *Capitalism and Freedom*. Chicago: University of Chicago Press.

Fukukawa, K. and Y. Teramoto (2009) 'Understanding Japanese CSR: The Reflections of Managers in the Field of Global Operations'. *Journal of Business Ethics*, 85(1): 133–46.

Haberberg, A. and A. Rieple. (2007) *Strategic Management: Theory and Application*. Oxford: Oxford University Press.

Ito, K. (2004) 'CSR ni yoru Koporeto Burando Keiei [Corporate Brand Management by CSR]', in *CSR – Kigyô Kachi wo dou Takameruka [CSR How to Heighten Corporate Value]*. Tokyo: Nihon Keizai Shinbun sha.

Iwai, K. (1999) 'Persons, Things and Corporations: The Corporate Personality Controversy and Comparative Corporate Governance'. *American Journal of Comparative Law*, 47(4): 583–632.

—— (2002) 'The Nature of the Business Corporation: Its Legal Structure and Economic Functions'. *Japanese Economic Review*, 53(3): 243–73.

—— (2005)*Kaisha ha Dareno Monoka [Who owns a corporation]*. Tokyo: Heibonsha Limited, Publishers.

Japan Society of Business Administration (JSBA) (ed.) (1975) *Kigyô no Shakaiteki Sekinin [Corporate Social Responsibility]*. Tokyo: Chikura-shobo.

Kamii, Y. and M. Nomura. (2004) *Japanese Companies: Theories and Realities*. Melbourne: Trans Pacific Press.

Keizai Dôyûkai (2007), *CSR Inobêshon [CSR Innovation]*. Tokyo: Keizai Dôyûkai.

Koike, K. (1996) *The Economics of Work in Japan*, translated by M. Saso. Macmillan.

Kuroki, F. (2003) 'Mochiai kaisho nimiru Kigyô to Ginko no Kankei [The Relationship between Corporations and Banks from the Viewpoint of Dissolution of Mutual Holding]'. *NLI Research Report*, 2003.10.

Lawrence, A. T., J. Weber and J. E. Post. (2005) *Business and Society: Stakeholders, Ethics, Public Policy*. Boston: MacGraw Hill.

Okamoto, D. and M. Umezu. (2006) *Kigyô Hyoka + Kigyô Rinri [Corporate Evaluation + Business Ethics]*. Tokyo: Keio University Press.

Okumura, H. (2000), *Corporate Capitalism in Japan*, translated by D. Anthony and N. Brown. Macmillan (originally published in Japanese in 1984).

Ravetz, J. R. (1971) *Scientific Knowledge and its Social Problems*. Gloucestershire: Clarendon Press.

Steiner, G. A. and J. F. Steiner(2000), *Business, Government and Society*. Boston: McGraw Hill,

Tanimoto, K. (2004) 'Changes in the Market Society and Corporate Social Responsibility'. *Asian Business & Management*, 3(2), 151–72.

—— (2005) 'Corporate Social Responsibility in Japan: Analyzing the Participating Companies in Global Reporting Initiative', with K. Suzuki. EIJS, Stockholm School of Economics, Working Paper 208, March 2005.

—— (2006) 'Evaluation of Corporate Social Responsibility (CSR) and the Market', in The

Japan Association for Comparative Studies of Management (ed.). *Business and Society.* Kyoto: Bunirikaku, 95–103.

—— (2007) 'Corporate Social Responsibility and Public Policy'. ADBI Conference: Best Practices in Corporate Social Responsibility in Asia, September 2007. http://www.adbi. org/files/session4_01_kanji_tanimoto_paper.pdf.

Toyo Keizai (1972–2000) *Kigyô Keiretsu Sôran [Keiretsu Data].*Tokyo : Toyo Keizai Shinposha.

—— (2006–2009) *CSR Kigyô Sôran [CSR Data].* Tokyo: Toyo Keizai Shinposha.

3 Perceptions of CSR and its adoption to business practice in the Thai context

Nooch Kuasirikun

Introduction

In recent years, corporate social responsibility (CSR)[1] has become a widely-discussed issue in Thailand, although this debate about CSR and its practice in Thailand is relatively unexplored in international literature. In order to shed light on Thai perceptions and practice of CSR, this chapter, first, outlines the contextual background of CSR in Thailand in terms of the Thai economy as well as the social and environmental problems confronting Thailand as a consequence of rapid economic change over recent decades. Secondly, the chapter draws on primary commentary in newspapers and government reports to investigate the concept of CSR and how corporate social and environmental responsibility is perceived in Thailand. Finally, the chapter examines how these perceptions of CSR have been translated into practice in Thai companies, and explores whether CSR practices in Thailand tend to be determined by or orientate towards Thailand's own social and environmental requirements.

Social and environmental problems and the Thai economy

Thailand, which is situated in Southeast Asia, has a total population of 65.28 million (2006) (Department of Labour Protection and Welfare 2007:15) occupying around 513,000 square kilometers of land. Since the Thai government initiated its strategic economic objective of developing Thailand towards a 'Newly Industrialized Country' (NIC) in 1945, the Thai economy has experienced a steady long-term growth rate indicated by a GDP of 9.1 per cent in the period from 1985–96 (Dixon 1999). Like many other Asian countries, however, Thailand suffered serious economic dislocation as a result of the Asian financial crisis of 1997. Ten years after this major economic setback, Thailand has slowly recovered as indicated by the steady growth of its GDP ranging from 4.5 per cent to 6.7 per cent over the years 2002 and 2007 (World Bank Thailand Office 2003–8). This growth has been sustained primarily by Thailand's export industries, such as electronics, vehicles and mechanical parts, and the increase in the price of agricultural commodities for export. In 2007, for example, export of agricultural commodities grew by 28.5 per cent due to a rapid price increase of 26.5 per cent. The main agricultural products that have enjoyed strong growth are rice, rubber and cassava (Office of the National Economic and Social Development Board (NESDB) 2008:5–6), although export of commodities like rice have been restricted in 2008 to prioritize local consumption needs.

In terms of a division in the workforce, in 2005 and 2006 around 40 per cent of the employed population was in the agricultural sector (Department of Labour Protection and Welfare 2007:15). Thus, regardless of the Thai government's efforts to promote Thailand as a NIC, a substantial proportion of the Thai workforce remains heavily reliant on agriculture. Due to this structuring of the Thai economy, most people who are categorized as 'poor' often live in rural regions outside Bangkok, with the poorest area being located in the northeast of Thailand (see Table 3.1).

Towards the end of the 1990s, poverty increased mainly due to the 1997 Asian financial crisis and economic downturn. This trend also continued into the early 2000s, but the data in subsequent years showed that the number of the population below the poverty line reduced in 2004 and 2006. The reduction appears, however, to be greater in the Bangkok area than in other regions: a reduction of 64.5 per cent (2004) and 44.05 per cent (2006) compared with, for example, the poorest region in the northeast of 18.09 per cent (2004) and 8.43 per cent (2006). As Table 3.1 shows, poverty is perceived quantitatively to be a predominantly rural phenomenon. This is despite the increased remittance of income to such rural areas by migrants who work in the larger cities, like Bangkok (World Bank Thailand Office 2003:5). Although urban poverty remains lower in quantitative terms, the standard of living and quality of life of some among the urban poor, especially migrant construction, wholesale or retail trade workers, is held to be worse than that of the poor in rural areas (World Bank Thailand Office 2006:16).

These migrant workers have nonetheless over the last few decades been a vital driving workforce in supporting the government's policy of developing Thailand into a NIC. Until recent years, cheap labour and relatively lax social and environmental legislation has enabled Thailand to compete effectively in international markets. Such rapid industrialization has, however, resulted in a variety of social and environmental problems. In social terms, many workers have had to live on precarious casual wages, as well as work in poor and unsafe working conditions (Komin 1989; Phongpaichit and Baker 1996). The issue surrounding working standards gained increased significance following the disastrous fire on 10 April 1993 at Kader Industrial (Thailand), a soft-toy manufacturer located in Nakornpathom province. This accident claimed 188 lives and injured nearly 500 workers (and featured on the front page of every Thai newspaper). As Kuasirikun and Sherer (2004) outlined, this type of accident is not isolated, although other similar accidents have tended to be on a smaller scale in terms of injuries and fatalities and therefore are not usually publicized to such an extent.[2] Although statistics of accidents at work are kept by the Department of Labour Protection and Welfare (formerly known as The Labour and Social Welfare Department), general public awareness of the labour situation has consequently been relatively low.

In 1998 the Labour Protection Act was passed in order to provide workers and employees with better protection in terms of minimum wages, suitable and safe working conditions, and maternity rights (Wilawan and Lengthaisong 1998;

Table 3.1 Number of population in poverty[a] by region and areas (in thousands)[b]

Region	Areas	1996	1998	2000	2002	2004	2006
Bangkok	Within municipality	73.5	75.8	106.9	144.5	51.3	28.7
	Total	**73.5**	**75.8**	**106.9**	**144.5**	**51.3**	**28.7**
Central Thailand	Within municipality	234.1	213.4	334.3	242.7	165.0	97.5
	Outside municipality	565.8	832.3	912.4	847.7	501.2	427.6
	Total	**799.9**	**1,045.7**	**1,246.7**	**1,090.4**	**666.2**	**525.1**
North	Within municipality	299.8	317.8	366.0	317.6	225.9	147.3
	Outside municipality	1,651.7	1,507.1	2,224.1	1,972.4	1,616.2	1,262.9
	Total	**1,951.5**	**1,824.9**	**2,590.1**	**2,290.0**	**1,842.1**	**1,410.2**
Northeast	Within municipality	465.3	557.6	683.5	464.2	428.7	319.4
	Outside municipality	4,423.6	5,652.6	6,598.2	4,362.8	3,525.0	3,301.1
	Total	**4,888.9**	**6,210.2**	**7,281.6**	**4,827**	**3,953.7**	**3,620.4**
South	Within municipality	117.0	115.8	104.2	88.3	62.0	85.0
	Outside municipality	661.6	970.5	1,225.9	695.2	443.4	387.2
	Total	**778.6**	**1,086.3**	**1,330.1**	**783.5**	**505.4**	**472.2**
Overall	Within municipality	1,189.7	1,280.4	1,594.9	1,257.3	932.9	677.9
	Outside municipality	7,302.7	8,962.5	10,960.6	7,878.1	6,085.8	5,378.8
	Total	**8,492.4**	**10,242.9**	**12,555.5**	**9,135.4**	**7,018.7**	**6,056.7**

Source: National Statistics Office (2006).

a Population in poverty is defined by the National Statistics Office as those whose consumption expenditure is below the poverty line. The average poverty line in the year 2006 for Bangkok, Central Thailand, North, Northeast and South are 2,020; 1,476; 1,266; 1,240; 1,340 and 1,386 baht per person per month respectively (National Statistics Office 2006).
b This data is collected every other year.

Table 3.2 Occupational injuries

Year	Total employees inspected	Death	Permanent total disability	Permanent partial disability	Number of adjudications Absence from work ≥ 3 days	Absence from work ≤ 3 days	Total	Total
1997	5,825,821	1,033	29	5,272	68,480	155,562	230,376	3.95%
1998	5,145,830	790	19	3,714	55,489	126,486	186,498	3.62%
1999	5,321,872	611	12	3,396	50,239	117,739	171,997	3.23%
2000	5,417,041	620	16	3,516	48,338	127,076	179,566	3.31%
2001	5,544,436	607	20	3,510	48,077	137,407	189,621	3.42%
2002	6,541,105	650	14	3,424	49,012	137,879	190,979	2.92%
2003	7,033,907	787	17	3,821	52,364	153,684	210,673	3.00%
2004	7,386,825	861	23	3,775	52,893	157,982	215,534	2.92%
2005	7,720,747	1,444	19	3,425	53,641	155,706	214,235	2.77%
2006	7,992,025	808	21	3,413	51,901	148,114	204,257	2.56%

Source: Department of Labour Protection and Welfare (1998–2007).

Wichianchom 1999). Despite this Act, however, the situation of workers in Thailand, especially with regard to health and safety conditions in the workplace, has not improved to a satisfactory level as statistics indicate that 2–4 in every 100 workers across this period suffered fatality or injuries as a result of unsuitable working conditions (see Table 3.2 below). Serious measures need to be taken in order to provide and enforce adequate protection for employees while at work.

Since the Kader factory incident in 1993, there were also other occupational health and safety-related cases with equally disastrous consequences. For example, on 13 August 1993 there was a fire at the Royal Plaza Hotel, which led to the death of 157 people and injured 200 more who were working or staying at the hotel. Similarly, on 11 July 1997, a fire at the Royal Jomtien Resort Hotel resulted in 91 deaths and 50 injured, and on 19 September 1999, a huge explosion at the Hongthai Kasedphuttana factory caused 36 deaths and seriously injured two of its workers. Moreover, due to the magnitude of the latter explosion, 571 houses, temples, schools and a hospital within a one kilometre radius were in varying degrees affected (Jareanled 2006). In the context of such cases, and in spite of occupational and safety inspections, it is alarming that more than 10 years after the Kader incident, statistics persistently indicate that many companies are still failing to provide adequate occupational standards and safety measures to protect the lives of their workers, customers and the wider community (Jaihao 2006).

Gender inequality is also a problematic issue in Thai society. Women workers, who in 2007 constituted approximately 17 million (48.57 per cent) of the total 35 million labour force in Thailand, have long experienced unequal treatment at work (*Matichon* 27 March 2007). Although it is recognized by the Labour Department that women workers, especially those who work in factories, experience unequal treatment at work compared to male counterparts in such matters as pay, employment rights and working facilities (*Krungthepthurakit* 9 March 2007), workplace inspections and surveys appear to show the contrary. In 2005, of 27,116 establishments inspected, only 73 establishments (0.27 per cent) were found to discriminate against female workers (Yearbook of Labour Protection and Welfare Statistics 2006:125). The Labour Department's inspection of female labour in 2006 revealed that of 37,988 establishments inspected (totalling 1,050,670 female workers), only 0.26 per cent (97 establishments) committed illegal actions, such as violation of working time (0.12 per cent) (46 establishments, 65 people), overtime (0.08 percent) (30 establishments, number of people unavailable), and sexual harassment (0.02 percent) (8 establishments, number of people unavailable). None committed gender discrimination (Yearbook of Labour Protection and Welfare Statistics 2007:125), although another survey conducted by the Labour Protection and Welfare Department in 2007 revealed that of 300,000 establishments investigated, only 0.02 per cent (67 establishments) provided in-house nursery facilities for their employees to enable the parent, especially the mother, to continue to work with no extra childcare cost (*Naewna* 9 August 2007). With limited and random government inspection of only around 6 per cent of the total female worker population annually, female labour in Thailand by and large remains vulnerable and exposed to exploitation.

In environmental terms, there have also been numerous problems in Thailand that have accumulated over its period of industrialization. Such problems as noise, water and air pollution are common environmental issues in Thailand. As Kuasirikun and Sherer (2004) elaborated, communities who live near industrial areas have had to suffer the environmental consequences of toxic air and contaminated water over the last few decades (see also Sangrudsameekul 2008a, 2008b).[3] Such areas as the Eastern Seaboard and Mabtaphud industrial estates are two prominent examples of how industrialization affects local people's lives. Phongrai (2008) reports that chemical pollutants released into the atmosphere by factories in the Mabtaphud area are at such high levels that 25 communities living around this industrial estate are affected by ill health. Yet, amid all the health scares, the government has granted permission to 12 more petro-chemical projects (Phongrai 2008). Notwithstanding the complaints of the local people themselves and attempts by the Eastern People's Network, who work on behalf of the affected communities to engage with the relevant local authorities and the Department of Industrial Works, environmental effects of air pollution to date remain a prominent health concern in Thailand (*Matichon* 3 October 2007).

In addition to air pollution, industrial waste also generates water pollution when toxic water from factories located along river banks is released into rivers. Water pollution is of particular concern as water from rivers is often not only a source of water for Thai people in their daily life, but these rivers are also the main water supply for agriculture, which is the livelihood of two-fifths of the Thai population (Kuasirikun and Sherer 2004). As rivers run through many towns across central Thailand, when the polluted water is released in one place, the toxin is carried along the river ways (Sangrudsameekul 2008b).[4] The Chao Phraya river,[5] for example, is 375 kilometres long and runs from north (Nakhonsawan province) across the central plains to Bangkok and the Gulf of Thailand in Samutprakan province. It was reported in July 2007 that there were 209 factories along the Chao Phraya river that released untreated water and solid wastes into the river (*Thansedthakit* 3 April 2008). Another river that is also severely affected by industrial waste is the Thajeen river, which passes through four provinces in central Thailand, namely Chainad, Suphanburi, Nakornpathom, and Samudsakorn provinces (*Post Today* 14 February 2008; *Naewna* 15 February 2008). Overall, there are over 6,000 factories situated along river banks in Thailand with high water consumption and waste discharge (*Phimthai* 9 April 2008). When considering the water contamination problem in relation to the importance of water supply from these rivers, the magnitude of water pollution in Thailand is immense (Sangrudsameekul 2008b; *Khomchudleauk* 21 March 2007; *Thansedthakit* 30 September 2007; *Business Thai* 29 February 2008).

Overall, the negative effects of Thai industrialization have become slowly recognized and relevant governmental agencies have begun to take measures to help deal with social and environmental issues. For example, there has been the introduction of the Labour Protection Act 1998 and the Environmental Act 1992, with the aim of creating socially and environmentally friendly business conduct. In spite of such government's efforts, however, social and environmental problems in Thailand do not appear to have been remedied to satisfactory levels. In recent years, therefore, and in part due to increased awareness of social and environmental issues in the global context, these concerns have gained increasing importance and are being discussed more widely among Thai academics and business practitioners in terms of the development of CSR.

The concept of CSR in Thailand

In the English-speaking context, various aspects of CSR have been extensively discussed in the literature (Aguilera *et al.* 2007; Bansal and Roth 2000; Buchholz 1991; Campbell 2007; Demirag 2005; Dunn 1991; Klonoski 1991; Lyon 2004; Maximiano 2007; Strike *et al.* 2006). In contrast, CSR in Asian countries has been investigated by a smaller if growing number of researchers, whose theorization of CSR practice in the context of different Asian countries has tended to stem from a variety of perspectives (Baughn *et al.* 2007; Frost 2006; Welford 2007; Chapple and Moon 2007). Some research such as that of Frost (2006) highlights exploitation problems in the nature of the supply chain in Bangladesh, Vietnam, Cambodia and China, and other research like that of Welford (2007) focuses on how corporate governance structures in Asian countries is affected where there is a lack of independence in the governance board due to close family business ties that can compromise CSR practice. Conceptualized in terms of these previous studies, Chapple and Moon (2007) point out that CSR issues in Asia are different and more fundamental than those in the West in that CSR issues in Asia encapsulate 'problems', such as the lack of or disparities in education, poverty, labour rates and standards, human rights, health care, corporate governance and vulnerability to natural disasters (Chapple and Moon 2007; see also Engle 2007; Frost 2006; Welford 2004, 2007; Welford and Frost 2006). Thailand often forms part of comparative analyses within these studies, however, the concept of CSR as perceived and understood among business practitioners in Thailand has rarely been elaborated in any significant detail.

Development of CSR in Thailand

Until recently the term CSR has been relatively unknown to corporations in Thailand. Research on Thai publication and press databases, such as the *Bangkok Post*, *Matichon* newspaper library and the NewsCentre, reveal there was very little written on CSR and corporate social and environmental-related issues before the year 2000. Within these newspaper databases, articles on CSR only began to appear in the media around 2005–6 with the focus on the impact of CSR on Thai exporters. The volume of news articles on CSR and CSR-related issues also increased dramatically in 2007. This increase from 2000 to 2007 seems to reflect an incremental change in attitude towards corporate social responsibility issues amongst the international business community in Thailand from the late 1990s to mid-2000s, as they slowly adopted a more holistic approach to the conduct of their business in response to international arguments that globalization has contributed to 'major environmental disasters' and 'scandals over child labor exploitation by multinational companies in developing countries' (Demirag 2005:11). As a consequence, companies and supply chains in Thailand, especially those trading with multinational firms, have gradually put in place relevant policies concerning their corporate social responsibility directed not only at their workers and the environment, but also the community at large (*Prachachadthurakit* 27 June 2005).

In this sense CSR is a concept understood to have been recently adapted from the West in order to describe and promote corporate social, environmental and community responsibility. Pressure from Western multinational business, which has become more concerned with how products and services are processed globally, appears to be one force that has engendered wider debate about CSR practices among the business community in Thailand. For example, in order to maintain its competitive edge in international markets from the end of the 1990s, Thai supply chain manufacturers for multinational companies were required to conduct their businesses in compliance with various international certifications concerning health and safety at work (ISO 18000), product quality management (ISO 9000) and environmental management (ISO 14000) (Fukui 1999). In particular, Thai garment exporters were required by their international trading partners to improve their social and environmental responsibility. As recognized by the director of the Thai Garment Manufacturing Association, 'CSR would play a significant role in the global supply chain, so Thailand should differentiate itself by highlighting the strength of Thai garment manufacturers' respect for human rights and workplace health and safety' (Thapanachai 2002:B1; see also Thongrung 2002). Nonetheless, it was not until 2004 when more general debate on the importance of corporate social and environmental responsibility started to gain sufficient momentum that the Stock Exchange of Thailand initiated a discussion forum on social and environmental issues. In this forum, it was pointed out that

> 'social issues and the environment have become added dimensions for exporting products around the world. With key importing nations – including the United Sates, Japan and Australia – paying attention to them ... we need to strive for international standards. Otherwise Thai businesses will face difficulties ... [as] investors are paying greater awareness to investing only in socially-responsible listed firms'.
>
> (*The Nation* 21 October 2004:2; see also Polkuamdee 2004;
> Chitsomboon 2005)

Overall, by 2007, it was realized in the Thai business community that CSR was here to stay and that all companies, especially those who traded internationally, would need to improve their corporate social and environmental policies if they were to compete effectively in international markets (Arunmas 2007a, 2007b).

Towards a Thai definition of CSR

Although international trade gave stimulus to the development of CSR in Thailand, the relevance of CSR to Thailand was quickly explored by various Thai professionals ranging from academics, government agencies, charitable organizations, business community and regulators (*Phujudkarnraisabda* 27 June 2005). In this respect, various forums, seminars and conferences have been organized in Thailand to facilitate the exchange of ideas that these different professionals have on CSR. Seminars on CSR often attract people from different backgrounds, profession and organizations who come together to explore the impact of CSR, how CSR strategy might be beneficial to Thai business and what the right strategy for CSR might entail. (Lancaster 2004). A seminar entitled 'Creating Sustainable Business through CSR' organized jointly by four organizations in 2006, namely the Research Fund Trust (governmental agency), the Thaipat Institute,[6] the Stock Exchange of Thailand and *Krungthepthurakit* newspaper, represents a good example of how collaborative CSR has become in Thai society (*Prachachadthurakit* 19 September 2005; *Krungthepthurakit* 19 June 2006). Moreover, support for CSR is also apparent among charitable organizations, such as the Magic Eye Association in their seminar in July 2006 entitled 'Catching up with Global CSR: Has Thai business started?' (*Prachachadthurakit* 24 July 2006). CSR has also been widely welcomed among the business community in Thailand with many attempting to define what CSR means in the Thai context (*Prachachadthurakit* 31 July 2006). 'The Power of CSR in the Changing Face of Globalization' was a topic chosen by one of the main business newspapers in Thailand, *Prachachadthurakit*, for its annual seminar in 2007 (Bangkokkian 2007). In 2008, in collaboration with the Corporate Social Responsibility Institute (CSRI) of the Stock Exchange of Thailand, the *Prachachadthurakit* newspaper also organized a seminar under the title 'Deep into CSR in Practice: Leading to Sustainable Organizations' (*Prachachadthurakit* 28–30 April 2008). This seminar aimed to provide participating organizations with knowledge of CSR in terms of compliance with standards and the implications of practicing CSR. Overall, therefore, given the amount of publicity and support that CSR has received, it is undeniable that CSR has come to play an important role in the way business people think and the ways in which business activities will be conducted in Thailand in the years to come (Lancaster 2004; Thongrung 2006a). In their different forms, these forums, seminars and debates have sought to discuss and adapt CSR to the Thai socio-economic context.

The main concerns of the seminars outlined above were not only to explore the underlying concept of CSR and discuss how it might be used proactively as a strategic approach to improve business performance, but also to explore the wider applicability of CSR in the Thai context for the amelioration of Thai society overall. With regard to the concept of CSR, the director of the Thaipat Institute thus stated that 'real CSR emerges from goodwill within the organization ... [and] ... is a commitment to behave ethically in order to build a sustainable economy by working with all relevant stakeholders to improve business and society at large' (Chitsomboon 2006a:B8). Other economists have called for companies to implement His Majesty The King's concept of a 'sufficiency economy' to create balanced and sustainable economic growth (Chitsomboon 2006b). This concept is premised on business' commitment to maintaining long-term performance without compromising the views of a wider range of stakeholders who represent the environment, society and future generations (Chitsomboon 2006b). Thus, CSR practice in Thailand has been formulated in the idea of a 'sufficiency economy' that aims to find a balance between responsible business and a healthy society (*Prachachadthurakit* 31 July 2006) in order to bring about sustainable development. In this sense, CSR as an initial response to global business pressure has evolved into a strategic approach to the holistic improvement of Thai business performance within the context of the wider socio-economic and developmentalist ethics of Thai society.

As CSR has become adopted as a business strategy, many commentators on CSR in Thailand have also stated that companies in Thailand have always practiced CSR in one form or another (Senanuch 2007; Thongthanakul 2007a; Yodprudtikan 2008) and have begun to identify existing practice under the CSR rubric. Private organizations have for many decades donated monies largely in the form of philanthropic gifts in support of, for example, education, cultural promotion, sporting events or relief of hardship, but also in some cases for sustainable community development (Thongthanakul 2007b; *Phujudkarnraisabda* 20 November 2006; *Prachachadthurakit* 26 June 2006, *Prachachadthurakit* 4 September 2006, *Prachachadthurakit* 23 July 2007). For other commentators, however, philanthropy is not regarded as meaningful CSR activity because in principle CSR activities must have a positive and practical impact on society with sustainable benefits (Chanchaochai 2007). CSR should not simply equate with executives donating their returns or companies handing out money. Rather more pertinently, CSR should be about how companies coexist with and support the environment and the communities around them in long-term policy terms. Engendering this harmonious coexistence might be facilitated by CSR activities, such as budgets to ensure that business activities are environmentally neutral and socially promotive, or that the contribution made to the community helps enhance the quality of life of the people in the company's local areas. Corporate contributions might be made in financial terms and/or in the form of human resources, volunteers or provision of technological expertise. Thus, in the Thai context, although it has been argued that historically many companies have practiced CSR, it is the advent of CSR from the West that has led the business community and their associated organizations and agencies to redefine and broaden their strategies and activities into more meaningful CSR terms.

The emergence of broad-based definitions of CSR in Thailand

Henriques (2007) has remarked that CSR is a concept that has no universal definition. In Thailand too, the concept of CSR and its indigenous forms have been the subject of growing debate in recent years, and the definitions provided by different academics and organizations vary in their detail. The most widely accepted definitions are, however, those provided by the Thaipat Institute, the Thailand Business Council for Sustainable Development (TBCSD)[7] and the Stock Exchange of Thailand through its CSR Charter.

The Thaipat Institute defines CSR as an organization's

'internal or external business activities that are concerned with the effects of that business on both proximate and distant levels of society. Such activities can be generated by the deployment of resources available within the organization or obtained from outside the organizations with the aim of creating a harmonious and peaceful way of living in society'.

(Yodprudtikan *et al.* 2006:3)

The TBCSD, on the other hand, has provided a more detailed definition of CSR as a company's continuous intention to manage its activities in a socially responsible way. The fundamental components of being socially responsible are perceived to be: (1) The company must have good corporate governance; (2) Its production process of products and services is safe and environmentally friendly; (3) It must have regards to human rights, labour rights and social equality; (4) It must build upon an organizational value of being transparent and honest; (5) It recognizes its responsibility to support the development of trade and investment in the community of which the organization is a part. This includes developmental activities relating to the education, health and well-being of the people within the community; (6) Socially responsible activities should be undertaken in close relation to the organization's business with a high level of employee involvement; and in addition to the above, (7) companies might make donations to the community in order to help create good corporate relations (Phaithoon 2007). Although the concept of CSR provided by the Thaipat Institute is broad in bringing together resources from within and beyond the organization, the TBCSD's concept of CSR indicates more specifically that companies should give priority to CSR activities that are closely associated with the actual processes of the business. Nonetheless, like the Thaipat Institute, the director of the TBCSD states that

'responsible business does not simply mean donations to the community or a communication process designed to create corporate good image. … [Rather CSR] needs to be understood and articulated from the top management team right across the broad spectrum of people working in the organization to help build the capacity of the community to improve its way of living and allow sustainable development … because in order for the business sector to survive, community, society and the environment need to survive as well'.

(Boonyakit 2007:33)

The significance of CSR in Thailand has been further enhanced by the establishment of the Corporate Social Responsibility Institute (CSRI) in 2007, under the auspices of the Securities and Exchange Commission, a regulatory body of the capital market in Thailand (*Phujudkarnraiwan* 22 March 2007; *Phujudkarnraiwan*

3 September 2007). Essentially, the CSRI supports socially responsible business practice in the private sector. It organizes activities that promote the knowledge and understanding of CSR in general. More specifically, the CSRI is a centre which disseminates the importance of CSR by encouraging business conduct with a high regard for social stakeholders' needs and the environment. The director of the Stock Exchange of Thailand stated in 2007 that 'social responsibility is a very important issue at present because it provides support for business to grow more strongly by enhancing the value-added of companies' (*Phujudkarnraiwan* 22 March 2007:30). From the point of view of the Stock Exchange of Thailand, CSR was initially significant in the current business climate as a result of the fact that it can be deployed to facilitate long-term business profitability and stability. However, following the establishment of the CSRI and in order to provide listed (as well as any interested non-listed) companies with CSR guidelines, the Corporate Social Responsibility Charter (CSRC) was subsequently introduced in 2007 by the CSRI. Under this Charter, the conceptualization of CSR was substantially broadened as:

> a contractual agreement with which corporations must comply with great care and consideration, good governance, and ethics. It aims at engendering sustainable growth with no negative impact. Moreover, corporations must also carry out socially and environmentally-related activities to enhance the people's standard of living, the community and society in general, and the environment. The contractual agreement should include internal and external stakeholders, namely shareholders, investors, chairpersons, managers, employees, workers and other people who may be affected by the company's activities, as well as those concerned about the environment. The ultimate aim is to improve the general well-being of society with monetary or non-monetary contributions which will create value-added and sustainable success to the company.
>
> (*Prachachadthurakit* 30 April 2007:42)

Overall, CSR, as defined by these three prominent Thai organizations, has come to a broad consensus that ethical and responsible business practice should encompass the needs of internal and external stakeholders with an aim of enhancing the social, economic and environmental well-being of these stakeholders whether they are directly (inside) or indirectly (outside) related to the organization. The main aim of CSR in the Thai context has therefore become the achievement of broad-based sustainable development for Thailand in social, environmental and economic terms, while at the same time allowing business to profit ethically from the socio-economic stability that such sustainable development brings. Longer-term emphases on a 'sufficiency economy' and the consequences of the 1997 financial crisis in many ways rendered Thailand fertile ground for the growth of this ostensibly imported but ultimately context specific conceptualization of CSR.

Implementation of CSR in Thai businesses: CSR as a good business strategy

Generally speaking, although conceptual awareness of CSR has been augmenting, the actual practice of it in Thailand among individual companies remains limited (Polkuamdee 2004). At present, CSR appears to remain largely associated with the donation of scholarships for education and sponsorship of sporting events, all of which are aimed at stakeholders outside the company. This strand of CSR has been widely adopted in the past by large companies in such industries as cement, petroleum or mining, but can really only be considered as complementary to the elaboration of environmental protection policies. Although provision of such funds for various purposes no doubt helps the needy to some degree, it is frequently argued that CSR in practice should mean much more than just philanthropy (*Prachachadthurakit* 19 February 2007). Consistent with the TBCSD's concept of CSR, meaningful CSR activities should embrace 'aspects of labor standards, community service, environment and good governance or accountability, ... (and) ... should form a core policy of the individual company. It must not be just paying lip service' (Kuntiranont 2004:O1).

As the broader Thai public and consumers have also begun to realize that economic performance should no longer be the sole measure of business success, companies in recent years have had to take wider social and environmental issues into consideration in their business strategy. On the one hand, some chief executives profess genuine concern about CSR, which is an integral part of good corporate governance policy and is therefore discussed at the board level (Rojanaphruk 2004a, 2004b). On the other hand, however, CSR has also become an effective marketing manoeuvre designed by companies to gain a competitive advantage and often deployed simply as a public relations exercise (Jitmongkol 2007). Regardless of the claim by some executives that it is conscience that drives CSR practice in their company (Rojanaphruk 2004a, 2004b), there has been some scepticism about the way CSR has been deployed in the Thai private sector, particularly in relation to its apparent use as a means of creating a good corporate public image. In this respect, the chief executive officer of a leading Thai bank expressed his view that 'listed companies are becoming increasingly concerned about CSR, but their activities focus ... more on public relations to build up their corporate image' (Parnsoonthorn and Chudasri 2007:B2; see also Prawee 2008). Whatever the mixed motivation behind the implementation of CSR, companies over the last few years have nonetheless become more explicit about their CSR policies and have come to regard CSR as a necessary 'modern' management strategy.[8]

Due to the growing public profile of CSR and the benefit to brand names that CSR engenders, many companies have in the last few years publicly declared their overall CSR activities. Some have claimed that CSR is a well-established policy that has been embedded in their wider business values and strategy for more than 10 years, including Bangchak (Limsamarnphun 2006), Merck (*Phujudkarnraisabda* 29 October 2007), Siam Cement Group (Niratpattanasai 2007b:B2), and Nestle (Thailand) (Chiangnoi 2007a:24, 2007b; Jiamrodjananont 2007; *Prachachadthurakit* 12 March

2007). Some, like the Mitrphol Sugar Group, have argued that CSR has been its committed corporate policy for over 50 years (*Prachachadthurakit* 22 October 2007:37). In order to emphasize that their business activities reflect the overall concept of CSR defined by TBCSD, the Mitrphol Sugar Group's management has stated in a newspaper interview that its main concern has always been the proper utilization of natural materials and business conduct that is friendly to the environment. In particular, this includes environmental management of sugar-cane production, environmentally friendly sugar-cane harvesting, the reduction of the usage of fertilizers and chemicals on farms and management of other social and environmental issues in their factories (*Prachachadthurakit* 22 October 2007:38). With this concern in mind, the company works very closely with local farmers in order to provide them with up-to-date knowledge and modern technology to help them improve productivity. This type of CSR is known in Thailand as CSR in-process and is contrasted with CSR after-process by means of scholarships, sponsorships and community donations. As CSR after-process is often a retrospective and remedial process that is frequently used as an attempt at corporate image management, CSR in-process emphasizes preventative measures integral to the production and operational processes to ensure that products and services create zero or minimal detrimental impact on employees, the environment and society at large.[9] CSR in-process is demonstrably of greater long-term value, although in public relations terms CSR after-process is much more effective as a marketing tool.

Similarly, Nestle's CSR in-process is based on their professed core value, namely 'being a part of society'. Its concern is to ensure that Nestle and local communities prosper hand in hand with good standards of living for the people in the surrounding community (Jiamrodjananont 2007:34). As Nestle's business is based on agricultural products, like the Mitrphol Sugar Group, Nestle has also worked together with local farmers, providing knowledge and technology to help improve the quality of the coffee beans that Nestle subsequently buys from them (Chiangnoi 2007b:24). This strategy is obviously to the advantage of Nestle, but also to some extent to the benefit of the farmers themselves. Moreover, it has been reported in the media that Nestle has taken serious environmental measures to improve the conditions of their factories, such as the recycling of water, making sure the water purifying system is properly operated and the waste from coffee production is recycled and used as compost (Chiangnoi 2007b). These two examples are indicative of how CSR in-process initiated by companies in Thailand can reflect the socio-economic and contextual needs of Thai society and the environment. Despite such efforts, however, social and environmental problems in Thailand remain significant and such measures represent the first steps in what might be done in broadening corporate social responsibility.

In addition to CSR in-process, both Mitrphol and Nestle also have CSR after-process programmes, which are detached from their main corporate business operations and reach out to wider groups of people in the community. These include the 'School of My Dreams' project, the provision of mobile medical units and a programme set up to help young people with drug problems (*Prachachadthurakit* 12 March 2007; 22 October 2007). Thus, these two companies implement both

CSR in-process and after-process in order to ensure that their business activities are sustainable in the sense that they are worker-friendly, environmentally efficient and community-empowering. When CSR in-process and after-process are undertaken systematically alongside each other, CSR activity can be rendered beneficial to even wider groups of stakeholders who are both directly and indirectly associated with the organization.

At present, the general trend among companies in Thailand is still to engage in CSR after-process. Nevertheless, CSR in Thailand seems to be moving gradually from philanthropic donations, which have been the main form of corporate social responsibility in Thailand for decades (*Prachachadthurakit* 27 June 2005), towards wider developmental projects, such as the establishment of schools or provision of school equipment in the provinces outside Bangkok (Asawanipont, 2006). In mining, oil, chemical and cement industries such projects have also begun to take the form of environmental collaboration with local communities through refor-estation and conservation programs (Thongrung 2006b; Chanasongkram 2006; Ongdee 2006). These forms of CSR, though requiring greater commitment and longer-term investment, still allow contributors more flexibility, since they appear to demand less long-term planning, are less expensive and can be discontinued if the financial situation of the companies does not permit such programmes in the future. Ultimately, amid the increasing popularity of CSR in Thailand, it is likely to be CSR in-process that will bring the most benefit in terms of sustainable develop-ment to the Thai population and business enterprise alike.

CSR activities as a reflection of the social and environmental needs of Thailand

Overall, in the wake of the international business community's concern over CSR issues, companies in Thailand have begun to adopt and pay more attention to their wider corporate social and environmental responsibility as part of a wider debate on sustainable development. The question increasingly asked of companies is not simply whether the company is profitable, but also how the profits are actually made and at whose expense. Some companies may have implemented measures that would render their production process more socially and environmentally friendly, others have continued to focus on making philanthropic contributions, and a few have simply deployed CSR as a business strategy for marketing purposes. Many more have yet to address the issue of CSR or have been selective in its imple-mentation. A main dilemma of Thai proponents of CSR pertains to the question of selectivity, namely how companies, which might donate a considerable sum to CSR after-process but employ child labour or pollute the river, can be regarded as 'responsible' (Yuraprathom 2006; Thongthanakul 2007a; 2007b, see also *Matichon* 12 October 2006). It has been voiced that CSR should not simply represent a set of partially fulfilled good intentions, but companies should demonstrate their full commitment, with long-term objectives, goals, strategies and accountabilities (Ekvitthayavechnukul 2006). A meaningful and well-integrated CSR policy should ensure that companies are not selective in their CSR contribution, and disclosure of their policies and achievements should be used to enhance transparency and accountability in the practice of corporate social responsibility. In this respect, CSR in Thailand still needs to be more effectively implemented and regulated with regard to the environmentally friendly nature of the corporate production process and in ensuring that internal stakeholders, such as workers and employees, are suitably treated in terms of pay, adequate facilities, equal male-female opportunities, childcare provision and safe working conditions. The limited nature of general or company-specific information on these fundamental issues of CSR indicates that companies are not as candid in these areas as they are in informing the public of their long-term CSR in-process commitments or their after-process CSR projects. On this basis, therefore, CSR activities as implemented by companies in Thailand still at best only partially respond to or reflect the social and environmental needs of Thai society.

Moreover, in 2010, ISO 26000 will be formally adopted by Thailand as an internationally accepted guideline for CSR practice. Notwithstanding the increased attention and publicity given to CSR in Thailand, a survey has shown that there are only a few multinational companies that have so far put in place CSR mechanisms that approximate to the recommendation of ISO 26000 (*Prachachadthurakit* 10–12 March 2008a). This could indicate that the adoption of ISO 26000 will not have the desired effect of bringing about beneficial change in the way companies conduct their business as many CSR advocates in Thailand might have hoped. According to the latest draft of ISO 26000, the public sector, manufacturers and business operators are encouraged to be socially responsible in terms of (1) organization governance, (2) human rights, (3) labour practices, (4) the environment, (5) fair operating practices, (6) consumer issues, and (7) contribution to the community and society (Arunmas 2007a; *Prachachadthurakit* 10–12 March 2008b). This guideline is doubtlessly useful as it provides future direction for organizations that wish to become more socially responsible, but the question clearly remains open as to the extent of corporate commitment to CSR in Thailand, however beneficial it is to the country's sustainable development and business environment.

Future agenda: How might CSR be improved in Thailand?

Ekvitthayavechnukul (2006) has appropriately suggested that for CSR to be successfully implemented, it is essential that organizations have long-term objectives, goals and strategies concerning CSR, which are set at the board or governance level. Corporate governance is regarded by the chief executive officer of a leading bank in Thailand as 'the key to ... [organizations] having responsibility to society and shareholders' (Parnsoonthorn and Chudasri 2007:B2). The significance of corporate governance to the development of CSR is further elaborated by the ex-Prime Minister of Thailand, Khun Anand Panyarachun, a founding member and currently president of TBCSD:

> Corporate governance is a multi-faceted subject ... [which] ... deals with issues of accountability and fiduciary duty. It is the set of processes and policies by

which companies are directed and controlled. ... Governance applies to everything; it applies to production, it applies to mindset, it applies to the business culture of that company, and of course it applies to the boardroom. ... Parallel to governance, ... [there is] ... corporate social responsibility, a concept that encourages companies to consider the interests of society. The two elements of corporate governance and corporate social responsibility are not directly connected, but ... [there is an] ... interaction between them. You cannot have a company that focuses only on corporate governance to the neglect of corporate social responsibility and vice versa. You cannot have a good company or a successful company focusing on corporate social responsibility and neglecting corporate governance. The two things go together; they run parallel with each other. ... There are some features of each that are similar, and the end goal is the same. This end goal is to be a responsible corporate citizen.

(Niratpattanasai 2007a: B2)

Undoubtedly, Khun Anand Panyarachun's model of governance represents an ideal framework where corporate governance and corporate social responsibility are developed alongside one another with the aim of responsible corporate citizenship in both financial and social terms. In reality, however, some companies, especially those listed on the Stock Exchange of Thailand, include corporate governance in their organizational structure in the absence of an equivalent requirement for CSR governance, but few companies have integrated CSR into their governance mechanisms. In addition to having good corporate governance, moreover, it is suggested by a chief executive officer of a leading Thai bank that a further key to creating responsibility to society as well as shareholders lies in the disclosure of accurate and timely information (Parnsoonthorn and Chudasri 2007: B2). Without disclosure of information, it would be very difficult to assess the performance and achievements of organizations in social and environmental terms. At present, social and environmental reporting is voluntary, and unlike financial information, there is no legal framework that obliges companies to report their corporate social and environmental responsibility information.[10] In the absence of such a framework, reporting of social and environmental issues among Thai companies lacks direction and the detailed information necessary to facilitate assessment of corporate social and environmental achievements (Kuasirikun and Sherer 2004; Kuasirikun 2005).

Overall, perceptions of CSR among businesses in Thailand have been positive. Even though certain indigenous forms of CSR have to some degree existed for some time, pressure from international trade has been an important stimulus in leading companies to conduct their business in more socially and environmentally responsible ways. At present, however, there is no universally accepted definition of CSR, although ideas of a 'sufficiency economy', the importance of local community and wider environmental sustainability have become the underpinning premises of the conceptualization of CSR in Thailand. Although CSR in its present forms appears to be influenced by concepts imported from the West, both CSR in-process and after-process activities in Thailand have essentially been initiated with the aim of promoting the indigenous socio-cultural and environmental needs of Thai society. The implementation of CSR nonetheless varies from company to company. Some companies have long established CSR in-process as well as more traditional after-process activities, while some opportunist companies have tended to employ CSR as a means of developing customer relations with the community and promoting corporate and brand image. Overall positive perceptions towards CSR and the varying attempts made by companies to implement CSR activities, however, have created a platform from which one can view with optimism the future development of CSR in Thailand in the years to come. Measures now need to be taken to ensure that CSR policies are discussed and incorporated as part of corporate strategy at the board level in terms of how companies are going to ensure that their profit-making process is socially, environmentally and community friendly. In order to facilitate an assessment of corporate CSR, there also needs to be a reporting mechanism which makes companies' CSR activities visible in terms of CSR objectives, targets and achievements in quantitative and/or qualitative forms. In the final analysis, only by making CSR information publicly accessible and formally assessable, can CSR practice avoid being used as a 'branding' exercise, and thereby, allow it to contribute to the sustainable development agenda for Thai business and society within which it has been conceptualized by its growing number of Thai proponents.

Suggested Further Reading

Christmann, P. (2004) 'Multinational Companies and the Natural Environment: Determinants of Global Policy Standardization'. *The Academy of Management Journal*, 47(5): 747–60.

Dahlsrud, A. (2006) 'How Corporate Social Responsibility is Defined: An Analysis of 37 Definitions'. *Corporate Social Responsibility and Environmental Management*, 15(1): 1–13.

Dunning, J. H. (2003) *Making Globalization Good: The Moral Challenges of Global Capitalism*. Oxford: Oxford University Press.

Forsyth, T. (2005) 'Enhancing Climate Technology Transfer Through Greater Public-Private Cooperation: Lessons from Thailand and the Philippines'. *Natural Resource Forum*, 29(2): 165–76.

Frost, S. and H. Ho. (2005) '"Going Out": The Growth of Chinese Foreign Direct Investment in Southeast Asia and its Implications for Corporate Social esponsibility'. *Corporate Social Responsibility and Environmental Management*, 12: 157–67.

Phongpaichit, P. and C. Baker. (1996) *Thailand's Boom!*. Chiang Mai: Silkworm Books.

Notes

1 The term CSR adopted in this chapter covers both social and environmental aspects of company activities and is therefore used interchangeably with corporate social and environmental responsibility.

2 Numerous examples of smaller scale accidents can be found in the Thai press. See, for example, *Matichon*, 2 December 2003 'Scaffolding Fell on Top of Workers, Many Injured'; *Phujudkarn*, 30 November 2004 'Furniture Factory Exploded, 3 Workers

Injured'; *Daily News*, 2 April 2005 'Gas Factory in Samudsakorn Exploded, Workers Hurt'; *Phujudkarn*, 26 July 2005 'Glove Factory in Hadyai Exploded, 7 Workers Injured'; *Komchadluek*, 1 March 2006 'Gas Factory Exploded in the Middle of Meaung Paknam'; *Phujudkarnraiwan*, 29 August 2006 'From "the Kliti Case" to the Investigation of Occupational Illness'.

3 Environmental problems are often reported in the Thai press. See, for example, *Post Today*, 16 October 2007 'Prime Minster Urged to Solve the Effects of Noise Pollution'; *Phujudkarn*, 16 October 2007 'Human Rights Committee Suggests Ways to Solve Noise Pollution at Suwannaphume Airport'; *Krungthepthurakit*, 18 March 2008 'Chakkramon Orders an Inspection of Factories with Pollution Risks'; *Banmeaung*, 18 March 2008 'Mayor of Mahachai Indicates Factories Are the Culprits in Causing Pollution as They Do Not Cooperate'; *Phujudkarn-online*, 20 March 2008 'Survey Shows Water Pollution Crisis 60% of the Bangkok Population Residing Near Factories Live with "Polluted Water"'; *Bangkok Today*, 27 March 2008 'Quality of Life in Rural Area'; *Siamrad*, 2 April 2008 'NGOs Demands that Prime Minister Assess the Environment'; *Post Today*, 2 April 2008 '*Mabtaphud* Not Wanted'; *Daily News*, 3 April 2008 'Pointing Out How Pollution Affects Town Development'; *Daily News*, 5 April 2008 'Water Crisis Life Crisis'; *Kaosod*, 9 April 2008 'An Easy Way for the Community to Monitor Environmental Quality'.

4 See also *Matichon*, 19 July 2005 'D-Day Investigate Pig Farms Polluting *Thachin*'; *Khomchudleauk*, 21 March 2007 'Inspection of 3 Industrial Factories in Angthong Needed to Determine the Cause of Polluted Water'; *Thansedthakit*, 30 September 2007 'Strict Control to Prohibit More Factories Being Built on the Chao Phraya River Bank'; *Kaosod*, 24 January 2008 'The Governor of Radburi Attempts to Solve the Polluted Water in Khlong Pradoo'; *Matichon*, 14 February 2008 'The Environment in Surin Is Reaching a \Critical Point as 10,000 Tons of Waste-Water Pollution Increases'; *Business Thai*, 29 February 2008 'The Mekhong River is Dying'; *Phimthai*, 17 March 2008 'The Governor of Samudsakhorn Points Out that Factories Are the Cause of Polluted Water, Foul Smell and Excessive Waste'; *Daily News*, 6 May 2008 'Strictly Regulated Waste Water Released from Factories into the Chao Phraya River'.

5 The cities along the Chao Phraya river are Nakhonsawan, Uthaithani, Chainat, Singburi, Angthong, Ayutthaya, Pathumthani, Nonthaburi, Bangkok and Samutprakan.

6 The Thaipat Institute is an affiliated organization of the Foundation for Thailand Rural Reconstruction Movement under Royal Patronage (TRRM). The Thaipat Institute was founded by a group of business people whose aim was to improve the social well-being of Thai society and promote corporate social responsibility in the private sector.

7 The Thailand Business Council for Sustainable Development (TBCSD) was established in November 1993. The objective of the TBCSD is to promote environmental awareness within the business sector under the concept of 'sustainable development'. Its current memberships constituted by business leaders from 28 companies both Thai and multinational (http://www.tei.or.th/tbcsd/about_tbcsd/index.html).

8 See, for example, *Phujudkarnraisabda*, 5 November 2007 'Catch Up with Modern Management "*Sermsuk*" Speeds Up to Prove Its CSR Direction'; *Prachachadthurakit*, 20 March 2006 'Creating Brand with CSR'; *Prachachadthurakit*, 28 May 2007 '"Good Citizen" D-Tec Introduces a Jigsaw to Build a Brand with a Difference'; *Prachachadthurakit*, 17 December 2007 'Building the "Good Citizen" Brand: A New Strategy by "RS" Managing Risks for "Artists"'; *Siam Thurakit*, 23 August 2007 'Branching Out with CSR: Stimulate Purchasing Demand/Brand Loyalty'; *Thansedthakit*, 11 October 2007 'Honda Hopes to Be "Brand-Liked by Thai People"'.

9 See, for example, *Prachachadthurakit*, 7 August 2006 'Successful "Thai Style CSR" Begins with Good Spirit … and Strategy'; *Prachachadthurakit*, 16 January 2006 'How to Distinguish Real from Fake CSR'.

10 Australia and Norway are the only two countries that have integrated the requirement of environmental information into corporate law. Bubna-Litic's (2006) study has

demonstrated that this mandatory environmental reporting requirement has improved disclosure of environmental information in companies operating in these countries.

References

English sources:

Aguilera, R., D. Rupp, C. Williams and J. Ganapathi. (2007) 'Putting the S Back in CSR: A Multi-level Theory of Social Change in Organizations'. *Academy of Management Review*, 32(3): 836–63.

Bansal, P. and K. Roth. (2000) 'Why Companies Go Green: A Model of Ecological Responsiveness'. *Academy of Management Journal*, 43(4): 717–36.

Baughn, C. C., N. L. Bodie and J. C. McIntosh. (2007) 'Corporate Social and Environmental Responsibility in Asian Countries and Other Geographical Regions'. *Corporate Social Responsibility and Environmental Management*, 14: 189–205.

Buchholz, R.A. (1991) 'Corporate Responsibility and the Good Society: From Economics to Ecology'. *Business Horizons*, July/August. 34(4): 19–31.

Bubna-Litic, K. (2006) 'Forcing Corporations to Be Better Environmental Citizen: Does it Really Work? In R. Welford, P. Hills and W. Young, *Partnerships for Sustainable Development: Perspectives from the Asia-Pacific Region.* Hong Kong: University of Hong Kong.

Campbell, J. (2007) 'Why Would Corporations Behave in Socially Responsible ways? An Institutional Theory of Corporate Social Responsibility'. *Academy of Management Review*, 32(3): 946–67.

Chapple, W. and J. Moon. (2007) 'Introduction: CSR Agendas for Asia'. *Corporate Social Responsibility and Environmental Management*, 14: 183–88.

Demirag, I, (2005) *Corporate Social Responsibility, Accountability and Governance Global Perspectives.* Greenleaf Publishing.

Dixon, C. (1999) *The Thai Economy: Uneven Development and Internationalisation.* Routledge: London.

Dunn, C. P. (1991) 'Are Corporations Inherently Wicked?'. *Business Horizons*, July/August. 34(4): 3–8.

Engle, R. L. (2007) 'Corporate Social Responsibility in Host Countries: A Perspective from American Managers'. *Corporate Social Responsibility and Environmental Management*, 14: 16–27.

Frost, S. (2006) 'CSR Asia News Review: April-June'. *Corporate Social Responsibility and Environmental Management*, 13: 238–44.

Henriques, A. (2007) *Corporate Truth: The Limit to Transparency.* London: Earthscan.

Klonoski, R. J. (1991) 'Foundational Considerations in the Corporate Social Responsibility Debate'. *Business Horizons*, July/August. 34(4): 9–18.

Komin, S. (1989) *Social Dimensions of Industrialisation of Thailand.* Bangkok: National Institute of Development Administration (NIDA).

Kuasirikun, N. and M. Sherer. (2004) 'Corporate Social Accounting Disclosure in Thailand'. *Accounting Auditing and Accountability Journal*, 17(4): 629–60.

Kuasirikun, N. (2005) 'Attitudes to the Development and Implementation of Social and Environmental Accounting in Thailand'. *Critical Perspectives on Accounting*, 16: 1035–57.

Lyon, D. (2004) 'How Can You Help Organizations Change to Meet the Corporate

Responsibility Agenda?'. *Corporate Social Responsibility and Environmental Management*, 11: 133–39.

Maximiano, J. M. B. (2007) 'A Strategic Integral Approach (SIA) to Institutionalizing CSR'. *Corporate Social Responsibility and Environmental Management*, 14: 231–42.

Phongpaichit, P. and C. Baker. (1996) *Thailand's Boom!*. Chiang Mai: Silkworm Books.

Strike, V., J. Gao and P. Bansal. (2006) 'Being Good While Being Bad: Social Responsibility and the International Diversification of US Firms'. *Journal of International Business Studies*, 37(6): 850–62.

Welford, R (2004) 'Corporate Social Responsibility in Europe and Asia: Critical Elements and Best Practice'. *Journal of Corporate Citizenship*, 13: 31–47.

Welford, R. (2007) 'Corporate Governance and Corporate Social Responsibility: Issues for Asia'. *Corporate Social Responsibility and Environmental Management*, 14: 42:51.

Welford, R. and S. Frost. (2006) 'Corporate Social Responsibility in Asian Supply Chains'. *Corporate Social Responsibility and Environmental Management*, 13: 166–76.

Thai sources

Department of Labour Protection and Welfare (1998–2007). *Yearbook of Labor Protection and Welfare Statistics*. Bangkok: Labour Standard Development Bureau, Department of Labour Protection and Welfare.

National Statistics Office (2006) *Survey of the Social and Economic Situation in Households*. Bangkok.

Office of the National Economic and Social Development Board (NESDB) (2008) *Economic Outlook Thai Economic Performance in Q4/2007 and Outlook for 2008*. Bangkok: NESDB.

Yodprudtikan, P., V. Preeyapant, S. Charoenngam, S. Trivithayanurak, S. Shrestha, K. Angkularad, P. Chansa, R. Yangprayong, J. Junson, P. Sophontanased and P. Laitae. (2006) *CSR Development in the Business Process: Phase 1: the Study of Attributes, Components and Tools for Development*. Bangkok: Thaipat Institute.

Wilawan, K. and S. Lengthaisong. (1998) *The Essence of the Labor Protection Act of 1998*. Bangkok: Thammasarn Co. Ltd.

Wichianchom, W. (1999), *The Labor Protection Act 1998*. Bangkok: Winyuchon Publishing Co. Ltd.

World Bank Thailand Office (2003–8) *Thailand Economic Monitor*. Bangkok: World Bank Thailand Office.

Newspapers (Thai):

Bangkokkian (2007) 'Phalung CSR juudpleanthodsawat' (The Power of CSR in the Changing Decades). *Matichon*, 6 June: 34.

Bangkok Today (2008) 'Khunnaphabcheewitthongthin' (Quality of Life in Rural areas). *Bangkok Today*, 27 March.

Banmeaung (2008) 'PhormeaungMahachai raburongngantuadee hedsangmollaphid cheemai ruammeau' (Mayor of Mahachai Indicates Factories Are the Culprits in Causing Pollution as They Do Not Cooperate). *Banmeaung*, 18 March.

Boonyakit, C. (2007) 'Kledlub 4 prakarn tham CSR haisumred' (Four Secrets to Successful CSR). *Prachachadthurakit*, 13 August: 33.

Business Thai (2008) 'Maenam *Khong* jahsinlom ...!' (The Mekhong River is Dying). *Business Thai*, 29 February.

Chanchaochai, D. (2007) 'CSR thideereamtonthiphainai (ton 1)' (Good CSR Begins Inside (Part 1))'. *Thansedthakit*, 28 June: 22.

Chiangnoi, N. (2007a) 'CSR bab Nestle win win bab mejitsumneukpheasungkhom (1)' (CSR Nestle's Style: Win Win With Social Conscience Responsibility (1)). *Thansedthakit*, 2 August: 24.

—— (2007b) 'CSR bab Nestle win win bab mejitsumneukpheasungkhom (jop) (CSR Nestle's Style: Win Win With Social Responsibility (End)). *Thansedthakit*, 5 August: 24.

Daily News (2005) 'ro. ngo. Gas Samudsakhorn rabeudkhonnganjeb' (Gas Factory in Samudsakorn Exploded, Workers Hurt). *Daily News*, 2 April.

—— (2008) 'Cheephawahmollaphidkrathobphutthanameaung' (Pointing Out How Pollution Affects Town Development). *Daily News*, 3 April.

—— (2008) '"Wikritnam Wiklitcheewit" boklaopanhamollaphidthangnam' ("Water Crisis, Life Crisis": Narrating Water Pollution). *Daily News*, 5 April.

—— (2008) 'Khumkhemthaenamsea ro.ngo. longmeanam *Chao Phraya*' (Strictly Regulated Waste Water Released from Factories into the Chao Phraya river). *Daily News*, 6 May.

Jaihao, D. (2006) '"Pho.Ro.Bo. sathabunkhwamplodphai" khonngan 10 pee hengkarn torsooyungrairongroy' ("Safety Institute Legislation" for Labour, 10 Years Fighting and Not Seeing Any Progress). *Krungthepthurakit*, 9 October.

Jareanled, W. (2006) 'Jaak "arayah" thangsedthakit soo "hayyanah" khonggangnganthai' (From "Civilized" Economy to "Destruction" of Thai Labour). *Phujudkarn online*, 1 May.

Jiamrodjananont, W. (2007) 'CSR "reabngai-daijai" (CSR "Simple and Meaningful"). *Krungthepthurakit*, 5 October: 34.

Jitmongkol, D. (2007) 'Konlayud "CSR" sangbrandhaiyungyeun' (CSR Strategy to Create Sustainable Brand). *Post Today*, 26 January: B4.

Kaosod (2008) 'Pho.Wo.Jo. Radburi rahdomkae namnaoklongpradoo' (The Governor of Radburi Attempts to Solve the Polluted Water in Klong Pradoo). *Kaosod*, 24 January, p. 26.

—— (2008) 'Karntidtamtraudsobkhunnaphabsingwedlomyangngaydoychumchon' (An Easy Way for the Community to Monitor Environmental Quality). *Kaosod*, 9 April.

Khomchadluek (2006) 'RongnganbunjugasklangmeaungPaknam rabeudthuukkhonngan jebsahud song' (Gas Factory Exploded in the Middle of Meaung Paknam, Two Workers Were Critically Injured). *Khomchadluek*, 1 March.

Khomchudleauk (2007) 'Truadrongnganudsahakam 3 rongAngthonghasahedprakobnamsea' (Inspection of 3 Industrial Factories in Angthong Needed to Determine the Cause of Polluted Water). *Khomchudleauk*, 21 March.

Krungthepthurakit (2006) '4 ongkornjudwetheesewwanaplukkrasae "CSR" (4 Organizations Arranged a Seminar to Promote CSR). *Krungthepthurakit*, 19 June: 39.

—— (2007) 'Krasuongrangngandun ko. mo. khumkhronglookjangying 17 lan' (Labour Department Pushes for Legislation to Protect 17 Million Female Employees). *Krungthepthurakit*, 9 March.

—— (2008) '"Jakmonthr" sungtruadrongnganseaungkormollaphid' (Chakkramon Orders an Inspection of Factories with Pollution Risks). *Krungthepthurakit*, 18 March.

Matichon, (1997), 'Rangngabying "Nawa Nakorn" yueakhongkwammaipenthamkhong kodmai rang-ngan' (Female Workers "Nawa Nakorn" Victims of Disadvantageous Act). *Matichon*, 27 March: 9.

—— (2003) 'Khronglekthalomthubkhonnganjebranow' (Scaffolding Fell on Top of Workers, Many Injured). *Matichon*, 2 December.

—— (2005) 'Dee-day traudfarmmootham "*Thanchin*" nao' (D-Day Investigate Pig Farms Polluting Thachin). *Matichon*, 19 July: 9.

—— (2006) 'TV phuudeechaetescochairangngandek borisudangsoblaewmaimeemoon' (English TV Accused Tesco of Child Labour Exploitation: After Investigation Tesco Found No Evidence and Rejected This Accusation). *Matichon*, 12 October: 20.

—— (2007) 'Klum anurukrongsanpokkrong jee ko.ko. singwedlomkhumMabtaphud' (The Conservative Group complains to the Administrative Court to push the *Mabtaphud* Environmental Committee), *Matichon*, 3 October: 9.

—— (2008) 'Singwedlom Surin khoakhunwiklit khayahwanlahmunton – namnaolam' (The Environment in Surin Is Reaching a Critical Point as 10,000 Tons of Waste-Water Pollution Increases). *Matichon*, 14 February: 9.

Naewna (2007) 'Sawaddikarntheechoybunthaopunhakarnchairangnganded (rainganphised)' (Welfare Department Helps Alleviate Child Labour Problem (Special Report)). *Naewna*, 9 August.

—— (2008) 'Khoopidrongnganmollaphid "*Suwit*" sung Ko.Ro.Ao. khumkhem–nen4 lumnamsamkhan' (Threaten to Close Down Factories Which Create Pollution: "*Suwit*" Orders the Department of Industrial Work to Strictly Monitor Factories Around 4 Important Rivers). *Naewna*, 15 February.

Phaithoon, A. (2007) 'CSR "Jubmaidai Laimaithun" (Chasing CSR)'.: <http://www.csrthai-center.com/csrwebsite/board/view.php?No = 6> (accessed 20 December 2007).

Phimthai (2008) 'Phoowa. Samudsakhorn chee rongngantonhedsangmollaphid namsea klin-men khayahlonmeaung' (The Governor of Samudsakhorn Points Out That Factories Are the Cause of Polluted Water, Foul Smell and Excessive Waste). *Phimthai*, 17 March.

—— (2008) 'KrasuongUtsahakamtidrabobtruadwadkhunnaphabnamuttanomud' (The Industry Department to Install an Automated Water Quality Monitoring System). *Phimthai*, 9 April.

Phongrai, J. (2008) 'Yonroy 1 pee monlaphitmabthaphud sukkhaphab singwedlommaime khamtob' (*Mabtaphud* Revisited 1 Year After: No Answers to Health and Environmental Problems). *Krungthepthurakit*, 2 January.

Phujudkarn (2004) 'Rongnganfurniturerabeudkhonnganjebthunthee 3 rai' (Furniture Factory Exploded, 3 Workers Injured). *Phujudkarn*, 30 November.

—— (2005) 'Rongngan phalidthungmeuyang Hadyai rabeud khonnganjeb 7 rai' (Glove Factory in Hadyai Exploded, 7 Workers Injured). *Phujudkarn*, 26 July.

—— (2007) 'Ko.ko. sitthimanudsayachon saneuneawthangthangkaekaimonlaphidseang Suwannaphume' (Human Rights Committee Suggests Ways to Solve Noise Pollution at Suwannaphume Airport). *Phujudkarn*, 16 October.

Phujudkarn-online (2008) 'Pholsamruadwikridsathankarnnam khonkrung banklairongn-gankwa 60 per cent chaicheewitkab "namnao"' (Survey Shows Water Pollution Crisis 60% of the Bangkok Population Residing Near Factories Live with "Polluted Water"). *Phujudkarn-online*, 20 March.

Phujudkarnraiwan (2006) 'Jaak "Khadee Kliti" thung "karnwinitchairokjakkarnthamngan"' (From "the Kliti Case" to the "Investigation of Occupational Illness"). *Phujudkarnraiwan*, 29 August.

Phujudkarnraisabda (2005) '"CSR" sungkomhengkarnhai karnjudkarnphanuaksang-phonkamrai' ("CSR" a Giving Community Combined Management to Create Profit). *Phujudkarnraisabda*, 27 June: D7, D8.

—— (2006) 'Peudneawthurakitpheausungkhom CSR thai sataifarung' (Open Business

Strategy for Society: Thai "CSR" in a Foreign Style). *Phujudkarnraisabda*, 20 November: D7, D8.

—— (2007) "'Merck" kohtid CSR nenlongngen-khrongkarntorneaung' (Merck Grips on CSR Emphasizing Investment-Continuity of Projects). *Phujudkarnraisabda*, 29 October: D1, D2.

—— (2007) 'Kohkrasaeborihanthunyuk "*Sermsuk*" rengphisoodsenthang CSR' (Catch Up with the Modern Management "*Sermsuk*" Speed Up to Prove Its CSR Direction). *Phujudkarnraisabda*, 5 November: D1, D2.

Phujudkarnraiwan (2007) 'TLT. Tungsathabunwijaipheautaladthun phromchoongan CSR tongteabtokhoo thurakit' (SEC Established SET Research Institute for Capital Market Emphasizing That CSR Must Grow Hand in Hand with Businesses). *Phujudkarnraiwan*, 22 March: 30.

—— (2007) 'CSR mungnasookhwamrubphidchobtosungkhom' (CSR: The Road to Social Responsibility). *Phujudkarnraiwan*, 3 September: 30.

Post Today (2007) 'Jeenayokkaepunhaphonkrathobthangseang' (Prime Minister Urged to Solve the Effects of Noise Pollution). *Post Today*, 16 October.

—— (2008) 'Khumkhem ro.ngo. ploynamsea' (Strictly Monitor Factories Which Release Polluted Water). *Post Today*, 14 February.

—— (2008) 'Maiaao*Mabtaphud*' (*Mabtaphud* Not Wanted). *Post Today*, 2 April.

Prachachadthurakit (2005) 'Thodrahud CSR "tonthun" reau "kamrai" khongongkorn' (Decoding CSR "Cost" or "Profit" of Organizations). *Prachachadthurakit*, 27 June: 50, 56.

—— (2005) 'Asian forum khrungthi 4 judphlu ... tham CSR babmeekonlayud' (4th Asian Forum Ignite ... CSR strategy). *Prachachadthurakit*, 19 September: 56.

—— (2006) 'CSR theam kap CSR thae dooyangrai' (How to Distinguish Real from Fake CSR). *Prachachadthurakit*, 16 January: 56.

—— (2006) 'Sangbrandduoy CSR' (Creating Brand with CSR). *Prachachadthurakit*, 20 March: 60.

—— (2006) 'Thodkrabuankarn CSR Banpoo "karnthumngen ... maidaisangsing deenai kwamroosuekkhon"' (Strip Banpoo's CSR Strategy: "Money Alone ... Does Not Create Good Feelings"). *Prachachadthurakit*, 26 June: 50.

—— (2006) 'Meau CSR klaypenpradenron' (When CSR Turns a Hot Topic). *Prachachadthurakit*, 24 July: 52.

—— (2006) 'Khonkhamtob "CSR sataithai" Healthy Society – Healthy Business' (In search of an Answer to a "Thai Style CSR" Healthy Society – Healthy Business). *Prachachadthurakit*, 31 July: 52.

—— (2006) 'Sookwamsumred "CSR sataithai" reamtonduoyjitwinyan ... thambabmee konlayud' (Successful "Thai Style CSR" Begins with Good Spirit ... and Strategy). *Prachachadthurakit*, 7 August: 48.

—— (2006) 'Yeanfungtawanorgmong CSR yeepun (jop) withiHonda ... jaakprudyasoo vision' (From an Eastern Perspective Looking at CSR in Japan (the eEnd): The Honda Way ... from Philosophy to Vision). *Prachachadthurakit*, 4 September: 52.

—— (2007) 'Maichaikhaeborijaakleawjopkan' CSR babchabub "Mead Johnson" ('Not Just One-Off Donations' CSR Mead Johnson Style). *Prachachadthurakit*, 19 February: 42.

—— (2007) 'Todrahud DNA "Nestle" phakrasaekrabuandarnsang CSR radubjitsamneuk (Decoding DNA "Nestle": Examining the Creation of CSR at Conscience Level). *Prachachadthurakit*, 12 March: 41, 42.

—— (2007) 'TLT. kickoff..kodbud CSR sangthurakitpheausungkhom' (SET Kicks Off

CSR Charter to Build Corporate Social Responsibility). *Prachachadthurakit*, 30 April: 41, 42.

—— (2007) '"Khondee" D-Tec torphabsangbrandthitektang' ("Good Citizen" D-Tec Introduces a Jigsaw to Build a Brand with a Difference) *Prachachadthurakit*, 28 May: 41, 42.

—— (2007) 'CSR sataithaithithooktongmohsom' (Appropriate Thai Style CSR). *Prachachadthurakit*, 23 July: 41, 42.

—— (2007) '"*Mitrphol*" CSR babthaithai bundaisoo "ongkornnawattakam" ("*Mitrphol*" Thai Style to Create an "Innovative Organization"). *Prachachadthurakit*, 22 October: 37, 38.

—— (2007) 'Sangbrand "khondee" soodmai "RS" borihankhwamsseaung "sinlapin" (Building the "Good Citizen" Brand: A New Strategy by "RS" Managing Risks for "Artists"). *Prachachadthurakit*, 17 December: 37, 38.

—— (2008) 'CSR in Movement', *Prachachadthurakit*, 28–30 April:32.

—— (2008a) 'Nubthoylangrubmeau "ISO 26000 "rabeudwela" lookmaikhong thurakit-thai' (Count Down to Adaptation of ISO 26000 New "Time Bomb" for Thai Business). *Prachachadthurakit*, 10–12 March: 33.

—— (2008b) 'Updaterang ISO 26000 chabublasud' (Update: Latest Version of ISO 26000). *Prachachadthurakit*, 10–12 March: 33.

Prawee (2008) 'Khodee 8 prakarnkhongkarntham CSR' (Eight Advantageous Points of CSR Practice), *Thai Post*, 9 January.

Sangrudsameekul, K. (2008a) 'Mapleankhayah … haipenprayodkandeekwa!' (Let's Convert Waste into Something Useful!). *Banmeaung*, 18 April.

—— (2008b) 'MaruamkankeunkwamsodsaihaimaenamChaoPrayakandeekwa!', (Let's Do Something to Revive the Chao Praya River!). *Banmeaung*, 2 May.

Senanuch, S. (2007) 'CSR bab thai thai: rawangkarnhailaekwamrubphidchob' (Thai Style CSR: Between Giving and Responsibility). *Prachachadthurakit*, 23 July: 42.

Siamrad (2008) '"NGO" jeeNayok pramensingwedlom' ("NGOs" Demands that Prime Minster Assess the Environment). *Siamrad*, 2 April.

Siam Thurakit (2007) 'Teknhortoryod CSR: plukdemandsea/phukdeebrandsinkha' (Branching Out with CSR: Stimulate Purchasing Demand/Brand Loyalty). *Siam Thurakit*, 23 August: 29, 30.

Thansedthakit (2007) 'Khumkhemhamtung ro.ngo. rim *Chao Phraya*' (Strict Control to Prohibit More Factories Being Built on the Chao Phraya River Bank). *Thansedthakit*, 30 September.

—— (2007) 'Hondawangkheunthan "brandthikhonthaichob"' (Honda Hopes to Be "Brand-Liked by Thai people"). *Thansedthakit*, 11 October: 55, 56.

—— (2008) 'Rudkhoopid 41 borisudkamjudkhonsea' (Government Threatens to Shut 41 Factories Because of the Nature their Industrial Waste Management). *Thansedthakit*, 3 April.

Thongthanakul, S. (2007a) 'CSR babphopheang' (Sufficiency CSR). *Phujudkarnraisabda*, 30 July: D1, D2.

—— (2007b) 'CSR Focus CSR maichaikhae "thambun"' (CSR Focus: CSR Is Not Just for "Merit"). *Phujudkarnraisabda*, 7 May: D5.

Yodprudtikan, P. (2008) 'Krasaebansadboriban (CSR) pe-nuu' (The CSR Trend in the Year of the Rat). *Krungthepthurakit*, 8 January.

Yuraprothom, A. (2006) 'Khokhorahakhong CSR' (Criticisms of CSR). *Prachachadthurakit*, 16 October: 48.

Newspapers (English):

Arunmas, P. (2007a) 'Exporters Must Boost Quality: New Standards Focus on Labour Rights'. *Bangkok Post*, Business Section, 13 June: B3.
—— (2007b) 'Trade Barriers to Cost 5000 Jobs'. *Bangkok Post*, Business Section, 22 August: B3.
Asawanipont, N. (2006) 'Amway Looks More to Health'. *The Nation*, Business Section, 7 November.
Chanasongkram, K. (2006) 'Maroot Mrigadat Talks About Helming an International Oil Company, Super Mods and the Importance of Forest Preservation in Thailand'. *Bangkok Post*, Real Time Section, 18 August: R15.
Chitsomboon, P. (2005) 'Every Corporation Has a Social Duty: Community Values Matter to Investors'. *Bangkok Post*, Business Section, 7 June: B2.
—— (2006a) 'Businesses Need More CSR'. *Bangkok Post*, Business Section, 1 July: B8.
—— (2006b) 'Ethics Make Good Business Sense. Firms Urged to Apply Sufficiency Principles'. *Bangkok Post*, Business Section, 26 July: B3.
Ekvitthayavechnukul, C. (2006) 'More Are Opting for Social Responsibility'. *The Nation*, 28 August: B2.
Fukui, M. (1999) 'Consumers Baulk at Sweatshop Goods, Factories Warned About Labour'. *The Nation*, Business Section, 22 November: 2.
Kuntiranont, W. (2004) 'Encouraging Big Business to Be More Socially Responsible Will Yield Many Benefits to Both Consumers and Society at Large – and Even the Companies Themselves'. *Bangkok Post*, Outlook Section, 4 November: O1.
Lancaster, I. (2004) 'CSR Is Here to Stay'. *Bangkok Post*, Business Section, 2 September, p. B3.
Limsamarnphun, N. (2006) 'Born Responsible: Anusorn Sangnimnuan says Bangchak Has Been Looking After Its Neighbours Since the Company Was Founded Back in 1985'. 24 September: 7.
Niratpattanasaim K. (2007a) 'The Role of Corporate Responsibility in Thailand'. *Bangkok Post*, 3 September: B2.
Niratpattanasai, K. (2007b) 'Recipe for Success at SCG'. *Bangkok Post*, 17 September: B2.
Ongdee, S. (2006) 'Banpu Sets Up an Environmental Rehab Fund'. *The Nation*, Business Section, 4 December: 3.
Parnsoonthorn, K. and D. Chudasri. (2007) 'Social Responsibility Must Be a Priority: CSR Is More ThanJ a Public-Relations Effort'. *Bangkok Post*, Business Section, 25 September: B2.
Polkuamdee, N. (2004) 'Social Responsibility Now Essential' *Bangkok Post*, Business Section, 30 October: B2.
Rojanaphruk, P. (2004a) 'Top Jeweler Aims for More Caring Society'. *The Nation*, Business Section, 7 July: 3.
—— (2004b) 'Corporations Embrace Good Citizenship'. *The Nation*, Business Section, 2 August: 1.
Thapanachai, S. (2002) 'Accountability Essential'. *Bangkok Post*, Business Section, 16 November: B1.
The Nation (2004) 'Corporate Social Responsibility Talk'. *The Nation*, Main Section, 21 October: 2.
Thongrung, W. (2002) 'Attitude Change Is Needed'. *The Nation*, Business Section, 16 November: 2.

—— (2006a) 'CSR Is the New Social Mantra'. *The Nation*, Business Section, 12 July: 4.
—— (2006b) 'Chevron Extends a Green Hand to Local Communities'. *The Nation*, Business Section, 7 August: 2.

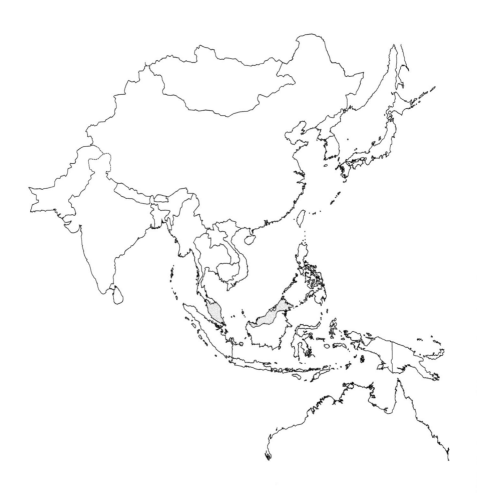

4 A multilevel assessment of corporate social responsibility disclosure in Malaysia

Roszaini Haniffa and Mohammad Hudaib

Introduction

The corporation's goal of generating wealth alone has increasingly been contested over the years, with growing recognition that corporations have broader social responsibilities. Corporate social responsibility (CSR), which is defined as 'the art of doing well by doing good' (*The Economist*, 2005) or 'the way in which a company's operating practices (policies, processes, and procedures) affect its stakeholders and the natural environment' (Waddock and Bodwell, 2004: 25), is a fast-growing concept embraced by corporations. The requirement to balance the needs and concerns of all those who impact or are impacted by the corporation's actions and performance, both in the short and longer term, is becoming an integral part of their business strategy to survive in an ever increasing competitive business world.

Engaging in CSR has been recognized as important in building favourable relations with the investment community, improving access to capital, enhancing relationships with employees and communities and strengthening reputation and branding. Hence, it is not surprising to find the number of corporations engaging in and communicating on their CSR initiatives and activities is on the increase. Various media are used for the purpose and over time, the extent and quality of corporate social and environmental disclosure (CSED) varies and the divergence across industries and countries may be attributed to the degree of internal and external pressures. Hence, an inquiry into the various internal and external pressures or factors affecting CSED is necessary to enhance our understanding on corporate's accountability management strategy. Our model addresses an important gap in the literature by incorporating internal factors at the micro (individual) and meso (organizational) levels and external factors at the macro (country) and supra (transnational) levels to explain possible determinants of CSED in the annual reports of Malaysian corporations. Our model and empirical findings make an important contribution to the literature in the area especially to other developing countries with similar political and socio-economic characteristics.

An underlying principle of our analysis is that corporations need not only be made accountable, but also to be seen to be accountable. Not least because corporations around the world play a big role in shaping the world economy and triggering social change as they control a large amount of wealth:

... the largest 500 companies control 42 percent of the world's wealth. Of the biggest 100 economies, half are now corporations and half are countries. ... Indeed, only 27 countries now have a turnover greater than sales of Shell and Exxon combined. Shell – the world's second – owns or leases some 400 million acres of land, which makes it larger than 146 countries. ... General Motors' sales revenues are roughly equal to the combined GNP of Tanzania, Ethiopia, Nepal, Bangladesh, Zaire, Uganda, Niger, Kenya and Pakistan

(Gray and Bebbington, 1998: 4–5)

Such levels of control and power enjoyed by corporations come with a big responsibility to 'account' for their actions. An important issue related to accountability that needs to be addressed is to *whom* corporations should be held accountable. It is now widely accepted that corporations are not only accountable to their shareholders but also to various stakeholders in the business environment within which they operate. These stakeholders can be an organization, a coalition of people or an individual who feels that they have a stake in the consequences of management's decisions and this 'stake' rests on 'legal, moral, or presumed' claims, or on the capacity to affect an organization's 'behaviour, direction, process, or outcomes' (Mitchell *et al.* 1997: 858). Similarly, stakeholders comprised of those who have the power to influence current or future decisions and whose support is essential or whose opposition must be negated if major strategic change is to be successfully implemented. Mitchell *et al.* (1997) identify three key attributes as indicators of the amount of attention management need to give a stakeholder: power, legitimacy and urgency. In short, identifying stakeholder groups is a critical aspect in explaining the nature of the relationships between corporations and their stakeholders in a particular business environment.

In order to hold the corporations 'accountable', we first need to be aware or conscious of them, and to be able to see them in some way. In other words, our ability to hold corporations to account is dependent on their organizational activities being transparent to us (Gray *et al.* 1997; O'Dwyer 2003). This requires a fundamental reform in accounting that allows for social and environmental impacts to be accounted in a more transparent and visible manner rather than treating them as 'externalities' that effectively allow corporations to deny accountability and hence, responsibility for such impacts.

Literature review on corporate social and environmental disclosure

A prerequisite in improving accountability is to understand the factors that influence CSED, specifically the extent and quality of disclosure by corporations and possible reasons for non-disclosures. Previous studies have looked at the relationship between CSED and possible determinants of disclosure, which can be broadly categorized into three groups (Adams 2002): (1) corporate characteristics, such as company size (Hackson and Milne 1996), industry group (Deegan and Gordon 1996), share trading volume and price (Patten 1990) and corporate age and risk

(Roberts 1992); (2) general contextual factors, such as country of origin (Adams and Kuasirikun 2000), social and political context (Hogner 1982; Burchell *et al.* 1985; Adams and Harte 1998), economic context (Guthrie and Parker 1989), cultural context (Haniffa and Cooke 2005), ethical relativism (Lewis and Unerman 1999), time and specific events (Burchell *et al.* 1985; Walden and Schwartz 1997), media cover (Brown and Deegan 1998) and stakeholder power (Roberts 1992); and (3) internal contextual factors, such as corporate governance and corporate values (Haniffa and Cooke 2005; Campbell 2003; Cowen *et al.* 1987). The results tend to vary across countries, industries and time.

Similarly, many theories have been espoused to explain CSED, of which, three are dominant: legitimacy, stakeholder and institutional theories. Legitimacy theory maintains that there is a social contract (Deegan 2002) between the corporation and its constituents, and corporate social disclosure is a method of responding to the changing perceptions of a corporation's relevant public. This contract compels the company to appear legitimate in the eyes of the wider society if it wishes to continue pursuing its activities. Thus, corporate social disclosure is one of the strategies employed by corporate entities to seek acceptance and approval of their operations from society. Through corporate disclosure, organizations communicate to all their stakeholders that they are abiding by the terms of the social contract, thus achieving legitimacy necessary for its continued survival (Preston and Post 1975). Seen in this light, CSED is a mechanism that is adopted in order to maintain that legitimacy. Many studies (Buhr 1998; De Villiers and Van Staden 2006; Deegan and Rankin 1997), including those from a longitudinal perspective (Deegan *et al.* 2002; Hogner 1982), provide support for legitimacy theory. However, studies by O'Dwyer (2002) and Campbell *et al.* (2003) do not find support for legitimacy theory.

Stakeholder theory, on the other hand, addresses not only the dynamic and complex relationship between the company and its surroundings (Gray *et al.* 1996), but also the ability of companies to balance the conflicting demands of their various stakeholders (Roberts 1992). There are two streams to the stakeholder theory: ethical and managerial (Deegan and Unerman 2006). The former, often prescriptive in nature, views all stakeholders as having equal rights to information about how an organization is affecting them and in turn, how the organization owes its accountability to all stakeholders without prioritizing any particular interest group. In contrast, the latter stream postulates that different stakeholders have different expectations and levels of relationship with an organization and as such must be managed accordingly based on their command of resources, regulatory power and access to influential media or consumer power. The study by Neu *et al.* (1998) provides evidence to support the latter theory.

Institutional theory, a powerful theoretical perspective that provides explanation as to how the mechanisms used by organizations to align perceptions of their practices and characteristics with social and cultural values became institutionalized, has been applied in the area of CSED (Rahaman *et al.* 2004; Unerman and Bennett 2004). The theory complements both stakeholder and legitimacy theories in understanding how organizations acknowledge and respond to changing social and institutional pressures and expectations in order to maintain legitimacy (Deegan and Unerman 2006). It also addresses how accounting influences and is influenced by a multiplicity of agents, agencies, institutions and processes (Miller 1994).

Although previous studies provide some closure on the debate as to why companies should be involved in CSED, who benefits from CSED, what issues CSED should address and how CSED should be communicated, contemporary practices have been criticized for not being genuine (Adams 2002; 2004), since corporations are given the privileged status of 'reporting entities'; in other words, CSED is assumed to be a domain managed and controlled by corporations themselves (Lehman 1999). The choice to report more on positive impacts (Adams 2004; Gray *et al.* 1996) but with minimal disclosures on the negative impacts of corporate activities (Deegan and Gordon 1996) suggests corporations adopt libertarian models of accountability as these enable corporations to legitimize their activities but not necessarily transform and make them accountable for the impacts of their activities. This situation is very common among corporations in developing countries including Malaysia due to a lack of awareness among stakeholders and intervention by the state and pressure groups in society.

Studies on CSED in Malaysia have received substantial attention since the 1980s. Teoh and Thong (1984) conducted a survey to elicit degree of awareness of participants in the social and environmental disclosure process and also analyzed the 1980 annual reports of 100 public listed companies in Malaysia. They found only 29 per cent of companies making such disclosure with the most popular theme being human resources. Andrew *et al.* (1989) studied 119 Malaysian and Singaporean public listed companies as at the end of 1983 and found only 26 per cent of companies disclosing such information, with the most popular theme again being human resources. They further concluded that social and environmental disclosures were associated with larger-sized companies and those in the financial and banking sectors. Che Zuriana *et al.* (2001) conducted a longitudinal study (1995–99) of a sample of 100 companies from various sectors. They found less than 30 per cent of the companies disclosed social and environmental information and most disclosures were related to human resources, findings similar to those by Andrew *et al.* (1989) and Teoh and Thong (1984). A study by Thompson and Zakaria (2004) indicated that firm size, financial leverage, industry membership and reporting awards were statistically related to the extent of social and environmental disclosure and the extent of disclosure was found to be generally low. Haniffa and Cooke (2005) considered corporate governance and cultural factors as possible determinants of CSED and their study concluded that some corporate governance factors influence disclosure but not cultural factors.

The studies by Teoh and Thong (1984) and Andrew *et al.* (1989) were conducted based on annual reports in the 1980s and may not reflect the situation in the early part of the 1990s where Malaysia enjoyed remarkable economic growth and received a steady inflow of foreign funds before being hit by the economic crisis in 1997. The studies by Che Zuriana *et al.* (2001) and Thompson and Zakaria (2004) considered the period after the financial crisis and incorporated more variables in the model to explain CSED. Haniffa and Cooke (2005) add a new dimension to the research by incorporating cultural and corporate governance variables in the model and provide empirical evidence regarding the potential influence of cultural and governance factors on CSED in the Malaysian context.

In this chapter, we extend the work of Haniffa and Cooke (2005) by including variables at four levels that may impact CSED and test the model in the context of Malaysia. The premise of our theoretical framework is that corporations are being pressured by external and internal forces to engage in CSED to meet rapidly changing expectations about business and its social responsibilities. The external forces can be further divided into two levels: supra (transnational) and macro (country). At the supra level, globalization and capital need theories play an important part in explaining CSED. Globalization is the process by which national economies become increasingly integrated (Bernhagen 2003), often as a result of power wielded by transnational corporations. Dependence on foreign direct investments may cause companies to emulate practices of their powerful counterparts. Capital-need theory suggests seeking funds at the lowest cost to help companies grow would cause them to engage in corporate social responsibility and adopt transparent reporting practices including CSED (Cooke 1989). Hence, activities of multinational companies (MNCs),[1] capital mobilization and foreign activities are some of the factors that push companies to engage in CSED. The motives could be instrumental in promoting business competitiveness and in aligning social and environmental policies with others globally.

At the macro level, the state can play an important role in CSED through enacting and enforcing rules or making known its aspirations related to CSED policies. The government's interest in establishing competitive business environments, promoting social cohesion and fostering collective responsibility for the betterment of society will lead them to push firms to engage in CSED especially if they have a substantial stake in the companies. Similarly, the accounting profession and the relevant bodies associated with listed companies, such as the Securities Exchange Authority and Institute of Directors, may encourage CSED by honouring companies that undertake and report their social and environmental activities. Political-economic theory could explain the role of the state and the profession in CSED (Cooper and Sherer 1984). Governments have a political and economic interest in having their flagship companies (or companies where they have substantial stakes) exhibit high standards of corporate social responsibility, and CSED is the mechanism used to help reduce the companies from becoming targets for reprisal and negative publicity. Similarly, related authorities have political and economic agendas to be seen as promoting transparency including CSED among listed companies to compete both locally and globally.

Internal forces influencing CSED can be divided into two levels: meso (organizational) and micro (individual). At the meso level, the top management has the most direct power to influence the firm's engagement in social and environmental activities by developing corporate strategy and allocating resources to different firm programmes and practices including CSED. In other words, directors who want the firm to become involved in social and environmental activities and CSED will need to have the power to put them on the agenda and to align the activities

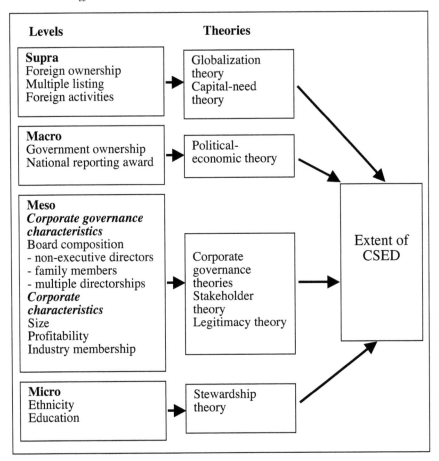

Figure 4.1 Factors influencing corporate social and environmental disclosure (CSED).

with the firm's strategic goals. Corporate governance theory may help explain the role of top management in pushing for CSED to protect the company's reputation and long-term competitiveness. Board composition and multiple directorships may provide top management with the power to initiate and commit the companies to be socially and environmentally responsible and to show accountability through CSED. Corporate characteristics, such as size, profitability and type of industry, may influence engagement in social and environmental activities and both stakeholder and legitimacy theories help explain the association between CSED and corporate characteristics. Large and profitable firms would attract the attention of both stakeholders and the media and as such, they need to pay attention to how their actions are perceived by others. Hence, CSED may be used as a mechanism to legitimize activities. Firms within a given industry are confined by the specific norms, values and beliefs of that industry and CSED may not only legitimize their activities by complying with industry norms, but also help in pre-empting bad publicity, avoiding institutional investor disinvestment, promoting suppliers' interests and employee welfare and ensuring the organization's long-term survival.

At the micro level, what is desirable, valuable and constitutes a good life in an organization is contingent on the cognitive and personal values of the community within the organization, as these will diffuse to the overall organizational values and business ethics. Unlike agency theory, which views managers as seeking to only maximize their own interest, stewardship theory suggests that organizational actors, especially top management, bring their personal morality-based values into the firm and act as good stewards in protecting the interest of the principals (Davis *et al.* 1997). Hence, it is not surprising to find them going beyond economic interests or self-fulfilment in managing the companies. Ethnicity and education may influence top management's desire to engage in CSED and demonstrate their accountability as good stewards. Figure 4.1 presents our multilevel framework of factors that may influence the extent of CSED. The next section will provide an insight into the Malaysian context and develop hypotheses from the framework.

Malaysia: Economic, political and social context

In this section we will not discuss the political and socio-economic context separately as they are interrelated. Hence, in developing our hypotheses, we will link them to the general context of the country.

External forces

Impact of forces at the supra (international) level: Globalization and the need for capital have affected business policies and practices in developing countries. After the First Malaysia Five-Year Economic Plan (1966–70), which emphasized infrastructure development, the subsequent plans concentrated on the establishment of import-substitution and export-oriented industries particularly with the enactment of the Promotion of Investment Act 1986, which provided many types of incentives for foreign direct investment (FDI). This has encouraged many foreign transnational corporations to set up subsidiaries in Malaysia as it has the right kind of infrastructure in place: stable government, good economic policies, abundant natural resources, both skilled and semi-skilled manpower and good business infrastructure. Export-oriented FDI provided the nation with valuable foreign exchange capital, which facilitated economic growth. Low interest loans, increasing access to foreign exchange and other incentives have contributed to the massive influx in the number of multinational companies setting up business in the country. This has important implications on reporting practices including CSED. Local firms as well as subsidiaries of those MNCs will tend to mimic their foreign counterparts' and parent companies' practices in order to attract investors and compete for funds.

Foreign ownership, multiple listing and foreign activities are proxies at the 'supra' level that may influence CSED. The flow of foreign funds into the capital markets may cause an increase in the demand for transparency due to higher perceived risk resulting from separation between management and owners geographically. In the context of Malaysia, foreign ownership may be an important determinant of CSED because a substantial fund in the capital market comes from foreign owners who may not want to take the risk of investing in companies that are not engaged in corporate social responsibility. Similarly, companies that are listed in more than one market may need foreign funds to help in their expansion strategy and must compete for funds with other companies abroad. CSED may be used as a mechanism to gain the confidence of ethical investors. Furthermore, when companies are listed in more than one market, they may need to comply with CSED rules in other countries. Although companies may not be listed abroad, they may still be involved in foreign activities via joint ventures and associates and, when they operate beyond their homeland, they will need to comply with CSED rules and regulations of the country in which they are operating. The experience gained in the preparation of accounting reports including CSED in foreign lands may encourage companies to adopt, if not adapt, practices locally. Hence, we hypothesize that:

H_{1a}: There is a positive relationship between CSED and concentration of foreign ownership.

H_{1b}: There is a positive relationship between CSED and multiple listing.

H_{1c}: There is a positive relationship between CSED and foreign activities.

Impact of forces at the macro (country) level: Besides globalization and capital need, the state and relevant authorities have political and economic interests in seeing that local companies and the stock market are able to compete internationally and attract funds into the country. Various elements in the five-yearly Malaysia Development Plans and the longer term Outline Perspective Plans as well as Vision 2020, indicate the Malaysian government is taking social and environmental issues seriously. It recognized that in order to achieve the status of a fully developed country, it would have to seriously consider its sustainability policies. This has important implications on companies that have significant government investments, as they would like to be seen as supportive of the government's aspirations including environmental and social policies. Furthermore, by virtue of their links with the government either through shareholdings or contracts, such companies are prone to scrutiny not only by the government but also other interested parties, both local and global. Hence, we hypothesize that:

H_{2a}: There is a positive relationship between CSED and government shareholdings.

As part of the strategy in encouraging transparency, Bursa Malaysia, the Malaysian Institute of Certified Public Accountant, Malaysian Institute of Management and Malaysian Institute of Accountants have taken the initiative to honour excellent corporate reporting among public listed companies through the National Annual Corporate Report Award. Such awards not only encourage companies to pay considerable attention to increase transparency, but also to enhance their reputation as part of good corporate citizenship. Thus, companies that are concerned with their reputations will take extra effort in producing reports to win the NACRA. Government shareholding and receipt of NACRA or other reporting awards are proxies at the macro level that may influence CSED. Hence, we hypothesize that:

H_{2b}: There is a positive relationship between CSED and the recipients of NACRA or other reporting awards.

Internal forces

Impact of forces at the meso (organizational) level, corporate governance and CSED: The strategies of the corporation should not only focus on making profit but also show accountability to their stakeholders. This could be addressed through corporate governance, which involves taking into account all factors that affect the viability, competence and moral character of an enterprise. Issues of governance include to whom and for what the corporation is responsible, and by what standards it is to be governed and by whom. Governance issues including CSED may be part of the remit of the board of directors, especially non-executives who are seen as the check-and-balance mechanism, not only in ensuring that companies act in the best interest of owners but also other stakeholders. In the context of Malaysia, corporations do indeed comply with the rulings of having a majority of non-executive directors on the board but the potential effectiveness of their role may not necessarily improve CSED due to the following reasons: 1) selection of non-executive directors are often based on friendship, political allies, business contacts etc., hence may not be totally independent to act in the best interest of stakeholders; and 2) some non-executive directors do not have any business and legal knowledge and experience including issues related to CSED, hence they end up acting as a 'rubber stamp.' As such, we hypothesize that:

H_{3a}: There is a negative relationship between CSED and boards dominated by non-executive directors.

Besides composition in terms of non-executive directors on boards, composition in terms of number of family members on boards may also influence disclosure practice. In the context of Malaysia, certain families have substantial equity holdings in the corporations causing little separation between those who own and those who manage. Most of the major decisions are made by the most senior person of the extended family, and the transactions tend to be highly personal and restricted to friends, members of the extended family or relatives. In such cases, corporate reporting including CSED will be minimal unless there is pressure for management to do so and if the benefits outweigh the costs. Hence, our next hypothesis is:

H_{3b}: There is a negative relationship between CSED and boards dominated by family members.

Multiple directorships may have important implications on disclosure practice because by sitting on more than one board, the directors concerned will be more aware of affairs in other companies including CSED. Experience gained from other companies' reporting may encourage such directors to ask the company's management to also consider certain social and environmental issues that may have been discussed in other boards. In the context of Malaysia, multiple directorships are common. Directors, who have previously experienced a social reporting issue and how it was dealt with, could share this knowledge in another company on which they sit especially if they felt that this would enhance the reputation of the company. Thus, our next hypothesis is:

H_{3c}: There is a positive relationship between CSED and boards dominated by directors with multiple directorships.

Corporate characteristics and CSED: Large companies undertake more activities and have greater impact on society. They also tend to receive more attention from various groups in society and therefore are under greater pressure to disclose their social and environmental activities to various stakeholders to legitimize their business. In the context of Malaysia, larger companies have the resources and experience to engage in CSED at a lower cost. Furthermore, due to their size and visibility, they would like to be seen as leaders in corporate citizenship and their disclosure practices are often emulated by others. Therefore, we hypothesize that:

H_{3d}: There is a positive relationship between CSED and size of company.

Companies with good news including profitability are more likely to engage in CSED to allow management the freedom and flexibility to undertake and reveal more extensive social responsibility programmes to stakeholders. They would like to demonstrate their contribution to society's well-being and not perceived as insensitive profit-making companies. This forms part of their legitimizing strategy. Hence, the next hypothesis is:

H_{3e}: There is a positive relationship between CSED and profitability of company.

Companies' disclosure of social and environmental information may be expected to be in line with the peculiarities of their respective industries. More labour intensive industries, such as manufacturing, may choose to disclose more information on employees compared to companies in the extractive and chemical industries, which may opt to disclose more environmental information to reflect sensitivity to environmental problems. Similarly, consumer-oriented industries can be expected to exhibit more social disclosure to enhance their corporate image among market consumers and other stakeholders. The existence of a nationally dominant firm heavily engaged in CSED within a particular industry may lead to a bandwagon effect on the levels of disclosure adopted by other firms in that industry including CSED. In short, the influence of industry type on CSED depends on how critical the effects of the economic activities are on the society. The increase in awareness of the citizens of matters pertaining to the environment, human resources and other aspects of social responsibility may force companies to highlight such information to demonstrate social accountability. As such, the next hypothesis is:

H_{3f}: There is a positive relationship between CSED and type of industry.

Impact of forces at the micro (individual) level: It will be hypocritical to discuss corporate social responsibility disclosure practices without considering the values, motives and choices of those people who are really involved in formulating policy and taking decisions in the organization or who have discretion over the firm's socially responsible (or irresponsible) actions and engagement in CSED. How a firm operates and reports will be influenced by the social values of the relevant publics within which it exists. In the context of Malaysia, the mind of Malaysian managers is influenced by ethnicity, education and the type of organization they work for (Chuah 1995). Ethnicity may be an important factor in influencing CSED due to divergence in cultural values within the nation resulting from ethnic polarization, partly attributed to the government's National Economic Policy (NEP), which is an affirmative action plan to eliminate the identification of race with economic function (Jomo 1986).[2] The NEP institutionalized positive discrimination in favour of *bumiputra*[3] by offering concessions in terms of grants, trade, education and certain jobs and as such, ethnicity defines the Malaysian ethos. It is a well-known fact that strong collusion exists between the government and some businessmen who benefit from the government's NEP (Jayasankaran 1997; *Far Eastern Economic Review* 1998). Since government is one of the relevant publics of the firm, developing a corporate reputation as being socially responsible via performing and disclosing social responsibility activities may be seen as part of a strategic plan in managing stakeholder relationships (Roberts 1992). Hence, it may be expected that firms run by management dominated by the government's favoured ethnic group, in this case the Malays or *bumiputras*, may choose to disclose more social responsibility information as a legitimization strategy in changing the perceptions and diverting attention of other stakeholders on their proximity to government as well as to continue to have an influential voice at both governmental and institutional levels. In other words, the intention of CSED by firms dominated by Malay directors is to legitimate their activities. Therefore, we hypothesize that:

H_{4a}: There is a positive relationship between CSED and boards dominated by Malay/*bumiputra* directors.

Companies headed by managers who have experience working with other foreign companies or receive qualifications from abroad normally have higher awareness of CSR and as such, may act as agents for change in CSED practices in their companies. In Malaysia, the attitudes of managing directors may be influenced by their educational background or organizations they work for. If they are exposed to foreign education or have worked in foreign organizations, they would be more conscious of the importance of such issues and the CSED practices adopted to gain legitimacy and act as good corporate citizen. Hence, our hypothesis is:

H_{4b}: There is a positive relationship between CSED and the qualification and experience of the managing director.

Research method

The sample population for this study was drawn from companies listed on the Bursa Malaysia. One hundred and twenty-three (123) companies were selected at random on a proportional allocation basis to ensure a representative sample from all industrial sectors for the year 2006. Although companies may use other media to demonstrate CSED, this study focuses on annual reports.

Dependent and independent variable: Content analysis, which is a method of codifying the text (or content) of a piece of writing into various groups depending on selected criteria (Weber 1988), was used to collect the necessary data. An essential element in content analysis is the selection and development of categories into which content units can be classified. As in most previous studies, the categories and items were drawn from previous research in the area and applicability to the Malaysian environment (Hossain *et al.* 1994; Haniffa and Cooke 2005). A list covering all items related to environment, employees, community, product and value added, was designed and adopted. Krippendorff's alpha, a test for reliability of the instrument, confirmed the reliability of the instrument. The final checklist instrument consisted of 41 corporate social and environmental disclosure items.

Two types of measure of CSED, an index score (CSEDI) and number of words (CSEDW),[4] were employed to capture the extent of disclosure made in each of the themes. The former measurement captures 'variety' of disclosure and the latter captures the 'extent' of CSED. Both measurements were adopted because the latter cannot capture pictures and graphics, which are potentially powerful and highly effective methods of communication (Beattie and Jones 1992, 1994; Preston *et al.* 1996) and excluding them may be considered a limitation. The approach to scoring items is essentially dichotomous in that an item scores one if disclosed and zero if it is not.[5]

The scores for each item were then added to derive a final score for the firm. The approach of scoring the firms is additive and equally weighted and was calculated as follows to give the final CSEDI:

$$CSEDI_j = \frac{\sum_{t=1}^{nj} X_{ij}}{n_j}$$

where

$CSEDI_j$ = corporate social and environmental disclosure index
n_j = number of items expected for j^{th} firm, $n_j \leq 41$
X_{ij} = 1 if i^{th} item disclosed and 0 if it is not disclosed, so that $0 \leq I_j \leq 1$

Items related to pictures and graphical presentations in the checklist were excluded when making a word count. This resulted in only 40 items being considered. The number of words were added together to compute the CSEDW. The independent

Table 4.1 Multilevel constructs of determinants of CSEDI and CSEDW

Levels	Explanatory variables	Measurement
Supra	Foreign ownership (FOROWN)	Proportion of foreign shareholders to total shareholders
	Multiple listing (LIST)	1 = multiple listings, 0 = single listing
	Foreign activities (FORACT)	1 = involved in foreign activities, 0 = none
Macro	Government ownership (GOVOWN)	Proportion of government shareholdings to total shareholdings
	National reporting award (AWARD)	1 = recipient, 0 = none recipient
Meso	Board composition – non-executive directors (NED)	Proportion of non-executive directors to total directors on the board
Corporate governance characteristics	Board composition – family members (FAM)	Proportion of family members on the board to total number of directors
	Multiple directorships (MULDIR)	Proportion of directors on the board with directorships in other companies to total number of directors
Corporate characteristics	Size (STA)	Proxy used is total assets
	Profitability (ROE)	Return on equity = earnings after tax/total equity.
	Industry membership (INDY)	Bursa Malaysia's classification: IT_1 = consumer, IT_2 = construction/property, IT_3 = trading/services, IT_4 = plantations/mining; IT_5 = industrial
Micro	Ethnicity – boards dominated by Malay directors (MALBOD)	Proportion of Malay directors to total directors on the board
	Education – qualification and experience abroad (MDQUAL)	1 = MD has qualification/experience abroad, 0 = local

variables representing the multilevel constructs used in this study are presented in Table 4.1.

Data analysis: The relationship between the various multilevel independent variables and the two measures of CSED was tested using multiple regression analysis.[6] The assumptions underlying the regression model were tested for multicollinearity based on correlation matrix as well as variance inflation factor[7] while analysis of residuals, plots of the studentized residuals against predicted values as well as the Q-Q plot were conducted to test for homoscedasticity, linearity and normality assumptions. In addition, normality tests based on skewness, kurtosis and Kolmogorov-Smirnov Lilliefors were also conducted.

Discussion of results

Table 4.2 presents the results of descriptive analysis of CSED by themes based on number of companies making at least one disclosure item (column 2), incidence figures, i.e. number of companies making at least one disclosure item as percentage of the total sample (column 3), amount of disclosure as measured by word count (column 4) and amount of disclosure as measured by word count to total words for all disclosures in the sample (column 5). It can be seen from the table that Malaysian listed companies, regardless of the measure used, tend to disclose more information on the product and employees and very little on value-added and environmental information.

Table 4.3 provides descriptive statistics for the continuous independent variables. It can be seen that the mean of CSEDI was 23 per cent and the range was from 4.6 per cent to 55.6 per cent, out of a possible score of 100. The mean of CSEDW was 287.4 words and the range was from 21 to 925 words. Both measures of dependent variables were not normally distributed as indicated by standard tests on skewness and kurtosis. As such, the dependent and continuous variables that

Table 4.2 Descriptive statistics for CSED measures in Malaysian listed companies

Themes	Disclosing companies making at least one disclosure	Disclosing companies as a % of total sample (incidence)	Number of disclosed words (amount)	Disclosed words as a % of all disclosed words	Mean	Std. dev.
Employee	122	99	10,890	31	2.74	2.16
Community	51	41	3,464	10	0.74	1.06
Environment	32	26	2,444	7	0.38	0.78
Product	122	99	17,020	48	3.20	1.46
Value-added	11	9	1,361	4	0.15	0.51

Note: Total sample of companies – 123.
      Total disclosed words – 35,179.

Table 4.3 Descriptive statistics for dependent and continuous independent variables

Variables	Mean	Std. dev.	Min.	Max.	Skewness	Kurtosis
CSEDI	23.02	11.20	4.63	55.63	1.060	0.934
CSEDW	287.45	178.63	21.00	925.00	0.962	0.535
FOROWN	14.90	10.12	0.00	43.13	2.16	-1.14
GOVOWN	6.903	12.556	0.000	80.560	3.732	16.208
NED	49.87	10.14	25.00	74.00	-1.20	-1.40
FAM	14.00	21.0	0.00	57.00	3.54	-0.39
MULDIR	8.56	2.14	0.00	15.53	0.36	2.14
STA	9589462	10592233	9529.00	91867584	4.214	21.826
ROE	10.39	8.25413	-8.17	36.79	0.098	0.681
MALDIR	46.22	23.22	0.00	100.00	0.567	-0.525

Notes: CSEDI= corporate social and environmental disclosure index; CSEDW = length corporate social and environmental disclosure; FOROWN = proportion of foreign shareholders; GOVOWN = government shareholdings; NED = proportion of non-executive directors on the board; FAM = proportion of family members on the board; MULDIR = proportion of directors on the board with multiple directorships, STA = size of total assets; ROE = profitability; and MALDIR = proportion of Malay directors on the boards.

were not normally distributed were transformed to normal scores before conducting regression analysis.

Table 4.4 presents the correlation matrix for the dependent and continuous independent variables in our framework. It can be seen that multicollinearity is not a problem. Similarly, an analysis of residuals indicates no problems of heteroscedasticity and linearity.

Table 4.5 summarizes the results for the multivariate regression models using the transformed data based on normal scores. The regression produced an adjusted R^2 of 0.453 for CSEDI and 0.438 for CSEDW. This means that 45.3 per cent and 43.8 per cent of the factors in the two regression models based on CSEDI and CSEDW respectively, explained CSED practices in the context of Malaysia.

Both of the regression models indicate positive relationship at the 1 per cent level between CSEDs and companies with multiple listing, companies that are recipients of awards, boards dominated by non-executive directors, profitable companies and Malay dominated boards, as predicted. The results support our hypotheses H_{1b}, H_{2b}, H_{3a}, H_{3e} and H_{4a}. However, both of the regression models indicate insignificant relationship between CSED and companies with foreign activities, family dominated boards, boards dominated by directors with multiple directorships, type of industry and managing directors with experience and/or qualification from abroad, thus not supporting hypotheses H_{1c}, H_{3b}, H_{3c}, H_{3f} and H_{4b}. Interestingly, foreign ownership (H_{1a}) and government ownership (H_{2a}) were found to be only significantly related to CSEDI at the 1% per cent and 5 per cent levels respectively but not in the case of CSEDW. Size was significantly related to both CSEDI and CSEDW, at the 5 per cent and 1 per cent level respectively.

In short, empirical evidence based on CSEDI found it to be significantly associated with two out of three constructs at the supra level, both constructs at the macro level, three out of six constructs at the meso level and one out of two constructs at the micro level, in the direction as predicted. On the other hand, empirical evidence based on CSEDW found it to be significantly associated with only one out of three constructs at the supra level, one out of two constructs at the macro level, three out of six constructs at the meso level and one out of two constructs at the micro level, also in the direction as predicted. The slightly different result between the two models is an important finding because it shows the measures used are important in drawing conclusions. In our case, CSEDI reflects the *variety* of information disclosed while CSEDW reflects the *extent* of information disclosed.

At the supra level, the significant association of CSED with multiple listing was consistent with prior studies and indicates in the absence of rules and regulations on CSED in the country, companies listed on both local and overseas stock exchange may do so in their annual reports due to better experience in handling information and in adopting legitimation strategies to reflect societal concerns in the global market, as explained by the globalization theory. At the macro level, companies that have received awards in the past, tend to engage more in CSED as this would continue to boost their image and 'capture' the interest and attention of stakeholders. At the meso level, the negative significant relationship between boards dominated by independent non-executive directors and CSED support our

Table 4.4 Correlation matrix of dependent and continuous independent variables

	CSEDI	CSEDW	FOROWN	GOVOWN	NED	FAM	MULDIR	STA	ROE	MALDIR
CSEDI	1									
CSEDW	0.940**	1								
FOROWN	0.258**	0.193*	1							
GOVOWN	0.036	0.141	0.018	1						
NED	-0.186*	-0.241**	-0.122	0.347	1					
FAM	-0.179*	-0.237*	-0.086	-0.02	0.054	1				
MULDIR	0.259**	0.219**	-0.074	0.197	0.366	-0.130	1			
STA	0.210*	0.195*	0.076	0.437	0.001	-0.056	0.288	1		
ROE	0.356**	0.333**	0.162	0.179	-0.164	-0.029	0.035	-0.046	1	
MALDIR	0.243**	0.216*	-0.144	0.135	0.066	-0.257	0.088	0.102	-0.109	1

Note:
* Correlation is significant at the 0.05 level (2-tailed).
** Correlation is significant at the 0.01 level (2-tailed).

Table 4.5 Multiple regression results using index CSEDI and CSEDW as the dependent variables

	Predicted sign	CSEDI		CSEDW	
		B coefficients	t–stats	B coefficients	t–stats
Intercept			−1.119		−1.147
Supra level					
FOROWN(H_{1a})	+	0.153	2.197*	0.088	1.192
LIST(H_{1b})	+	0.288	4.115**	0.305	4.298**
FORACT(H_{1c})	+	0.156	1.809	0.143	1.561
Macro level					
GOVOWN(H_{2a})	+	0.173	2.854*	0.044	0.731
AWARD(H_{2b})	+	0.310	5.259**	0.315	5.438**
Meso level					
NED(H_{3a})	−	−0.205	−3.085**	−0.193	−2.867**
FAM(H_{3b})	−	−0.122	−1.267	−0.048	−0.929
MULDIR(H_{3c})	+	0.107	1.195	0.139	1.036
STA(H_{3d})	+	0.188	2.584*	0.232	3.141**
ROE(H_{3e})	+	0.278	3.759**	0.211	2.817**
IT1(H_{3f})	+/−	0.043	0.580	0.084	1.110
IT2		0.124	1.542	0.076	0.927
IT3		0.068	0.803	0.169	1.971
IT4		−0.104	−1.113	−0.018	−1.194
Micro level					
MALBOARD(H_{4a})	+	0.359	5.005**	0.273	3.745**
MDQUAL(H_{4b})	+	0.010	0.193	0.089	1.562
Adjusted R^2		0.453		0.438	
F–statistic		9.164		8.688	
p		0.000		0.000	

Note:
* Correlation is significant at the 0.05 level (2-tailed).
** Correlation is significant at the 0.01 level (2-tailed).

contention that in the context of Malaysia, non-executive directors play a limited role in influencing CSED policy and practice perhaps due to lack of experience, power and also an indifferent attitude towards societal concerns or that such companies may feel that having more non-executive directors to monitor business activities was a sufficient substitute for public social and environmental disclosures. Size and profitability were also found to be significant in explaining CSED. Large companies engaged in more CSED due to reasons of accountability and visibility as outlined in legitimacy theory, and CSED is used by companies as an avenue to publicize their image and also legitimize their activities especially during good times. At the micro level, Malay dominated boards were found to be statistically related to CSED. Existence of a policy of positive discrimination on business opportunities based on ethnicity affects corporate behaviour including its disclosure practice. Being the government's favoured ethnic group, boards dominated by the Malays may adopt a legitimating strategy to change the perceptions and divert the attention of its various stakeholders on the close relation it shares with the government and to continue to have an influential voice at both governmental and institutional levels by increasing their CSEDs.

Summary and future agenda

The current study has attempted to increase our understanding of corporate social and environmental disclosure (CSED) practices in the annual reports of Malaysian listed companies. Our starting premise has been that, by considering internal and external pressures at four levels, we are in a better position to understand the potential effects they may have on CSED in annual reports. We investigated CSED practices in Malaysian annual reports by classifying the external forces into two levels: supra or international level and macro or country level; and the internal forces also into two levels: meso or organizational level and micro or individual level. We then identified constructs at the various levels and developed our hypotheses in the context of Malaysia and tested our framework based on two measures of CSED using multiple regressions. We found support for most of the hypotheses except for companies' involvement in foreign activities, boards dominated by family members, directors with multiple directorships, type of industry and experience/qualification of the managing director.

Given the exceedingly complex nature of the business environment, there are inherent limits in the ability of positive empirical research to capture all dimensions that influence CSED policy and practice in our framework. Hence, an in-depth survey from the supply side, i.e. companies, would be useful to determine more precisely the reasons and motives to support the findings in this study and also to build upon our model by considering other independent variables based on responses from the companies.

Suggested further readings

Global Reporting Initiative. (2002) *Sustainability Reporting Guidelines on Economic, Environmental and Social Performance*. Amsterdam: GRI.

Gray, R. and J. Bebbington.(2001) *Accounting for the Environment*, 2nd edn. London: SAGE.

Haniffa, R. M. and T. E. Cooke. (2002) 'Culture, Corporate Governance and Disclosure in Malaysian Corporations'. *Abacus*, 38(3), 317–49.

Mathews, M. R. (1997) 'Twenty-five Years of Social and Environmental Accounting Research: Is There a Silver Jubilee to Celebrate?' *Accounting, Auditing and Accountability Journal*, 10(4), 481–531.

Unermann, J., J. Bebbington and B. O'Dwyer. (eds) (2007) *Sustainability, Accounting and Accountability*. London: Routledge.

Notes

1 MNCs (multinational companies) and TNCs (transnational companies) are used interchangeably as they both refer to corporations involved in business in at least two countries.

2 The National Economy Policy was introduced in 1970 following the racial riot in 1969 due to economic dominance of Chinese amid the poverty of the Malays (Jayasankaran and Hiebert 1997). See Haniffa (1999) on discussion of NEP and its implications on the business environment.

3 *Bumiputra* refers to both Malays and other indigenous ethnic groups in East Malaysia (Malaysia 1991). However, for the purpose of this study, *bumiputra* refers to only the Malay group.

4 Different volume measurement has been employed in previous studies and each has its advantages and limitations. Number of pages (Patten 1992; Deegan and Rankin 1997) and proportion of page (Guthrie and Parker 1990; Gray *et al.* 1995a) reflect amount of total space given to a topic and by inference, the importance of that topic (Krippendorff 1980). However, such measurements may be affected by font size, margins and treatment of blank parts of a page. The use of number of words (Zeghal and Ahmed 1990; Deegan and Rankin 1997; Deegan and Gordon 1996) is more practical and easily categorized but may be affected by concise and verbose styles of writing (Hackston and Milne 1996). Number of sentences (Tsang 1998; Hackston and Milne 1996) has the advantages of being more easily identifiable, less subjective to interjudge variations, problems of allocating based on proportion of page and standardizing number of words, but is more suitable in inferring meanings (Krippendorff 1980). In this study, both word and sentence counts were considered but due to high correlation between the two, only word count will be reported in the paper.

5 Use of dichotomous procedure is considered a limitation because it treats disclosure of one item as equal to a company that makes 50 disclosures and does not indicate how much emphasis is given to a particular content category but the advantage is that it gives coders less choice (Hackston and Milne 1996: 88). However, the use of word count partly accommodates this problem. The scores for each item were then added to derive a final score for the firm as follows:

$CSEDI = \beta_0 + \beta_1 \text{ FOROWN} + \beta_2 \text{ LIST} + \beta_3 \text{ FORACT} + \beta_4 \text{ GOVOWN} + \beta_5 \text{ AWARD} + \beta_6 \text{ NED} + \beta_7 \text{ FAM} + \beta_8 \text{ MULDIR} + \beta_9 \text{ STA} + \beta_{10} \text{ ROE} + \beta_{11} \text{ IT}_1 + \beta_{12} \text{ IT}_2 + \beta_{13} \text{ IT}_3 + \beta_{14} \text{ IT}_4 + \beta_{15} \text{ IT}_5 + \beta_{16} \text{ MALBOD} + \beta_{17} \text{ MDQUAL} + \in_{it}$

$CSEDW = \beta_0 + \beta_1 \text{ FOROWN} + \beta_2 \text{ LIST} + \beta_3 \text{ FORACT} + \beta_4 \text{ GOVOWN} + \beta_5 \text{ AWARD}$

$+ \beta_6$ NED $+ \beta_7$ FAM$+ \beta_8$ MULDIR $+ \beta_9$ STA $+ \beta_{10}$ ROE $+ \beta_{11}$ IT$_1$$+ \beta_{12}$ IT$_2$ $+ \beta_{13}$ IT$_3$ $+ \beta_{14}$ IT$_4$ $+ \beta_{15}$ IT$_5$ $+ \beta_{16}$ MALBOD $+ \beta_{17}$ MDQUAL $+ \in_{it}$

where:

CSEDI = corporate social and environmental disclosure index
CSEDW = length of corporate social and environmental disclosure
FOROWN = proportion of foreign shareholders to total shareholders
LIST = multiple listing
FORACT = foreign activities
GOVOWN = government ownership
AWARD = recipient of reporting award
NED = proportion of non-executive directors to total directors
FAM = proportion of family members to total directors
MULDIR = proportion of directors on the board with multiple directorships
STA = size based on total assets
ROE = profitability based on return on equity
IT1 = consumer
IT2 = industrial
IT3 = trading/services
IT4 = plantations/mining
IT5 = construction/property
MALBOARD = proportion of Malay directors to total directors
MDQUAL = managing director has qualification/experience from abroad
$\beta_0, \ldots , \beta_{12}$ = coefficients to be estimated
$\in_{it}$ = disturbance term

6 The Variance Inflation Factor indicates a problem if the factor exceeds 10 (Neter *et al.* 1983; Kennedy 1992).
7 See Cooke (1998) for discussion of advantages and disadvantages of different transformations in disclosure studies and why normal scores are considered appropriate for regression analysis in disclosure studies.

References

Adams, C. A. and G. Harte. (1998) 'The Changing Portrayal of the Employment of Women in British Banks' and Retail Companies' Corporate Annual Reports'. *Accounting. Organizations and Society*, 23(8): 781–812.

Adams, C. A. and N. Kuasirikun. (2000) 'A Comparative Analysis of Corporate Reporting on Ethical Issues by UK and German Chemical and Pharmaceutical Companies'. *European Accounting Review*, 9(1): 53–80.

Adams, C. A. (2002) 'Internal Organizational Factors Influencing Corporate Social and Ethical Reporting; Beyond Current Theorizing'. *Accounting, Auditing & Accountability Journal*, 15(2): 223–50.

—— (2004) 'The Ethical, Social and Environmental Reporting Performance Portrayal Gap'. *Accounting, Auditing & Accountability Journal*, 17(5): 731–57.

Andrew, B. H., F. A. Gul, J. E. Guthrie and H. Y. Teoh. (1989) 'A Note on Corporate Social Disclosure Practices in Developing Countries: The Case of Malaysia and Singapore'. *British Accounting Review*, 21: 371–76.

Beattie, V. and M. J. Jones. (1992) 'The Use and Abuse of Graphs in Annual Reports: Theoretical Framework and Empirical Study'. *Accounting and Business Research*, 22(88): 291–303.

—— (1994) 'An Empirical Study of Graphical Format Choices in Charity Annual Reports'. *Financial Accountability and Management*, 10(3): 215–36.

Bernhagen, P. (2003) 'Is Globalization What States Make of it? Micro-Foundations of the State-Market Condominium in the Global Political Economy'. *Contemporary Politics*, 9(3): 257–76.

Brown, N. and C. Deegan. (1998) 'The Public Disclosure of Environmental Performance Information – A Dual Test of Media Agenda Setting Theory and Legitimacy Theory'. *Accounting and Business Research*, 29(1): 21–41.

Buhr, N. (1998) 'Environmental Performance, Legislation and Annual Report Disclosure: The Case of Acid Rain and Falconbridge'. *Accounting, Auditing & Accountability Journal*, 11(2): 163–90.

Burchell, S., C. Clubb and A. Hopwood. (1985) 'Accounting in Its Social Context: Towards a History of Value Added in the United Kingdom'. *Accounting, Organizations and Society*, 110(4): 381–413.

Campbell, D., B. Craven and P. Shrives. (2003) 'Voluntary Social Reporting in Three FTSE Sectors: A Comment on Perception and Legitimacy'. *Accounting, Auditing & Accountability Journal*, 16(4): 558–81.

Che Zuriana, M. J., A. Kasumalinda and M. Rapiah. (2002) 'Corporate Social Responsibility Disclosure in the Annual Reports of Malaysian Companies: A Longitudinal Study'. *Social and Environmental Accounting Journal*, 22(2): 5–9.

Cooke, T. E. (1998) 'Regression Analysis in Accounting Disclosure Studies'. *Accounting and Business Research*, 28(3): 209–24.

—— (1989) 'Voluntary Corporate Disclosure by Swedish Companies'. *Journal of International Financial Management and Accounting*, 1(2): 1–25.

Cooper, D. J. M. J. and Sherer. (1984) 'The Value of Corporate Accounting Reports: Arguments for a Political Economy of Accounting'. *Accounting, Organizations and Society*, 9: 207–32.

Cowen, S. S., L. B. Ferreri and L. D. Parker. (1987) 'The Impact of Corporate Characteristics on Social Responsibility Disclosure: A Typology and Frequency-Based Analysis'. *Accounting, Organizations and Society*, 12(2): 111–22.

Davis, J. H., F. D. Schoorman and L. Donaldson. (1997) 'Toward a Stewardship Theory of Management'. *Academy of Management Review*, 22(1): 20–47.

De Villiers, C. J. and C. J. Van Staden. (2006) 'Can Less Environmental Disclosure Have a Legitimising Effect? Evidence from Africa'. *Accounting, Organizations and Society*, 31(8): 763–81.

Deegan, C. and B. Gordon. (1996) 'A Study of the Environmental Disclosure Practices of Australian Corporations'. *Accounting and Business Research*, 26(3): 187–99.

Deegan, C. and M. Rankin. (1997) 'The Materiality of Environmental Information to Users of Annual Reports'. *Accounting, Auditing & Accountability Journal*, 10 (4): 562–83.

Deegan, C. and J. Unerman. (2006) *Financial Accounting Theory*. London: McGraw Hill.

Deegan, C., M. Rankin and J. Tobin. (2002) 'An Examination of the Corporate Social and Environmental Disclosures of BHP from 1983–97: A Test of Legitimacy Theory'. *Accounting, Auditing & Accountability Journal*, 15 (3): 312–43.

Deegan, C. (2002) 'Introduction: The Legitimizing Effect of Social and Environmental Disclosures – A Theoretical Foundation'. *Accounting, Auditing & Accountability Journal*, 15 (3): 282–311.

The Economist. (2005) 'The Good Company: A Survey of Corporate Social Responsibility'. January 22: 1–22.

Far Eastern Economic Review. (1998) Survey Results, June 18: 36.

Gray, R. and J. Bebbington. (1998) 'Accounting and the Soul of Sustainability: Hyperreality, Transnational Corporations and the United Nations'. *Proceedings of 2nd Asian Pacific Interdisciplinary Research in Accounting Conference*, 1: 326–44.

Gray, R. H., C. Dey, D. L. Owen, R. Evans and S. Zadek. (1997) 'Struggling with the Praxis of Social Accounting: Stakeholders, Accountability, Audits and Procedures'. *Accounting, Auditing & Accountability Journal*, 10 (3): 325–64.

Gray, R. H., D. L. Owen and C. A. Adams. (1996) *Accounting and Accountability: Changes and Challenges in Corporate Social and Environmental Reporting*. Hemel Hempstead: Prentice Hall.

Gray, R., R. Kouhy and S. Lavers. (1995a) 'Corporate Social and Environmental Reporting: A Review of the Literature and a Longitudinal Study of UK Disclosure'. *Accounting, Auditing & Accountability Journal*, 8(2): 47–77.

Guthrie, J. E. and L. D. Parker. (1989) 'Corporate Social Reporting: A Rebuttal of Legitimacy Theory'. *Accounting and Business Research*, 19(76): 343–52.

Guthrie, J. E. and L. D. Parker. (1990) 'Corporate Social Disclosure Practice: A Comparative International Analysis'. *Advances in Public Interest Accounting*, 3(2): 159–76.

Hackston, D. and M. J. Milne. (1996) 'Some Determinants of Social and Environmental Disclosures in New Zealand Companies'. *Accounting, Auditing & Accountability Journal*, 9(1): 77–108.

Haniffa, R. M and T. E. Cooke. (2005) 'The Impact of Culture and Governance on Corporate Social Reporting'. *Journal of Accounting and Public Policy*, 24(50): 391–430.

Haniffa, R. M. (1999) 'Culture, Corporate Governance and Disclosure in Malaysian Corporations'. Unpublished thesis, University of Exeter.

Hogner, R. H. (1982) 'Corporate Social Reporting: Eight Decades of Development at US Steel'. *Research in Corporate Performance and Policy*, 4: 243–50.

Hossain, M., M. L. Tan and M. B. Adams. (1994) 'Voluntary Disclosure in an Emerging Capital Market: Some Empirical Evidence from Companies Listed on the KLSE'. *International Journal of Accounting*, 29(4): 334–51.

Jayasankaran, S. (1997) 'Hit the Brakes'. *Far Eastern Economic Review*, 18 December: 14–15.

Jayasankaran, S. and M. Hiebert. (1997) 'Malaysian Dilemmas'. *Far Eastern Economic Review*, 4 September: 18–20.

Jomo, S. K. (1986) *A Question of Class: Capital, the State, and Uneven Development in Malaya*. Singapore University Press.

Kennedy, P. (1992) *A Guide to Econometrics*. Boston: MIT Press.

Krippendorff, K. (1980) *Content Analysis: An Introduction to its Methodology*. London: SAGE.

Lehman, G. (1995) 'A Legitimate Concern for Environmental Accounting'. *Critical Perspectives on Accounting*, 6: 393–412.

Lewis, L. and J. Unerman. (1999) 'Ethical Relativism: A Reason for Differences in Corporate Social Reporting'. *Critical Perspectives on Accounting*, 10(4): 521–47.

Malaysia (1991) Second Outline Perspective Plan 1991–2000. Kuala Lumpur: National Printing Department.

Miller, P. (1994) 'Accounting as Social and Institutional Practice: An Introduction', in A. Hopwood and P. Miller (eds). *Accounting as Social and Institutional Practice*. Cambridge: University of Cambridge Press, 1–39.

Mitchell, R., B. Agle and D. Wood. (1997) 'Toward a Theory of Stakeholder Identification and Salience: Defining the Principle of Who and What Really Counts'. *Academy of Management Review*, 22(4): 853–86.

Neter, J., W. Wasserman and M. Kutner. (1983) *Applied Linear Regression Models.* Homewood, IL: Richard D. Irwin.

Neu, D., H. Warsame and K. Pedwell. (1998) 'Managing Public Impressions: Environmental Disclosures in Annual Reports'. *Accounting, Organizations and Society*, 23(3): 265–82.

O'Dwyer, B. (2002) 'Managerial Perceptions of Corporate Social Disclosure: An Irish Story'. *Accounting, Auditing & Accountability Journal*, 15(3): 406–36.

O'Dwyer, B. (2003) 'Conceptions of Corporate Social Responsibility: The Nature of Managerial Capture', *Accounting, Auditing & Accountability Journal*, 16(4): 523–57.

Patten, D.M. (1990) 'The Market Reaction to Social Responsibility Disclosures: The Case of the Sullivan Principles Signings'. *Accounting, Organizations and Society*, 15(6): 575–87.

Patten, D. M. (1992) 'Intra-industry Environmental Disclosures in Response to the Alaskan Oil Spill: A Note on Legitimacy Theory'. *Accounting, Organizations and Society*, 17(5): 471–75.

Preston, L. E. and J. E. Post. (1975) *Private Management and Public Policy.* Englewood Cliffs, NJ: Prentice-Hall Inc.

Preston, A., C. Wright and J. Young. (1996) 'Imag(in)ing Annual Reports'. *Accounting, Organizations and Society*, 21(1): 113–37.

Rahaman, A. S., S. Lawrence and J. Roper. (2004) 'Social and Environmental Reporting at the VRA: Institutionalised Legitimacy or Legitimation Crisis?' *Critical Perspectives on Accounting*, 15(1): 35–56.

Roberts, R. W. (1992) 'Determinants of Corporate Responsibility Disclosure'. *Accounting, Organizations and Society*, 17(6): 595–612.

Teoh, H. Y. and G. Thong. (1984) 'Another Look at Corporate Social Responsibility and Reporting: An Empirical Study in a Developing Country'. *Accounting, Organizations and Society*, 9(2): 189–206.

Thompson, P. and Z. Zakaria. (2004) 'Corporate Social Reporting in Malaysia'. *Journal of Corporate Citizenship*, 13 (Spring): 125–26.

Tsang, W. K. (1998) 'A Longitudinal Study of Corporate Social Reporting in Singapore: The Case of the Banking, Food and Beverages and Hotel Industries'. *Accounting, Auditing & Accountability Journal*, 11(5): 624–35.

Unerman, J. and M. Bennett. (2004) 'Increased Stakeholder Dialogue and the Internet: Towards Greater Corporate Accountability or Reinforcing Capitalist Hegemony?' *Accounting, Organizations and Society*, 29(7): 685–707.

Waddock, S. and C. Bodwell. (2004) 'Managing Responsibility: What Can Be Learned from the Quality Movement'. *California Management Review*, 47(1): 25–38.

Walden, W. D. and B. N. Schwartz. (1997) 'Environmental Disclosures and Public Policy Pressure'. *Journal of Accounting and Public Policy*, 16(2): 125–54.

Zeghal, D. and S. A. Ahmed. (1990) 'Comparison of Social Responsibility Information Disclosure Media Used by Canadian Firms'. *Accounting, Auditing & Accountability Journal*, 3(1): 38–53.

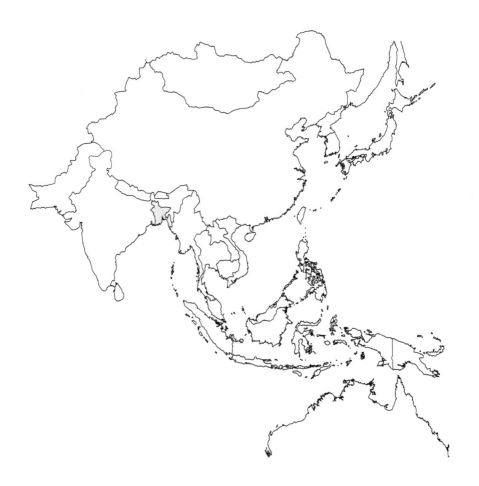

5 Exploitation of labour in Bangladeshi ready-made garment sector

Who is responsible?

Samia Ferdous Hoque and Abdullah Al Faruq

Introduction

Liberalization of economies and rapid growth of information technology have encouraged companies from developed countries to make investment in and/or outsource to developing countries. Consequently, the entrepreneurs of the developing economies have set up production facilities to produce low-cost goods for retail and consumption in Europe and North America. With this trend of offshore manufacturing, a new concern arises regarding the integration of ethically responsive initiatives within the global supply network. The companies of well known brand names have immense power; even some companies' revenues are more than the national income of many least developed countries (LDCs). For instance, the revenue of Wal-Mart is more than the GDP of China; the economy of General Motors is larger than that of Thailand (Mongabay 2005). A large number of small suppliers from different developing countries compete to be a part of the supply chain of these powerful corporations and for this they struggle to offer the lowest possible price sacrificing minimum working standards. Recently, these eminent corporations have been facing strong criticism from the media, consumers and pressure groups for encouraging poor wages, poor working conditions, poor environmental protection and poor health and safety standards in the supply chain. Bangladesh, being one of the most important suppliers from Asia, is also affected by these issues.

Textile, garment and knitwear products are the prime export products of Bangladesh. It has been supported by the World Trade Organization's Multi Fiber Agreement (MFA), which governed the world trade in textiles and garments from 1974 to 2004 by imposing quotas on the amount developing countries could export to developed countries. During this period, and certainly since the 1980s, Bangladeshi entrepreneurs have invested in this sector. Bangladesh earns 78 per cent of its export earning from ready-made garment (RMG) export. The sector's contribution towards the country's steady GDP growth (of 5 per cent) has been measured as 10.5 per cent (Awal 2005). Nevertheless, the sector has been facing serious criticism locally and internationally for the exploitation of its labour force. Considering the significance of this sector and magnitude of unethical activities happening in the industry, this chapter discusses corporate social responsibility (CSR) in Bangladesh in light of the RMG sector. The chapter begins by highlighting current trends in CSR activity according to different businesses in Bangladesh. It then discusses the current condition of the RMG sector. Finally, the chapter analyzes the reasons contributing towards the prevailing situation and concerns over exploitation.

The concept of CSR in Bangladesh

CSR, though a relatively new concept, is receiving attention from Bangladeshi entrepreneurs. Crane and Matten (2004) define CSR as 'the economic, legal, ethical and philanthropic expectations placed on organization by society at a given point in time' (43). Carroll (1991) has categorized the CSR activities of business into four stages. The first stage relates to economic responsibilities, which stresses the basic economic duties of the company, for instance, paying wages, ensuring profit for shareholders, selling products at a fair price etc. The second stage refers to legal responsibilities, which stem from the laws and regulation of a country. Complying with the first two stages is mandatory for every company, large or small. The third stage introduces ethical responsibilities, which are expected by society but are not obligatory. The fourth stage is of philanthropic responsibilities, which are desirable for society, and motivation relates to a sense of conduct for 'the good of the society'. CSR encompasses all four responsibilities. The applicability of this definition of CSR, however, needs to be analyzed in the context of the developing world. In most literature, CSR is defined from an American and European perspective, which may not be applicable in the context of developing countries. Prieto-Carrón *et. al.* (2006) have argued that in developing countries mandatory responsibilities are often confused with voluntary responsibilities. For example, even though paying a living wage and securing healthy and safe working conditions are basic economic responsibilities in the developed world, in the developing countries such provision can come under ethical responsibility, since most of the companies struggle to comply with even mandatory responsibilities. Conducting ethical and philanthropic activities are expensive and hence untenable for small firms from developing countries, which lack capital and expertise needed for carrying out these activities.

In Bangladesh, the concept of CSR is still limited to charitable activities. However, as noted above, CSR is not only about philanthropic or charitable work, rather it refers to taking responsibility of all aspects of a corporation's conduct. The focus of CSR activities vary based on type, size, sector and even geographical region of business. For example, small capital constrained firms may only meet economic and legal responsibilities, but large resourceful firms will also be able to manage philanthropic and ethical responsibilities. In Bangladesh, several resourceful multinational and local companies conduct CSR activities, however, their motives vary. Although multinational companies (MNCs) conduct CSR activities internally driven through their corporate culture and strategy, local companies of Bangladesh do not conduct CSR activities unless externally forced by foreign buyers, mainly Western contractors (Mondol 2007). Notably, in labour-intensive sectors of Bangladesh, including the RMG sector, violation of labour rights is rampant. Allegations are made that garment factories do not pay a living wage, working conditions are poor and workers are exploited. Hearson (2008) reveals the suppliers of BHS, House of Fraser, Levi Strauss and many other Western-owned fashion brands do not accept the principles of a living wage, and in many cases they do not even comply with the legal minimum. Therefore, at this point, the social responsibility of these suppliers would be to first comply with the mandatory responsibilities of Carroll's four-part model. By fulfilling their legal and economical responsibilities they may not score highly in terms of philanthropic activity, however, they can at least reduce the burden on their stakeholders.

Blowfield and Frynas (2002, as cited by Prieto-Carrón *et al.* 2006) give a broad definition of CSR: companies are responsible for the impact of activities on society and environment; companies have responsibility to the people with whom they do business; and corporations need to manage the relationship with society or to add value to society. This definition is perhaps more applicable for the small firms from the developing world. For example, regarding the current situation of the RMG industry in Bangladesh, the actions of garment factories have immense impact on the society and environment. Exploitation, such as low wages and long working hours, affect the physical and mental well-being of the workers. In line with Blowfield and Frynas' (2002) definition, if they were to stop such exploitation, it would mean an attempt to pursue social responsibility by reducing negative externalities. However, this cannot be expected since these small local firms are too capital-constrained to conduct activities beyond achieving economic sustainability. Yet, it is not that firms in Bangladesh do not exercise any social responsibility to their society. Historically, the small firms of Bangladesh have engaged in different philanthropic activities, such as giving donations to the poor, religious institutes and charitable organizations. That is to say, CSR in Bangladesh could be seen to take different forms in comparison to CSR as understood in the West. Unlike MNCs who have formal CSR policies and culture, small Bangladeshi firms conduct community development in the form of charity without any formal CSR agenda, policy or budget. With globalization has come the demand for more and more policy initiatives. Of course, the establishment of policies does not necessarily mean a company actually makes a contribution to society. Some MNCs are genuinely implementing CSR policies to stop exploitation in their global supply chains, while others are arguably using mission statements, policies and codes of conduct for public relations purposes, to combat pressure from the media, NGOs and other stakeholder groups. It is worth noting, policies have helped MNCs to foster an ethical image externally and internally and also take opportunity of the increasing trend of ethical consumption. Overall, there are important reasons to suggest the concept and perception of CSR is different in developed and developing economies. It is necessary, then, to look more closely at the specific business context in Bangladesh in order to present a more nuanced understanding of current

CSR activity – and the difficulties in achieving CSR in Bangladesh, particularly in the RMG industry.

Current condition of CSR activity in Bangladesh

According to Akkas (1999), the concept of social responsibility has received little attention in Bangladesh. He interviewed different stakeholder groups of firms and found the stakeholders perceive Bangladeshi businesses to be insincere and indifferent about social responsibilities. Tax evasion, adulteration, creation of artificial scarcity to increase commodity price, exploitation of employees and consumers are common practices. It is the tendency of almost every business to evade tax by falsifying information or bribing the public authorities. The markets are flooded with infringed products. Even, sub-standard medicines are sold on the market causing death to many people. In 1998, seven patients died in Rangpur Medical College Hospital for consuming expired medicines. The expiry dates of medicines, food items and cosmetics are often hidden by local manufacturers or retailers. The prices of necessity items such as rice, salt, baby food and vegetables are increased by forming cartels and by the creation of artificial crisis. At least 80,000kg of formalin-treated fish enters the country on a daily basis from Myanmar, posing a serious health hazard to millions of consumers (Ayon 2007). Due to this massive adulteration of fish, Bangladesh lost its fish export market in Europe and North America. However, the stories of unfair activities are even more scandalous in the textile and ready-made garment sector, from which Bangladesh earns most of its national income. In essence, managers in Bangladesh are driven by profit-making and workers are placed mainly on minimum wages. A majority of the country's population suffers from poverty and is not educated, which gives rise to ongoing exploitation. Thus, any advancement in CSR management in Bangladesh will contribute a lot to the society. The issues that can be considered to be important in relation to CSR in Bangladesh are the minimum wage, quality of working conditions, sexual harassment, discrimination and the lack of freedom of association.

Bangladesh is the world's third largest employer in the textile sector and sixth largest employer in the clothing industry. Bangladeshi garment workers are the lowest paid and most shockingly exploited in the world (Hearson and Morser 2007). The recently revised minimum wage is TK 1662, which is just 44 per cent of what is considered to be the living wage in the country (Bangladeshnews.com 2006a). Some economists in Bangladesh estimate that just the cost of rice accounts for 60 per cent of this minimum wage, and garment manufacturers are even reluctant to implement this minimum wage. According to the president of the Garment Workers Unity Forum, only 20 per cent of the 4,000 factories have implemented the minimum wage (AFP 2007). Some of the factories are fined for irregular salary payment and in some cases no payment at all. And even though 71.1 per cent of the company owners and executives think that workers are duly paid for overtime, over 90 per cent of the workers and civil society members complained of underpayment for extra work and 11 per cent of the employees complained they received no extra payment for overtime shifts (CPD 2003: 7). Recently, workers revolted against these issues of the wage structure through several violent upris-ings. In late May through to June 2007, there was a wave of labour unrest in the industry. Around 4,000 factories in Dhaka went on strike, 16 factories were burnt down by strikers and hundreds more ransacked and looted, pitched battles were fought against police and main roads were blocked. In three days, three workers were shot dead, thousands were injured and several thousands were jailed. Almost 20,000 workers formed an angry procession on the highways of the country. At the end, to tackle the unrest, the Bangladesh Rifles, a paramilitary force mainly associ-ated with guarding the borders of the country, was called from their normal duties and deployed across the areas of unrest (libcom.org 2007). In another incident on 7 May 2008, workers of the three garments factories in the port city Chittagong rioted in relation to issues of pay. They vandalized 50 vehicles and looted several shops (*Daily Star* 2008).

Along problems over the wage structure, working conditions are also a serious concern in the garment factories. Yet, these factories produce products for emin-ent multinational companies. To exemplify, research by WOW (2006), conducted on the workers of six Bangladeshi suppliers of Tesco, Asda and Primark, reveals that the workers' average monthly payment ranges from £7.54 to £8.33, which is not enough to cover their cost of food, rent and medicine. These suppliers force their workers to work in 16-hour shifts without proper compensation for overtime. They maintain a seven-day working week with no regular holidays, no paid sick leave and no maternity leave. The workplace is congested, hot, and lacks proper ventilation and fire exits. Workers face physical assault and female workers particularly are more prone to sexual harassment and obscene gestures by their mid-level staff. The same situation is prevalent in almost all factories. Due to the lack of proper health and safety measures accidents frequently occur. The four most recent incidents – three fires and the collapse of a factory – occurred less than a year after a major disaster at the Spectrum factory, which collapsed in April 2005 killing 63 workers, injuring over 70 more and leaving hundreds unemployed (LBL 2006). Exploitation is also taking place in many of the factories producing merchandise for different eminent universities of the US and UK, despite scholars at these institutions frequently discussing the unethical practices of corporations in less developed countries.

Sexual harassment, physical and verbal abuse and discrimination are also com-mon practices in the industry. Research by SDNP (2006) discloses 40 per cent of all workers in Bangladesh and 80 per cent of non-export processing zone (EPZ) gar-ment workers reported the use of sexual expletives in their workplace. Sexualized vocabulary, body language, hostile and a sexually charged work environment are commonly faced by workers. Supervisors, linemen, line chiefs and production man-agers practice hair pulling, stroking and kissing of workers sitting at machines. A worker at one of Gap's subcontractors said she suffered ear pinching and slapping from her supervisor, but knew she could not fight back for fear of losing what little income she had. The Gap workers who were interviewed said the factories they work in can be dangerous places, and they have experienced injuries including cuts, needle punctures, loss of digits, burns, severe respiratory illness, kidney infections and extreme temperatures (UNITE 2002). Furthermore, even though these garment factories hire mostly female workers, they pay more salary to male workers, another clear signal of gender discrimination. Trade union activities were prohibited within the EPZ area until late 2006. Even now, however, with this prohibition eliminated, there exists considerable restriction on the freedom of association, which indirectly prevents workers from collective bargaining. The managers of the companies claim that trade unions are manipulated by the political parties to satisfy their interests (Perman *et al.* 2004). Critics claim the recent unrest arose due to the conspiracy by Indian RMG lobby groups, who were seeking to undermine the garment industry of Bangladesh and so reduce international competition. They manipulated the trade unions of Bangladesh through exaggerated information about labour abuse in factories that initiated the conflict (Kumara 2006).

As per Carroll's (1991) model, it falls under the legal and economic responsibilities of companies to ensure standard working conditions, proper health and safety measures and proper wages. Yet, as the foregoing description outlines, Bangladeshi companies, particularly those involved in the labour-intensive cost-focused sectors, are still struggling to implement the first two stages of Carroll's model, regarding legal and economic duty, let alone the further stages of ethical and philanthropic responsibilities. According to Crane and Matten (2004), there is an area of overlap between law and ethics, following which we might consider executing legal responsibilities that can help organizations to maintain some of their ethical duties as well. Ahmed (2007) has noted that some of the textile and garment factories of Bangladesh have recently conducted community development activities, albeit on a limited scale. However, his research findings suggest that a lack of interest and awareness of the firms, as well as the community they might serve, are the most significant constraint in conducting CSR activities. Companies reported that they failed to gain the cooperation of the community while conducting these activities. The drivers of current unethical practices in the RMG industry are mainly initiated by three parties: Bangladeshi suppliers, foreign buyers and the Bangladeshi government. The behaviours of these parties are influenced by various factors shaping the current condition. The factors related to each of these parties are discussed below. Factors relating to suppliers and the government are obviously discussed in terms of their specific context in Bangladesh. However, it is worth noting, foreign buyer-driven factors are initiated by the MNCs that outsource their production in LDCs and hence are not only limited to the Bangladeshi context, but can be applied to the wider global context. By analyzing all these factors together, a better understanding of the current situation in Bangladesh can be drawn up, which in turn helps looking towards a future agenda of CSR management in Bangladesh.

Foreign buyers

According to Nicholls (2002) companies implement ethical standards in their global supply chain by taking proactive and defensive initiatives. Defensive strategies are guided by legal minimums and avoid buyer engagement in the implementation process; proactive strategies are supra-legal and include buyer engagement in the implementation process. Foster and Harney (2005) argue that defensive initiatives primarily target economic benefit whereas proactive initiatives target achieving social and environmental sustainability for business and community, besides economic benefits. Therefore, companies following defensive strategies impose pressures on suppliers regarding price, deadlines (which force suppliers to exercise low wages) and overtime (which generally violates established codes of conduct). Evidence suggests companies adopting a proactive strategy are more successful in achieving sustainability for the business and its stakeholders than those adopting defensive strategies. For instance, Gap, Disney and Wal-Mart all have well-designed codes of conduct that they use as a defence against negative publicity. However, depending merely on a code of conduct without proper implementation and monitoring is not enough. That is why exploitation is said to be rampant in these companies' supply chains and they are still associated with 'sweatshop' activities (LBL 2003). Contrarily, companies such as Sainsbury's, a UK-based supermarket chain, seek to prevent imposing undue pressure on suppliers; they actively engage in the implementation of standards over the protection of children, health and safety, working conditions and wages. Such proactive initiatives confirm their reputation, supplier efficiency and sales and thus ensure sustainability for the business and its stakeholders (Jones *et al.* 2005). However, proactive strategies are expensive to implement, which discourages companies. Moreover, Blowfield (2000) highlights that it is difficult to measure the impact of such initiatives, which is another reason for MNCs' reluctance in conducting proactive initiatives.

Bowie (1988) has argued when MNCs are guided by an absolutist philosophy and they encourage no differentiation in terms of wages and working standards between host and home country. However, the primary motive for MNCs to conduct international business with LDCs is to gain a cost advantage. Hence, following absolutism would mean a failure to ensure cost advantage, which would undermine any motive to go to LDCs. As such, absolutism is likely to lead to unemployment and seemingly raise poverty, given that the growth of foreign direct investment is likely to decline as existing MNCs start divesting. In this case, MNCs are undermining developing nations' rights to participate in global business and also disrespecting the moral obligations of MNCs to participate in the development process of LDCs and consequently, contravening the new development philosophy, 'Trade not aid' (*Guardian* 2002).

By contrast, when MNCs believe in relativism philosophy they consider the host country's context and comply with the local practices regarding wages and labour conditions. However, where existing wages and conditions provide an unacceptable and even inhumane, standard of living, this principle equates to encouraging these practices, which goes against sustainability (Perman *et al.* 2004). Bowie (1988) has argued that MNCs taking a relativist position believe that they are following ongoing practices of a host country and therefore doing nothing unethical. Moreover, Crane and Matten (2004) suggest MNCs follow relativism considering they have no right to interfere with wage structure and working conditions of a country and thus respecting their culture. Child labour and long working hours, among other things, may seem unethical in the Western context but considering the poor economic condition of the LDCs it can be lucrative to the workers as an additional source of income. Thus, it can be argued that relativism reduces the cost of doing business, which in turn makes organizations more profitable. This creates employment for greater numbers of people in LDCs and contributes to development (UNCTAD 2002). Additionally, Barrientos (2000) has argued that the recent trend in low-cost labour has created employment for marginal groups such as women and minority workers, who would have otherwise remained unemployed. Comparing the impact of absolutism and relativism, it can be argued that where absolutism can lead to the complete destruction of industry and unemployment, relativism at least ensures employment and participation of LDCs in international business and consequently, encourages development. Considering all these issues buyers sometimes intentionally maintain a relativist philosophy accepting that some exploitations will occur in the supply network.

Most MNCs have codes of conduct that set standards too high, making it difficult for suppliers from third world countries to implement and simultaneously be cost efficient; or more fundamentally, they lack sufficient capital to implement these expensive standards. Some MNCs also require their suppliers to implement international standards such as SA 8000 (Social Accountability Standard 8000), established by the US-based Council on Economic Priorities (CEP), which is too sophisticated and complex for small entrepreneurs to implement. Implementing set standards is possible in concentrated industries like the auto industry, but difficult for the textile industry, which has a relatively complex supply chain. According to Graafland (2002), only 15 to 20 per cent of suppliers can successfully implement such high standards. Arguably, then, these standards are simply unrealistic. Furthermore, MNCs sometimes put forward codes of conduct that are contradictory to the law of the country, which means they will fail to be implemented. For example, in Bangladesh, collective bargaining cannot be encouraged as trade unions are legally prohibited inside the EPZ. Even outside the EPZ, workers do not cooperate with trade unions as they are highly politicized and leaders mainly prioritize their own interests. Therefore, to prevent exploitation, codes need to be practical and also compliant with the culture and laws of the host country.

Most MNCs monitor compliance with a code of conduct through internal auditing. However, it is very difficult to execute, coordinate and maintain the same standards of auditing globally. Monitoring in the clothing industry is even more complex as the retailers source products from a wide variety of countries. According to the network model of the stakeholder theory (Rowley 1997), corporations' responsibilities are no longer limited within their immediate stakeholder groups rather it is extended towards the stakeholders' stakeholders. Therefore, in the supply chain a retailer has a business responsibility towards sub-suppliers along with their immediate supplier (Crane and Matten 2004). However, Fearne *et al.* (2005) have argued that due to globalization, companies have a long supply network involving suppliers from different countries. So it is complex and expensive to ensure implementation and monitoring of code compliance and also implement other CSR activities within the supply chain. As a result, companies are limiting their business responsibilities towards first-tier suppliers only.

Roberts (2003) argues that efforts to monitor compliance diffuses as the buyers move down the stages in the supply chain. Hence, exploitations happening in the sub-suppliers' factories go unnoticed and unmonitored. And inevitably, the lack of proper monitoring opens up opportunities for exploitations. Recently, to ensure more effectiveness, companies have adopted independent monitoring systems. For example, some companies require their suppliers to have certificates from an independent body that ensures suppliers are implementing standards properly (for example, adaptation of SA 8000). In Holland, aid agencies, trade unions and retailers' associations are negotiating to set up the Fair Trade Charter Foundation. This would have representation from all three constituencies to oversee the implementation and monitoring of a uniform code for the garment industry. Finally, some companies have hired outside organizations to monitor compliance in all of their global operation. For example, C&A, a Dutch clothing retailer, has hired the Service Organization for Compliance Audit Management (SOCAM) to conduct unannounced inspections of suppliers around the world. In 1997, SOCAM made 1,000 inspections. Based on the inspection reports C&A suspended 80 suppliers, 30 of whom were reinstated after providing a satisfactory corrective plan to the company (CAFOD 1998). Nevertheless, until now most companies are relying on in-house monitoring or no monitoring at all, which encourages exploitation.

Of course, initiatives undertaken to improve the working conditions of suppliers may be undervalued if codes of conduct and other related initiatives are buyer-driven and ignore the priorities of the suppliers. To improve the living standards of suppliers from different countries with different economic backgrounds the buyer needs to take diverse initiatives, which increases management complexity. For instance, while ensuring transport, health and education facilities are important for improving living standards of suppliers from Ghana, initiatives are likely to be very different for European suppliers (Blowfield and Jones n.d.). Some expectations of the suppliers may even prove to be contradictory to the ethical values of companies. To exemplify, as MNCs actively work towards eliminating child labour, the local community of a particular supplier may want more working opportunities for their children, since limited educational facilities lead parents to think that by working their children can at least contribute money to their low-income family (Tariquzzaman and Kaiser 2007). However, considering these limitations many companies are designing and implementing initiatives in partnership with suppliers to prioritize their needs and reduce complexity. For example, C&A has a dialogue strategy through which they consult with the suppliers when developing codes of conduct and designing initiatives for their improvement (Graafland 2002). John Lewis, a UK-based retailer of home appliances, also has a partnership programme with their suppliers to ensure their participation in the code-designing process (Buckley 2004). However, giving priority to suppliers' demand is not always possible due to government legislation. Additionally, cultural pressures (e.g. in highly patriarchal societies it is expected that men will receive more pay than women workers), unstable currencies and high inflation rates limit the scope of maintaining diversified CSR activities in worldwide supply networks (Bowfield and Jones n.d.).

Bangladeshi suppliers

According to Graafland (2002), the production cost of garments is only 1 per cent of the retail price, which is received by the owner of the supplier's factory. In contrast, the brand owner/buyer gets 25 per cent of the retail price as their profit. Therefore, the profit is insignificant for the garment factory owners from what they pay as salaries to their employees and spend for improving working conditions. As a result, employees get the lowest possible salary and poor working conditions. Furthermore, compliance with the codes increases the cost of production and thus makes suppliers incompetent compared with other local and international competitors. If the buyers do not simultaneously implement codes in their worldwide supply chain, then one becomes less competent than the other. This fear stimulates suppliers to avoid compliance with codes.

The enforcement of a code of conduct is sometimes hindered by a supplier's effort to falsify records on wage and working conditions (Foster and Harney 2005) and prevents buyers from realizing the state of the actual conditions. Factories conduct deceptive practices in very creative ways. They maintain fake records of payrolls, working hours and overtime payments. Workers are trained to behave in a certain way while auditing. Some factories have dedicated employees for maintaining these false records and training employees. Recently there has been a trend of hiring flexible workers, i.e. part-time, temporary, home-workers and employing marginal groups. The reason behind this is that the company has reduced responsibility towards flexible workers compared with full-time workers. Moreover, these workers are of more marginalized minorities, which reduces the possibility of whistle blowing, particularly, during auditing (Barrientos 2000).

In the garment industry, MNCs have a concern for their reputation and image, whereas the garment factories are small local businesses with limited concern for their image. In being less vulnerable to issues of reputation, these suppliers lack the urge to implement codes. They know if there is negative publicity in the media, no one will accuse them, but rather the buyers' brand image will be at stake (Roberts 2003). Furthermore, a single supplier has multiple buyers from Europe and America with different standards and requirements. The suppliers face difficulties in complying with different contradictory standards (Berthiaume 2006), which increase the complexity and cost of doing business. There is a need, arguably, for standardizing the codes across countries and companies (CAFOD 1998). However, in labour-intensive industries, the buyers are usually the most powerful among other members of the supply chain. An abundance of suppliers from different parts of the world want to compete for only two prime markets: US and Europe. The buyers have plenty of options and enjoy low switching costs. Subsequently, failing to offer the lower quote implies losing the contract for suppliers. This competition has become intense after the phase out of the Multi Fiber Agreement (MFA) in 2005. Bangladeshi suppliers are now competing not only with other local suppliers but also with suppliers from China, India, Indonesia and Pakistan etc. Compliance with codes of conduct and pressure to improve working conditions increase the cost of production and make the suppliers uncompetitive. Therefore, suppliers are struggling to offer the lowest possible price by sacrificing all to standards (or their falsification) so as to survive in the severe international market. Crane and Matten (2004) described this situation using the phrase 'race to the bottom'.

Bangladeshi government

Lack of good governance in Bangladesh is one of the prime reasons for a poor CSR culture. Bangladesh has endorsed seven of the eight labour conventions on collective bargaining, discrimination and equal remuneration, child labour and forced labor. However, serious violations are happening in all these areas due to the lack of proper enforcement of laws. The reason behind this situation is lack of monitoring, and bureaucracy and corruption in the public sector. For example, during 1997 to 2005, garment manufacturers and exporters signed four agreements with the government to solve labour exploitation in factories, yet to date none of those have been implemented (ICFTU 2006). Furthermore, in most developing countries national minimum wage is not enough for employees to maintain a decent living standard. Hence, multinationals, even after complying with the minimum wage standard, fail to ensure social and economic sustainability for their employees and their stakeholders (Blowfield and Jones n.d.). Similarly, in Bangladesh, although the national minimum wage was recently revised by the government and settled at Tk 1662, it still cannot be considered a living wage. The inflation rate has increased the cost of living up to 46 per cent. According to Islam (2006), to live a decent life fulfilling all the basic human needs a rural worker in Bangladesh needs to be paid Tk 5000 a month and urban worker Tk 9000. The National Garments Workers' Federation is demanding that the government should announce a rise in the minimum wage to Tk 3000 (BangladeshNews.com 2006b).

Not unlike other developing countries' governments, the Bangladeshi government is rather relaxed in regarding the implementation of labour laws and standards, fearing that too much strictness will result in increased costs of production and leave the export sectors lacking competitiveness. Not all factories have the capital and expertise to implement international standards. Strictness regarding compliance would mean shutting down these factories, which would then lead to significant unemployment in the area. The director of the Bangladesh Garments Manufacturers and Exporters Association has commented: 'human rights could never be honored if the semi-skilled and unskilled masses are forced to unemployment' (CPD 2003: 12). Thus, governments sometimes instruct external auditors to be lenient, otherwise fearing the negative effect from honest auditing on the national economy (Iwanow *et al.* 2005). To summarize, exploitation in the RMG industry is rampant in Bangladesh (as well as in other LDCs) because of MNCs' concentration on cost efficiency, unrealistic codes of conduct, lack of monitoring and unfair distribution of profit. These factors combined with Bangladeshi suppliers' tendency to falsify information, obligations to meet the differing needs of multiple buyers and finally the Bangladeshi government's reluctance to enforce labour laws are responsible for the current condition of the industry.

The above discussed factors are summarized in Figure 5.1, which as shown,

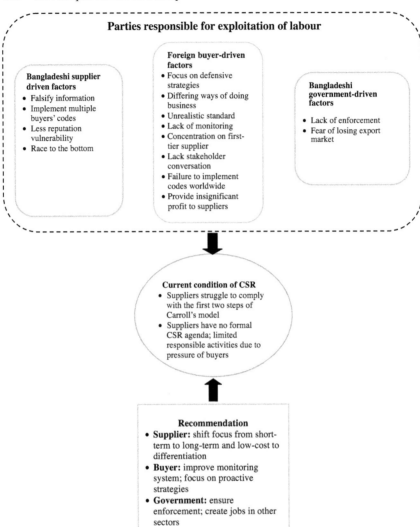

Figure 5.1 The current situation of CSR activities in the Bangladeshi RMG industry and the parties responsible.

lead to the current condition in which suppliers struggle to comply with even the first two stages of Carroll's (1991) model of CSR (i.e. economic and legal responsibilities). As a result, suppliers have no formal CSR agenda and only limited options to develop one. However, there are certain recommendations and new developments that may offer opportunities for positive change. Recently, due to the growth in information technologies (most notably the Internet), there has been a considerable amount of negative publicity and criticism regarding the unethical practices in the supply chain of high profile corporations. This in turn has raised the concerns of these corporate houses. Furthermore, ethical consumerism is now on the rise. A Europe-wide survey (MORI 2000), conducted on consumer attitudes, revealed that a company's commitment to social responsibility was an important factor when buying a product or service for 70 per cent of the respondents. The value of the fair trade market in UK is approaching towards 70m from 4m in 1994 (Crane and Matten 2004: 334). Appreciating the impact and significance of these ongoing issues, companies are increasingly trying to incorporate ethical sourcing initiatives in supply chains and change existing supplier practices. According to the *New Nation* (2007), US buyers Wal-Mart and Hanes and UK buyers Marks and Spencer, Primark, Tesco and Asda were recently criticized by their stakeholders because their Bangladeshi suppliers are not paying a living wage to the workers. In response, these retailers threatened to cancel all orders if the Bangladeshi suppliers did not comply. However, this defensive approach of the MNCs may not solve the problem in the long run. Indeed, cancelling the order would mean the creation of unemployment, which would deepen the problem. Arguably, then, the best practice needs to be some form of partnership with the suppliers to provide them some assistance, whether in the form of financial help or guidance.

Along with the actions of buyers, the Bangladeshi government is also taking several steps to encourage companies to improve the working conditions. Recently, a business fair was arranged by the Bangladeshi government exhibiting health and safety equipment to be used in garment factories. The motive behind arranging such an event was to create awareness among garment factory owners and their stakeholders. Moreover, the government has arranged meetings with stakeholders from the directors of the Bangladesh Garments Manufacturers and Exporters Association and the Bangladesh Knitwear Manufacturers and Exporters Association to discuss the issues regarding compliance in factories. The government has also decided to engage different firms to lobby in the US and Europe for improving the negative image created among the buyers (*New Nation* 2007). A study by Quazi (2002) is promising, revealing the attitudes of Bangladeshi managers are now positive towards consumerism. Managers believe consumerism is pro-business and appreciate proactive self-regulation where there is lack of enforcement from the government. They believe consumerism is at the early growth stage in Bangladesh, so at this point self-regulatory practices like superior product standard, compliance with industry codes of conduct or international guidelines etc. can prove to be tools for differentiating themselves and an important strategy to survive in business. This attitude undoubtedly contributes to improving the culture of CSR in Bangladesh.

Conclusion

Rossouw (1994) has focused on three phases through which moral development happens in developing countries: a survival, reactive and proactive phase. In the survival phase, business houses compete fiercely and struggle to earn their minimum income for survival; as the author puts it: 'bread first, morals later' (p. 46). Hence, at this stage corporations get involved in immoral activities just to sustain business. At a later stage, companies do not fight for survival rather they become stable and respond to the demands of the society and behave accordingly. However, by the third stage, businesses conduct ethical activities proactively, without waiting for the demands of society.

Immediately after the MFA phase-out, Bangladeshi suppliers lost their guaranteed market in the US and Europe and faced fierce international competition, particularly from China and India. Following Rossouw (1994), it can be argued that at this time the main focus of Bangladeshi suppliers was to survive in this new competitive era. In this circumstance, they found offering lowest possible prices the best way to sustain. To achieve low cost, they got involved in all sorts of unethical and inhumane practices. However, the situation has now changed. It has been observed that after the MFA phase-out the export of RMG products from Bangladesh has actually increased (ADB 2005). Nevertheless, garment manufacturers are still continuing to conduct unethical practices. As argued by Rossouw (1994), even when the survival phase is over, business houses continue to engage in immoral activities, first, because they were previously doing it and it has become habit. Secondly, if the society permits businesses to continue to practice unethical behavior then it is reasonable to suggest they will never change. This argument is applicable to what is currently happening in the Bangladeshi RMG sector. The owners of the factories previously exploited workers to survive and earn marginal profit. Now it has become their habit. Moreover, the relaxed legal structure of the government and pressures and/or inconsistencies from buyers has further intensified the problem.

It is critical that the suppliers change their focus from short-term profit gains to socially responsible activities. They must realize that in today's world to get better market access and acceptability among the local and international stakeholders compliance is necessary. Compliance can offer these garment factories a basis for upgrading and avoiding the low-cost route to competition, typically depending on cheap labour (Abdullah 2004). To stop exploitation, the government and the MNCs must also play a more critical role. The reason being that (1) government has a responsibility towards the well-being of all its citizens and is accountable to more people compared with a single garment supplier; similarly (2) the MNCs have more power and reputation vulnerability than the suppliers. The government needs to enhance capacity-building in the RMG sector so that small firms can comply with the codes of conduct. Furthermore, the government has to ensure enforcement without fearing the loss of export markets. Many buyers have long-term relationships with Bangladeshi suppliers and in the international market, Bangladeshi RMG products are perceived to be of a higher quality than those of China and India (ADB 2006). So compliance does not necessarily mean losing out to international competition; rather in the long run, considering the rise of ethical consumption, Bangladesh might lose its position in the market if unethical practices are *not* stopped. The threat of US and UK companies to Bangladeshi suppliers, mentioned in the previous section, is one such indication. Additionally, the government has to ensure that both local and foreign investment enters other sectors, so that manpower is not concentrated in the RMG sector. If the labour force is more flexible, then the supply of cheap labour will reduce, making it more difficult for employers to exploit their workers. The MNCs will also have to focus more on proactive strategies. However, proactive strategies are costly to implement and hence, are not appropriate to all companies. As such, reactive strategies could be acceptable if compliance with codes is monitored properly instead of it simply being a defence mechanism in face of media pressure. To avoid complexity of in-house monitoring, independent auditing agencies should be employed, as undertaken by the likes of Nike and C&A. Finally, given that MNCs are often perceived to take a significant share of profit unjustifiably, they should perhaps consider cutting their share of the profit and invest it the betterment of the suppliers.

Future agendas

Akkas (1999) has highlighted the problem of conducting research in the area of business ethics in Bangladesh. According to him, Bangladeshi companies are very conservative about disclosure of information. Mondol (2007) has also highlighted the problem and mentioned he could not interview officials because of their unwillingness to cooperate. In fact, the current authors made an attempt to collect primary data in order to examine in more detail how the various factors discussed here relate to the cause of exploitation in Bangladesh's RMG industry. However, the survey could not be conducted as the factory owners refused to talk about ethical issues. In large part, due to the existence of the recent military-backed government and ongoing labour unrest in the industry, businesses do not want to talk about ethical issues. Hence, having the difficulty of collecting primary data, the current discussion is limited, based on existing literature and publicly available information. Nevertheless, the opportunity remains for future researchers to conduct fieldwork and identify which of the above discussed factors are the most significant to explain the current situation of CSR activities in the Bangladeshi context.

Suggested further reading

Blowfield, M. (1999) 'Ethical Trade: A Review of Developments and Issues'. *Third World Quarterly*, 20(4): 753–70.

Emmelhainz, M. A., and R. J. Adams. (1999) 'The Apparel Industry Response to "Sweatshop" Concerns: A Review and Analysis of Codes of Conduct'. *Journal of Supply Chain Management*, 51–57.

Kung, H. (1997) 'A Global Ethic in an Age of Globalization'. *Business Ethics Quarterly*, 7(3): 17–31.

Nielsen, M. E. (2005) 'The Politics of Corporate Responsibility and Child Labor in the Bangladeshi Garment Industry'. *International Affairs*, 81(3): 559–80.

Phillips, R. (2008) 'European and American Perspectives on Corporate Social Responsibility'. *Business Ethics: A European Review*, 17(1): 69–73.

Takahashi, A. (1997) 'Ethics in Developing Economies of Asia'. *Business Ethics Quarterly*, 7(3): 33–45.

Yamaji, K. (1997) 'A Global Perspective of Ethics in Business'. *Business Ethics Quarterly*, 7(3): 55–70.

References

Abdullah, A. Y. (2004) 'Post Multi Fiber Agreement Era and Bangladesh RMG Sector'. *Journal of Business Administration*, 30(3/4): 91–113. Bangladesh: Jahangirnagar University.

ADB: Asian Development Bank. (2005) *Quarterly Economic Update Bangladesh: June 2005*. <http://www.adb.org/Documents/Economic_Updates/BAN/2005/dec-2005.pdf>.

—— (2006) *Quarterly Economic Update Bangladesh: February 2006*. <http://www.adb.org/Documents/News/BRM/brm-200601.asp>.

AFP: Associated Foreign Press. (2007) '*25,000 Textile Workers Protest Poor Wages in Bangladesh*. <http://afp.google.com/article/ALeqM5jDC4DNFzw_5Fqem0V3xkuLqGEFNw>.

Ahmed Q. M. (2007) 'Community People's Involvement in the CSR Agenda of Textile and Garment Industry in Bangladesh: Opportunities and Challenges', in *Proceedings of the 9th South Asian Management Forum: Management for Peace, Prosperity and Posterity*. Association of Management Development Institutions in South Asia (AMDISA) and North South University (NSU), Dhaka, 132.

Akkas, M. A. (1999) 'Social Responsibility of Business: The Bangladesh Perspective'. *Journal of Business Research*, 2: 43–53.

Awal, M. A. (2005) 'Bangladesh Strategy in Post-MFA Environment'. Unpublished paper delivered at Post-MFA Environment conference, 2 June 2005. Dhaka: Bangladesh Textile Mills Association.

Ayon, K. I. (2007) '80,000 kg Formalin Fish Enter Country Every Day No Policy for Fish Import Yet'. *Daily Star*. <http://www.thedailystar.net/2007/03/02/d7030201022.htm>.

BangladeshNews.com (2006a) 'RMG Workers' Minimum Wage Fixed at Tk 1,662'. <http://www.bangladeshnews.com.bd/2006/10/06/rmg-workers-minimum-wage-fixed-at-tk-1662/> (accessed 7 April 2008).

—— (2006b) 'RMG Workers Agitate forTk 3000 Minimum Wage'. <http://www.bangladeshnews.com.bd/2006/09/16/rmg-workers-agitate-for-tk-3000-minimum-wage/>.

Barrientos, S. (2000) *Globalization and Ethical Trade Assessing the Implications for Development*. John Wiley & Sons Ltd, Proquest Database.

Berthiaume, D. (2006) 'Reebok's Sourcing Strategy Places Ethics First. *Chain Store Age*, 32A-33A.

Blowfield, M. (2000) 'Ethical Sourcing: A Contribution to Sustainability or a Diversion? Natural Resources and Ethical Trade Programme'. Natural Resources Institute, University of Greenwich. <http://www.ethicaltrade.org/Z/lib/2000/other/nret-susdev.pdf#search='Ethical%20Sourcing%3A%20%20A%20contribution%20to%20sustainability%20%20or%20a%20diversion%3F'> (accessed 11 June 2006).

Blowfield, M. and K. Jones, K. (n.d.) 'Ethical Trade and Agricultural Standards – Getting People to Talk'. Natural Resources and Ethical Trade Programme, Natural Resources Institute, University of Greenwich. <http://www.nri.org/vinet/pub/publications/ETAgStd.pdf> (accessed 11 June 2006).

Bowie, N. (1988) 'When in Rome, Should You Do as the Romans Do? Relativism and the Moral Obligations of Multinational Corporations', in T. L. Beauchamp and N. E. Bowie (eds) *Ethical Theory and Business*. 6th edn. New Jersey: Prentice Hall.

Buckley, B. (2004) 'Responsible Sourcing'. Unpublished paper delivered at TIFCON Conference. John Lewis, 21 October 2004. <http://www.texi.org/events/O4Tifconpapers/John%20Lewis.ppt> (accessed 11 June 2006).

CAFOD: Catholic Agency for Overseas Development. (1998) Email attachment to A. Faruq re. Policy Papers: The Asian Garment Industry and Globalization, 4 February2008.

Carroll, A. B. (1991) 'The Pyramid of Corporate Social Responsibility: Toward the Moral Management of Organizational Stakeholders'. *Business Horizons*, July-August: 39–48.

Cassel, D. (2001) 'Human Rights and Business Responsibilities in the Global Marketplace'. *Business Ethics Quarterly*, 11(2): 261–74.

CPD: Center for Policy Dialogue. (2003) 'Report No-54: Corporate Responsibility in Bangladesh: Where Do We Stand?' <http://www.cpdbangladesh.org/publications/dr/DR-54.pdf>.

Crane, A., and M. Matten. (2004) *Business Ethics: A European Perspective*. Oxford: Oxford University Press.

Daily Star. (2008) 'Chittagong RMG workers on Pay-Hike Riot', 7 May 2008: 1.

Fearne, A., R. Duffy and S. Hornibrook. (2005) 'Justice in UK Supermarket Buyer-Supplier Relationships: An Empirical Analysis'. *International Journal of Retail & Distribution Management*, 33(8): 570–82.

Foster, L. and A. Harney. (2005) 'Why Ethical Sourcing Means Show and Tell'. *Financial times*, 22 April 2005: 17.

Graafland, J. J. (2002) 'Sourcing Ethics in the Textile Sector: The Case of C&A'. *Business Ethics: An European Review*, 11(3): 282–94.

Guardian. (2002) 'Trade Not AID'. <http://www.guardian.co.uk/analysis/story/0,3604, 722840,00.html>.

Hearson M. and A. Morser. (2007) 'Let's Clean Up Fashion 2007 Update'. Labour Behind the Label and War on Want. <http://www.labourbehindthelabel.org/images/pdf/lcuf2007.pdf>.

Hearson M. (2008) 'Let's Clean Up Fashion: The State of Pay Behind the UK High Street 2008 Update'. Labour Behind the Label. <http://www.labourbehindthelabel.org/images/pdf/letscleanupfashion2008.pdf>

ICFTU: International Confederation of Free Trade Unions. (2006) 'Internationally Recognised Core Labour Standards in Bangladesh'. <http://www.icftu.org/www/pdf/corelabourstandardsbangladesh2006.pdf>.

Islam, K. A. (2006) 'Employers Continue to Underpay Workers: National Minimum Wages Remain Distant Reality'. *Daily Newage*, 29 April 2006: 1–2.

Iwanow, H., M. G. McEachern and A. Jeffrey. (2005) 'The Influence of Ethical Trading Policies on Consumer Apparel Purchase Decisions: A Focus on The Gap Inc.' *International Journal of Retail & Distribution Management*, 33(5): 371–87.

Jones, P., D. Comfort, D. Hillier and I. Eastwood. (2005) 'Corporate Social Responsibility: A Case Study of the UK's Leading Food Retailers'. *British Food Journal*, 107(6): 423–35.

Kumara, S. (2006) 'Widespread Unrest Erupts Among Textile Workers in Bangladesh'. *International Committee of the Fourth International.* <http://www.wsws.org/articles/2006/jun2006/bang-j19.shtml>.

LBL: Labour Behind the Label. (2003) 'Wear Fair'. <http://www.labourbehindthelabel.org>.

LBL: Labour Behind the Label/ (2006) 'Tragedy in Bangladesh'. <http://www.labourbehindthelabel.org/images/pdf/bulletin25.pdf>.

Libcom.org. (2007) 'Garment Workers Revolt in Bangladesh'. <http://libcom.org/news/article.php/bangladesh-garment-revolt-140706>.

Mondol E. P. (2007) 'CSR-Corporate Social Responsibility: The Context and Cases of Bangladesh', in *Proceedings of the 9th South Asian Management Forum: Management for*

Peace, Prosperity and Posterity, Association of Management Development Institutions in South Asia (AMDISA) and North South University (NSU), Dhaka, 33–37.

Mongabay. (2005) 'Corporations Among Largest Global Economic Entities, Rank Above Many Countries – Corporations Make Up 63% of 150 Largest Global Economic Enterprises'. <http://news.mongabay.com/2005/0718-worlds_largest.html>.

MORI. (2000) *The First Ever European Survey of Consumers' Attitude towards Corporate Social Responsibility and Country Profiles.* London: MORI and CSR Europe.

New Nation. (2007) 'Propaganda Against Bangladesh RMG: Steps Taken to Meet Compliance Issue'. <http://nation.ittefaq.com/artman/publish/article_35144.shtml>.

Nicholls, A. F. (2002) 'Strategic Options in Fair Trade Retailing'. *International Journal of Retail and Distribution Management,* 30(1): 6–17.

Perman, S., L. Duvillier, N. David and J. E. S. Grumiau. (2004) 'Behind the Brand Names Working Conditions and Labour Rights in Export Processing Zones'. <http://www.icftu.org/www/PDF/EPZreportE.pdf#search ='Behind%20the%20Brand%20names>.

Prieto-Carrón M., P. Lund-Thomsen, A. Chan, A. Muro and C. Bhusan. (2006) 'Critical Perspectives on CSR and Development: What We Know, What We Don't Know, and What We Need to Know'. *Journal of International Affairs,* 8(2): 977–87.

Quazi, A. M. (2002) 'Managerial View on Consumerism: A Two-Country Comparison'. *European Journal of Marketing,* 36(1/2): 36–50.

Roberts, S. (2003) 'Supply Chain Specific? Understanding the Patchy Success of Ethical Sourcing Initiatives'. *Journal of Business Ethics,* 44(2/3): 159–70.

Rossouw, G. J. (1994) 'Business Ethics in Developing Countries'. *Business Ethics Quarterly,* 4(1): 43–51.

Rowley, T. J. (1997) 'Moving Beyond Dyadic Ties: A Network Theory of Stakeholder Influences'. *Academy of Management Review,* 22(4): 887–910.

SDNP: Sustainable Development Networking Programme. (2006) 'International Women's Day 2004 and Bangladesh'. <http://www.sdnpbd.org/sdi/international_days/women_day/2004/women_workers.htm>.

Tariquzzaman, S. K., and E. Kaiser. (2007) 'Employers' Perceptions of Changing Child Labor Practices in Bangladesh'. *BRAC Monograph Series,* no.35, BRAC, Dhaka.

WOW: War on Want. (2006) 'Fashion Victims'. <http://www.waronwant.org/campaigns/supermarkets/fashion-victims>.

UNCTAD: United Nations Committee on Trade and Development. (2002) 'Multinational Corporations (MNCs) in Least Developed Countries (LDCs)'. <http://www.globalpolicy.org/reform/2002/modelun.pdf#search = 'MNCs%20create%20employment%20in%20LDCs> (accessed 15 June 2006).

UNITE. (2002) 'The Gap's Global Sweatshop: A Report on the Gap in Six Countries'. <http://www.behindthelabel.org/pdf/Gap_report.pdf#search ='A%20Report%20on%20the%20Gap%20in%20Six%20Countries'> (accessed 16 June 2006).

6   CSR – a virtuous Circle. But which circle? And whose 'virtue'?

John Kidd and Frank-Jürgen Richter

Introduction

There is little doubt expressed when some extol the virtues of working within the guidelines of corporate social responsibility (CSR). Firms working in this way manage their staff carefully and they in turn respond by adhering to policies, ethically arranging new accounts and illustrate their personal well-being by lowering their turnover rate. The firm's products or services are of high quality, made ethically and efficiently and thus customers and clients look to this firm to accept more of their business, hence profits grow, but not at the expense of the suppliers. Through transparent accounting and being able to view compliant declarations, the ethical investors will turn to the firm as it exhibits such good qualities. But dig deeper and we find the suppliers at the second and deeper tiers may be less perfect, and customers too may put the (ethical) products to darker uses. However, the world is not perfect. Once one deconstructs the euphoria about CSR it is possible to observe dissent. We are all products of our own cultural context and histories, which determine our identities and world view. Thus, by differing one with another we will not necessarily perceive matters in the same ways; we will even reject some behaviour as being inappropriate to our situation – to the surprise of others.

There is an important message here about the local/global problematic of CSR. CSR in part is a 'system' of being responsible (to whom, by whom, we may ask …) that by its very nature can be translated globally, and what is more, the global marketplace is making it more and more important for participants from differing contexts to find a way to operate in accordance with their codes of conduct. However, we may draw out, there will always be differing perspectives based on local needs and customs. Inevitably, the relative differences in perception, obfuscation of declarations, and the subsequent distortion of analyses will alter our view of CSR. And depending on where we are in the globe, and whether we are working for a subsidiary of a multinational or a supplier or acting as a consumer, we will be living and working in a different circle; and to others we may not seem virtuous at all. Consider the potential difficulty of Nokia having its home base in 'clean and incorrupt' Finland as it deals with the working environment in China or Vietnam, which are 'dirty and corrupt' (Transparency International 2008); or the angst of Nike managers as the Western world of 'do-gooders' proclaimed against the employment of child labourers in Asian sweatshops producing the trainers that we all wish to wear.

It would seem a crucial element is about the differing modes of trust individuals are willing to assign to others who may influence their lives, be it as a subordinate or as a customer: somehow we need to 'trust in trusting' – i.e. to accept that some aspects of exchange will not easily fit in with one's own perspective or needs, but if an understanding can be made, then it is possible to trust in the differing processes that are perceived in the others' realm. In this 'trusting' there is an element recognizing that we need to be 'responsible' towards the others – who now embrace more than the dyad above, but includes a cascade of workers, suppliers and customers in 'our' concept of CSR. According to the Modern Language Association definitions, 'responsibility' is often characterized as a form of trustworthiness:

> 'Responsibility'
> 1 the social force that binds you to the courses of action demanded by that force; "we must instil a sense of duty in our children"; "every right implies a responsibility; every opportunity, an obligation; every possession, a duty" – John D. Rockefeller Jr [syn: duty]
>
> 2 the proper sphere or extent of your activities; "it was his province to take care of himself"[syn: province]
>
> 3 a form of trustworthiness; the trait of being answerable to someone for something or being responsible for one's conduct; "he holds a position of great responsibility" [ant: irresponsibility].
>
> (MLA 2009)

This chapter will illustrate the difficulties of over-eager leaning towards universality. There can be no singularly acceptable CSR mode, since we have to learn how to perceive others and their differing views of disclosure, gift-giving and ethics; and while doing so, be willing to compromise our own ideals through an understanding of those others. There ought to be little dissent on the viewpoint that manufacturing ought to transform raw materials to finished goods in the most efficacious manner possible: this is our responsibility in using our limited global resources. But to make this work we have to look to how and where we pollute, and whom we exploit in the enactment of our strategies. CSR is being forced to reassess itself in the light of many of the global leader's attitudes towards climate change, and by other reports showing global disparities of wealth and human rights. But if one is starving and proffered a job should one demand CSR be applied in the workplace, or simply grasp the wages? Hence our basic question – to whose virtuous circle ought we to adhere?

CSR and moral economy

We suspect we are currently facing a CSR-bubble in the West and believe many enterprises think the end justifies the means since there are a myriad of references (at least from the English language press) that advocate the benefits of CSR – asking, in effect, why are *you* not doing it? If we were to argue that many Western firms just show CSR in order to 'shine', it then follows that Asian firms should not rush to copy a 'Western model' but try to use their own traditional elements of CSR in their respective business cultures, e.g. the old Confucian inclination to 'care for each other'.

We have to note a paradox if we incline towards letting Western and Eastern firms adopt a CSR regime that reflects their own specific history and cultural inclinations. CSR as it is often construed is about letting 'others' outside of the immediate context of a given firm know about their protocols and practices. This 'telling' does not mean the firm really acts according to its story though we hope it does; and it begs the question of how others view this information. Seemingly, there needs to be some form of consensus in how these protocols and practices are valued and judged. If CSR is based completely upon local understanding and systems of meaning, a question arises as to whether a consensus is possible – whether it is possible to share information and to derive a deep appreciation of knowledge, even 'wisdom' that transcends local conceptual boundaries.

There are philosophical concepts to be understood at this stage – data may be shared and viewed at little cost to anyone, even quickly shifting it round the globe via the Internet has little cost; but transforming it to knowledge requires a model of data transformation that is personally derived from our historical precepts. Therefore, perhaps, proffered CSR data from a firm may be construed differently across the globe. We know, for example, that China, despite its significance for and engagement with multiple markets around the globe has become the world's greatest manufacturer of fake goods that are bought, not only by tourists, but by organization's purchasing staff globally (we give some examples later in this chapter). This manufacturing base has contributed to China's wealth and analysts believe piracy contributes a third to China's GDP (IBLS 2008). Obviously this large production base gives work to many directly and indirectly in the supply chain, but to support fake production is unethical – so what line should be taken, and by who?

A willingness to 'fake' and dishonestly use other's intellectual capital reflects that in some ways managers in modern China have a dearth of 'community feeling' as shown by their reaction to philanthropy.

One of the reasons that [multinational companies] MNCs and Chinese companies act differently on community investment is they understand corporate citizenship in different ways. Although the term 'corporate citizenship' entered academic vocabulary in China a long time ago, most Chinese companies don't perceive the idea of being a corporate citizen. This is even less likely for private-owned business.

Business owners tend to think that their business is only responsible for making profits for shareholders. It is understandable that business owners think this way; after all, they have worked hard to build a business. Why should they bother to be responsible for the whole society? CSR comes last on their agenda, and in many cases CSR is not on their agenda at all. CSR and charitable initiatives are only a bonus adding to successful operation and good reputation.

(Chen 2009)

We might modify the words of Chen to suggest the managers in China do not follow the old precepts of 'honour' to spread benefits across a wider community preferring instead a narrow view of capitalism, of 'me-ism', and supporting the firm's shareholders. It is worth pointing out, however, in the report Chen is discussing charitable donations – which both individuals and corporations seem unwilling to make in modern China, except in times of great national stress as occurred following the Sichuan earthquake.

CSR, then, ought to be understood and set against a complex understanding of differing cultural contexts and no doubt a longer historical view. One might hope Chinese managers working together with 'ethical' Westerners might learn how and what CSR might do for their indigenous firm, but one wonders, as some of the constructs are rarefied. Take for example the concept of '*Noblesse oblige*', noted since the mid-1800s (originally found in Balzac's *Le Lys dans la vallée* written in 1836). This refers to the social responsibilities that come with the possession of wealth, power and prestige (i.e. the personal ability to change matters) that may easily be equated to our notion of 'community feeling'. *Noblesse oblige* is used to suggest a certain moral economy, wherein privilege must be balanced by duty towards those who lack such privilege or who cannot perform such duty. Today the term can be applied to the idea of public responsibility as exhibited by the rich and powerful elite, who provide examples of good behaviour, who are seen, for example, to go beyond minimal standards of decency. For instance, we may note Bill Gates (Bill and Melinda Gates Foundation) or earlier US benefactors Ford, Rockefeller, Mellon and Carnegie, who all gave generously of their commercially derived wealth to benefit others. In many respects we all may incline towards *noblesse oblige* as we can express and act on our concerns for others less well off – but the example quoted above from modern China's corporate world might suggest otherwise.

If one looks to the literature surveys undertaken by academics reviewing business ethics one finds they inevitably react towards the after-effects of the corporate scandals of Enron, WorldCom, Tyco International (and others) – their problems undoubtedly created huge losses in real value as well as a loss of investor confidence in massive corporations. Yet at the time, the literature supported the 'large corporation' viewpoint and their efficiencies and their managers were lauded. For instance, Enron's 2000 financial report extols 'Outdistance the Competition' showing its overall financial position rushing upwards enhancing its past growth trend (see http://picker.uchicago.edu/Enron/EnronAnnualReport2000.pdf). Generally, researchers have looked towards Western ethical behaviour to create a basis for global comparisons, and subsequently we see an emphasis upon Western corporate identity as the 'correct' model to adopt. Indeed, we – the authors – acknowledge from our own European backgrounds, that we all seem to understand the general concept of 'the Enron problem' and we all agree it needed to be tightened up, especially as we have seen CEOs more frequently taken to the courts for their infringement of corporate rules. Nor are we alone; see for instance Brazelton and Ammons (2002). However, given that 'foresight' is 'hindsight looking backwards' it is very difficult to draw attention to true deviation in time to catch errors or to stop leaders from milking their corporations or their other stakeholders. That being so we continue to see the 'Enron problem' as per its glowing review of progress in 2000 and its implication of good corporate behaviour. Thus accountants sign-off the accounts of these firms each year, the financial press laud the firms' efforts and academics note their trends with respect to their implied CSR. We can thus reasonably assume the Western context has generated the bulk (if not all) of the theory and positions taking on CSR (and of course this is the underlying premise of this book, as outlined in the Introduction). Berron *et al.* (2007) offer a good example of the kind of frameworks put forward:

> ... first we define the ethical component of the corporate identity construct with a concept we call corporate ethical identity (CEI). Relying on the notion of corporate identity we define CEI as 'the set of behaviours, communications and stances that are representative of an organisation's ethical attitudes and beliefs'. This narrowly defined concept encompasses two aspects: corporate revealed ethics (CRE), which comprises the communication of a firm's ethical attitudes and beliefs, and corporate applied ethics (CAE), which comprises the firm's behaviours – actions that can be considered ethical.
>
> (Berrone *et al.* 2007: 36)

They proceed to question the role of stakeholders in the machinations of the (ethical) firm concluding that stakeholders gain greater value from a tangible ethical action than they do from a simple ethical revelation in contrast to the Chinese example given above. It may seem that 'stakeholders' are pursuing personal self-gain as they manage the ethical behaviour of the firms in which they are involved as managers, suppliers or purchasers. But it is difficult to really discern what they actually could alter in the operations of the questionable firm as their focus is diffuse. A further problem is that it is often easier to illustrate issues when looking at non-conformance:

> ... the business ethics literature demonstrates patterns of interest in negative phenomena. Many scholars have provided significant insights into incongruence, misconduct, and unethical behaviour in areas such as leadership, reward systems, decision processes, formal and informal structures to constrain unethical behaviour, organizational culture, climate regarding ethics, and moral development of the organization. This negative focus creates a gap in our understanding of organizational ethics above and beyond industry norms, practice norms, or societal expectations of general business principles.
>
> (Verbos *et al.* 2007: 20)

Arguably, then, it is worth getting beyond such constrictions, to provide positive routes towards a comprehensive universal CSR, even if, as we earlier asserted – universality may not be achievable, and the evolution of modernity and its attitudes invalidate the principles to which we allude as being good – that of (Western) *noblesse oblige* or (Asian) Confucianism.

Stakeholder issues

There is a specific issue with the concept of the Western view of stakeholder when placed within the Asian context. Recently, debates have focused on state-owned firms or the use of sovereign wealth funds since both have opaque goals. Many authors grapple with definitions of CSR and of the stakeholders involvement, such as Buchholz and Rosenthal (2005), and there are definitions such as –

> ... any individual or group who can affect or is affected by the actions, decisions, policies, practices, or goals of the organization
>
> (Carroll 1996: 74)

or

> ... those persons or interests that have a stake, something to gain or lose, as a result of its (the corporation's) activities.
>
> (Clarkson 1995: 92)

A stakeholder, then, is an individual or group that has some kind of involvement in what a business does and may also be able to affect the organization in some way. But does this concept translate well into the Asian context? Who, for example, is the stakeholder within Asian culture? Can we assume they are able to affect the goals of the organization? Can they assume a prime stake in the organization? ... and so on.

This is certainly not the case for the majority of Asian workers who are striving to earn money, and for whom any level of recompense in an urban sweathouse is better than potential starvation in their village (see, for example, Chapter 5 on the ready-made garment sector in Bangladesh). They are not allowed to utter dissent, nor would they wish to do so due to personal fears of losing their job, and they will not necessarily even know they are making fakes – to them 'it's just a job'. Even so, the 'average Chinese peasant' who may frequently face starvation will be surprised to note that in a list of firms compiled by the Boston Consulting Group (BCG) having turnovers of greater than $1 billion in 2007 (i.e. 10^9 in US nomenclature) there were 41 Chinese firms; and of these, 16 were owned by a branch of the Chinese military (*The Economist* 2007b). Chen (2009) notes that managers are busy in making money for their shareholders and are not interested in CSR. Are ex-rural workers a part of the stakeholders group of China Inc.? Set against the definitions noted above, it is unlikely. Therefore 'stakeholder' in the Chinese context becomes a confusing concept, especially as we recognize that the

Communist Party still rules strongly even though many Western observers forget this fact (McNally 2002).

There is an old Confucian principle allowing the 'head of the household' to be the real decision maker in China that is broadened within the Chinese family enterprise to include the direct and subsidiary managers who are blood relatives or, to a lesser extent, relatives by marriage. Naturally, this raises the issue of nepotism, but it is not one that is uniquely Chinese or Asian as there are others, for instance in South America, who uphold the same principles, saying 'family members can be better trusted'. Indeed, arguably, it is not in opposition to the idea of 'good' corporate identity and cases can be found *across* cultures, which complicate preconceptions we might have due to Western-inspired CSR frameworks. There is a case, for example, in Los Angeles:

> ... Farmers Insurance Inc. has an affinity for hiring family members – a practice the company isn't skittish about admitting after 75 years of business. In an economy riddled with instability, the Los Angeles-based insurer seeks strength in the very people that work for the company. That's because many of those employees bring the bedrock foundation of family life to the workplace. Several generations of *Farmers* families pass each other on a daily basis in the halls of the company's 66-year-old art deco headquarters on Wilshire Boulevard, or in its large regional claims centre in Simi Valley. Brothers and sisters, moms and dads, grandmothers and grandchildren – they are all working for *Farmers*.
>
> ... Jeffrey Beyer, *Farmers'* chief communications officer, said he thinks the more family members working for the company the stronger the culture. "It helps make people feel energized about the corporation" he said, "I don't think that anyone would argue against that."
>
> (Pondel 2003)

Indeed, they themselves quote an old premise –

> Our co-founder John C. Tyler once said, "The measure of our worth is not what we have done for ourselves, but what we have done for others." *Farmers* agents, district managers and employees make up what we call the *Farmers Family*, and as a family we're proud to give back to our communities.
> (http://www.farmers.com/FarmComm/about_farmers.html.
> Accessed 7 February 2009)

Family businesses are managed in a variety of ways. In China we see the extended hierarchical bloodline family; in Taiwan there is a similar arrangement, but often now because of taxes and untoward investigations by the police the family juniors are expected to split from the parent and to run a start-up (which may be complementary or may be a competitor to the older business); the Japanese hierarchical businesses are also family managed, but they will actively arrange marriages to bring in new blood if that person, often a man, has desirable business acumen;

but in Korea, although the leader may be seen as a family man, his managers are often professionals hired for their ability. A detailed exposé of Asian management issues is given by Min Chen (2004), other views are offered by Kidd and Richter (2002).

The variations in management styles, preferences and behaviours across Asia – quite often involving 'gift giving' – are subsumed in the general construct of 'corruption' and are perceived as aspects of inequality. An acute problem for developing countries at present is to create conditions of equal opportunity for all, and Asia is no exception. The neoclassical model of optimum utilization of resources through market forces is not always applicable in a developing economy on account of the presence of socio-economic rigidities and barriers, with corruption being a major (if mostly hidden) factor. To a great extent, for example, China is trapped in these rigidities in so far its successive governments have had to grapple with massive social problems – its once fast expanding and still huge population, its huge distances across its regions, its poverty and its large status gradients.

Eradicating 'inequality traps' and opportunity gaps are thus espoused as the main objectives of economic development of any developing country at present. These factors are stressed by the UN/World Bank in its *World Development Report* (UNDP 2006). The anonymous authors of the report discuss why income distribution matters for the reduction of poverty:

> In a mechanical sense the rate of income poverty reduction in a country is a function of two things: the rate of its economic growth and the share of any increment of growth that is captured by the poor. Other things being equal, the larger the share of income captured by the poor the more efficient the country is in converting growth into poverty reduction. Holding income distribution patterns constant and projecting current growth rates into the future, it would take three decades for the median household in poverty to cross the poverty line in Mexico. Doubling the share of the poor in future income growth would cut this time horizon by half. Or, for Kenya, the time horizon would be reduced by 17 years, from 2030 to 2013 – a transition that would bring the country within touching distance of an otherwise unattainable Millennium Development Goal target of halving income poverty.
>
> (UNDP 2006: 228)

As noted above, variations in cultural context will alter the perception, declaration and subsequent analysis of CSR. Variations will depend upon where we are in the globe, but also where we are situated within a country and within its cultures. The transition of data via mental models to knowledge depends on our received learning. Thus, in Figure 6.1, we assume the urban Shanghai person must feel more at ease than the rural peasant in the south western Guizhou province given their potential of receiving better education and having better access to news and informed commentary. In terms of the Human Development Index spanning a global context, the UNDP allows us to presume a variance of CSR perception that at one extreme upholds an inability to react against inequalities or malfeasance on

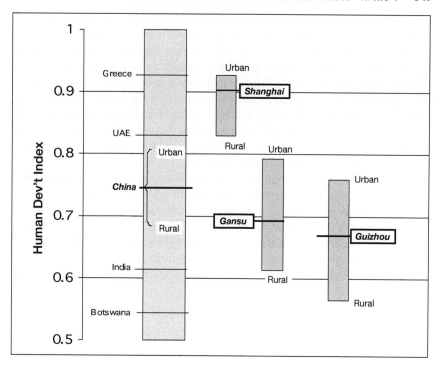

Figure 6.1 Comparisons of scores on the Human Development Index.
Source: Following UNDP (2006: 226)

two counts. First, there is a simple need to receive income, even if working in a 'sweathouse', since the cash, of which some may be sent home as a remittance, keeps many people from starvation; and secondly, the lack of information about general global mechanisms conditions the poor and ill-informed not to consider CSR as it applies to the firm's management or indeed to the workers themselves. If the managers are only interested in their own profits it may behove them to consider working in Guizhou rather than Shanghai. We see the opportunity to work based on the achieved level of education and skills, health, and also the extent of property rights are all factors contributing to individual and societal gains (Kidd 2007). That said, such arguments crash against some of our idealistic Western views of CSR that says we ought to give decent wages to our workers, which patently does not occur in the depths of a sweathouse.

Jeffery Sachs comments on this in terms of the economists' 'convergence theory' in which developing nations rapidly absorbs 'best of the world practices' as they buy into the production processes and lifestyles of the developed world. Clearly, this is how coastal China has developed through the ages as local entrepreneurs' absorbed foreign methodology, rules and equipment permitting local firms to gain greater economic benefits compared to the inland regions (Bernstein 2008). Such 'convergence' allows more poor people to be gainfully employed, and by earning they raise their family benefits (Sachs 2008: 18). However, according to Sachs, work is not the only need of the poor; primarily it is the co-related need to have better health care and also to have smaller families. Upgrading these two factors allows the poor family to better feed fewer mouths and so increase their family stability. At present the very high infant mortality in many regions 'forces' women into high birth rates, but not necessarily high infant survival rates, as the family is too poor to feed itself well enough. Western governments have all pledged towards the Millennium Goals (UN 2007) but have not delivered their cash in assured quantities – so even at a high level CSR does not work well: neither in terms of *noblesse oblige* nor in terms of Confucianism.

It would seem that historical drivers towards a universal view of CSR or at least a convergence towards a reasonable view of CSR are not working. It is not adhered to at UN levels, nor in 'go getting' firms managed by profit-orientated chiefs be these in the US, Europe or China. Given all the variations in CSR we might identify in general, but also key concepts such as managers and stakeholders, it is perhaps necessary to consider an entirely different basis of sharing in the ideals of CSR – which arguably simply requires developing a greater sense and awareness of trust.

Trust as the basis for CSR

Each year the World Economic Forum focuses on a topic deemed to be of the greatest interest to the greatest numbers of people globally. In 2003 it unveiled a survey on 'perceptions of trust' prior to its annual meeting in Davos: its conference theme was 'Building Trust'. The survey clearly shows that the level of trust worldwide is fading:

> … we are more distrustful than ever of our leaders and our [elected] governments whether it be as a parliament or a congress. It follows generally that we do not think we are being governed by the 'will of the people' … the highest levels of trust worldwide are enjoyed by the armed forces, non-government organisations, and the United Nations.
>
> (Updated by the World Economic Forum in 2005)

Their original survey of 20,000 persons, mainly in the 'Group of 20' countries, shows further disturbing evidence of deterioration in trust levels – here is a sample:

- Leaders generally were given lower trust ratings than the institutions they lead – 'not doing what they say' is the most often quoted failure of a leader.
- Citizens have as much trust in the media and in trade unions as they have in their nationally (mostly elected) governments.
- Leaders of non-government organisations (NGOs) were trusted in most countries.
- Leaders in the UN and spiritual leaders are the next most trusted.

- Global companies as well as large domestic companies were not trusted to operate for the best interests of society.
- The World Trade Organisation (WTO), World Bank and the International Monetary Fund (IMF) have almost as many people distrusting them as trusting in their probity to work for society's best interest: the WTO is the best trusted of the three.
- Most people in the survey said 'the world is not going in the right direction'.

(WEF 2005)

These findings show – at least according to the sample – that the modern world is one fraught with perceived dangers; and if not explicit, then danger is implied through our growing distrust of our leaders and our major institutions. The World Economic Forum notes that oddly we trust our armed forces, though perhaps this is due more to their role in security and anti-terrorist manoeuvres than in absolute terms.

The conflicts of interest illustrated in the above list link in with the failure of an American philanthropic venture – the Pallotta TeamWorks – which organized 'walking for charity' across the US. Their 350 officers were accused of giving themselves too great a remuneration, their clients withdrew and they were closed down. In fact, the great problem was of understanding how a profit-making organization could be a fund-raising operation. Their CEO, Dan Pallotta, has recently robustly challenged the US mentality (indeed, all our views) saying that the charitable sector should embrace capitalism since

> 'Charity is no longer an exchange between the non-needy and the needy. It is an exchange between the non-needy (donors) and the non-needy (the charity workforce) to provide services for the needy. It is thus an exchange between equals to help the needy'.

(Pallotta 2008)

He suggests the charitable sector should be structurally reformed to utilize the best business methods, to recruit top people and actively seek to make a profit while governed by the same transparencies and CSRs that direct (normal) businesses – which is in agreement with the views expressed in *CSR Asia* by Chen (2009) mentioned earlier. We see in this US example our unwillingness to trust in others where the outcome is unclear. We are giving to whom, the charity to fritter it away in overheads, or to the recipients nominated by the charity? Perhaps this is simply an occasion in which we need to learn to trust in trust.

It is rather too simplistic to opine that 'in trusting we will solve most problems' since the ways in which 'we' trust very much depends on our social and cultural context. Those raised in war zones will not easily trust and must keep their eyes open for the enemy, whereas those raised in relative isolation (like animals on an island) will be overly trusting: they have not experienced cheats or death threats and it is not a concept in their experiential vocabulary. In discussing corporate social responsibility we suggest the interaction mode within business networks must be one of mutual trust – that which is perceived to be long-term and generated through commitment (Jarillo 1988). This seems to work in Asian business circles since 'trust' is often said to be a substitute for legally binding contracts, as most emergent problems are resolved between the economic agents through negotiation rather than resorting to law and litigation (Fukuyama 1995). Indeed, as Asian nations still offer relatively weak laws, and as these are interpreted freely by the executive, business people know they have no recourse to the law. This causes some angst for the incoming Westerner who usually knows the 'force of law' supports business relationships back in the West. Generally speaking, relationships in Asia – business, political and professional – are based on personal considerations, not on the kind of objective reasoning and contracts preferred by Westerners, and the lack of an independent judiciary is one reason why the presence of lawyers is not nearly as common in East Asia as they are in the US or Europe. Traditionally, business arrangements in Asia were based on verbal commitments backed by interpersonal trust, which, unlike detailed contracts, allows for considerable flexibility in their interpretation and management as circumstances change – on both sides we might add if the partners are all Asian, who thus understand the nuances of the agreements and potential easements, as well as the bindings against default. These are generally all unstated and not written up but hidden in the *guanxi* (relationship). The Asian considers himself to be honest and able to be flexible, whereas the written Western contract covering many pages in its attempt to be 100 per cent rigid allows no easements, even when obviously needed as circumstances change.

We acknowledge the contrast between the 'Eastern' and 'Western' concepts of trust at an individual level. For instance, a Westerner in negotiation might fall back on a morality stemming originally from Judaeo-Christian beliefs (McClelland 1961); whereas an Easterner (in particular, a Chinese person) may rely on the ethics of *yi* (justice) and other internalized ethics derived from the edicts of Confucius (Luo 1997). Yet each person may believe they are projecting 'trustworthy images'. So the overt (even if unspoken) 'trust me' of the Westerner may be perceived as arrogant or immodest by the Easterner. And conversely the Easterner, even if truly 'expert', may appear too humble or self-effacing in the Westerner's eyes.

Historically, the essence of trust in Asia revolves around the Confucian principle *ren* – which refers to the way people relate to each other. One cannot exist alone and one must be able to interact with others. *Ren* can, therefore, be understood as being able to handle interpersonal or inter-organizational relationships personally: having *renqing* – human feelings. Trust as a corporate interaction mode is always based on a long-term commitment. Therefore in this fast-moving world it is not easy for managers in a supply chain to bridge cultures, especially when the chain alters quickly in form and allegiance. Supply chains are one form of network, but in China there are *guanxi* networks (which refers to interpersonal processes) that may involve gift-giving and some would say corrupt bribe exchanges (Nojonen 2003). Gift-giving has long been frowned upon in the Western business operations, and now in the West there are views expressed against excessive stock options (also viewed perhaps as a form of interpersonal bonding at a high level in the organization) offered to European and US managers: these are said to be corrupt or corrupting. Hence, the development of regulatory instruments and of the 'US Public Company Accounting Reform and Investor Protection Act' of 2002, more often referred to as 'SOX' following the names of its two principle authors Sarbanes and Oxley (SOX 2002; Kidd *et al.* 2008).

Importantly, we note that mutual trust is not pursued for charitable reasons, nor is it altruistic in intent (Kao and Sek-Hong 1993; Pellotta 2008). However, the self-interest in Japan lies in *hatake zukuri* (literally: ploughing the field) thereby guarding future eventuality. You never know when you have to become indebted to others (*osewa ni naru*) and so long-term relationships survive in environments where laws are poorly drafted and contracts are not easily enforceable by law (Luo 2000). Mutual trust and inter-organizational relationships manifest themselves in a variety of different forms. On the interpersonal level, Japanese *nomunication* and Chinese *guanxi* relationships are the best known. In Japan the tradition of *nomunication* (a conjoining of the Japanese *nomu*: to drink, with the English: communication) manifests in the informal meetings that take place at the end of the work day having the aim of building up a mutual group identity, thereby amplifying a spirit of *uchi* (in-group identity). Japanese 'salarymen' drink *sake* together in one of the many bars that specially cater for these groups of people. Thus, staff members grow closer to each other and more trusting by sharing experiences and explicitly talking of worries. *Nomunication* may include business partners from suppliers, customers and members of the same *keiretsu* (family of affiliated companies) to which the companies belong. This tradition is, however, changing under the severe economic pressure in Japan, and also due to the lack of its understanding by business partners from outside Japan – who are in attendance for a 'jolly good drinking session' but without the serious intent of the Japanese salaryman to build social coherence. Westerners are arguably wanting to do business too quickly for this traditional relationship building, and fear becoming involved or corrupted. They require instead an 'arm's length approach' by which they hope to be unsullied by accusations of bribery, corruption or nepotism – and they know 'there are no free lunches'. In a manner similar to the Japanese, when a Chinese entrepreneur seizes a business opportunity, he prefers to make a 'deal' based on previously established *guanxi* rather than seeking the anonymity of the market. Such a deal is based on opportunities arising through *guanxi*, engaging with privileged contacts and using non-publicly available information. Once, to conclude the deal, the value of the Chinese handshake was regarded to be high and invulnerable – this was based on Chinese trust (Fang 1999, 2004; Luo 2000). We should note that an introduction of a new person to the (*guanxi*) group by a trusted insider gives this new person almost the same level of *guanxi* as the introducer. This means the introducer has the responsibility to guarantee the debts of the new person if that person hints at defaulting. But, it also means the new person has great pressure brought on him by the group as a whole to behave honestly (I-Chuan Wu-Beyens 2000). Chen and Chen (2004), drawing from indigenous Chinese literature and relevant English publications, offer a fuller account of the intricacies of Chinese guanxi.

Trusting in trust

If people behave in socially responsible ways, they trust and will have taken the steps that Möllering (2006) considers are based in reason, in routines and in reflexivity. Of course, we all have to grasp how to trust each other and learn with whom we must interact in the course of our life be they lovers, passers-by, or co-workers in our own rule-bound institutional framework. We will have developed our reasoning about trust from ongoing routines even though we may reflect on their assumptions from time to time. Yet, at some stage, as Möllering points out, we will have to take on new relationships and have the need to make a 'leap of faith' in order to progress to an unknown future rather than remain locked in an unresponsive catatonia. He notes:

> ... it is crucial to recognise how the leap of faith interacts with reason, routine, and reflexivity in trust. It is not merely the case that trust rests on imperfect bases which leave a residual gap that needs to be crossed. Rather, by success-fully crossing the gap, trust also validates those bases. In other words, the leap of faith helps to generate and maintain the reasons, institutions and processes from which it first springs and, hence, it is truly crucial for our understanding of trust and its bases. If this is generally recognised, then I have high positive expectations as to the future benefits that trust research can bring to the social sciences.
>
> (Möllering 2007: 198)

We understand that the US, the UK and much of the Western-trained world is 'outcome and achievement oriented', which automatically creates conflict with staff who try 'to get it right' for the majority. Given the differences and uncertain-ties embedded in the minds of decision makers about 'those from over there ...' we might be forgiven of our despair in believing that nothing will ever be agreed, or international accords will not be struck between the Western and the Eastern nations. However, Fu *et al.* (2006) have suggested the 'new' Chinese firms are able to accommodate *guanxi* if they take care to remember its precedents depending on prior associations (of family, of township, of schooling etc), and that a similar form of social networking may allow both East and West to converge if the Westerner will also acknowledge their networks or fraternities are similar to *guanxi* nets. But there are differences, as the fraternity net does not carry such significant lifetime bindings as does a *guanxi* net once a Chinese person is bound by its association.

The modern 'achievement' society does not lend itself well to the slow build-up of trust through simple tests – initial contracts finalized correctly, aid given when none was requested, and so on – which will reinforce the trusting processes listed by Möllering. Such a build-up develops trust between the parties as we begin to note 'they think like us, so we will trust them more and more'. But from the beginning we have to come to a fundamental understanding of others. Bogenrieder (2006: 205–214) argues:

… differences between specialists in a multi-functional team […] can not be interpreted as only cognitive differences in knowledge. They are more fundamental than that […] it is argued that the causality should be the other way round. Specifically, that common understanding and validation criteria [of knowledge] should be seen as the result of co-operation, rather than a necessary condition.

This is an important argument, since people grouping together to exchange ideas simply cannot initially have an agreed goal, nor even agreed criteria for evaluating how to proceed as they are 'without knowledge of the other'. And, as we have said earlier – in carrying our fundamental cultural differences to new lands – we must be willing to suspend our judgements of 'them', since the others have very different views on CSR than us. All have to agree to compromise ideals to achieve cooperation, but before this point is achieved each has to incline towards trusting others – 'we have to engage, each of us in leaps of faith' as Möllering suggests. Or, as we are arguing herein, we have to not just learn 'to trust in trusting' but also act out that concept in practical ways. This will be very difficult since our behaviour is strongly determined by our social and cultural history and years in the home, in school and in our jobs as indicated by Fu *et al.* (2006), and other researchers of culture such as House *et al.* (2004) or Hofstede (1991). It is too emphatic and over-simplified to say we are Eastern or we are Western. Yet, we do rely upon a world view and established forms of behaviour based upon certain shared learning specific to our own cultural context. These behaviours are not always apparent to oneself or to an outside observer (not least since we frequently operate in a global culture), but nonetheless can manifest in our presentations of acceptable CSR:

We move. We dance. We shake hands. We bow. These behaviours become part of who we are and we cannot change them. Nor can we quickly learn new ones or abandon those we've acquired over our lives. Culture may more resemble tacit knowledge—it may inaccessible to our conscious mind. The ability to be German, just like the ability to play water polo, may defy explication. Our focus on behaviour allows us to imagine people as bundles of linked behaviours. Each behaviour can create external effects with others. A core insight from this behavioural bundling will be that consistency and complementarities prove advantageous. Acquiring a new behaviour that builds from existing behaviours is much simpler than starting from scratch. Having said all this, behaviour in strategic contexts depends crucially on beliefs. But just as beliefs can drive behaviours, so too can behaviours influence beliefs. People can expect others to behave consistently. Our behavioural models link behaviour to cognition. We rely on an automaton model to capture the encoding of behaviours inside peoples heads.

(Page and Bednar 2006)

We, the authors, consider that we are all pushed to some extent to believe, and maybe act according to the 'Asian Way' especially after the Japanese commercial success in the US and across Europe from the 1960s onwards (Kidd and Richter 2004). This can not be as we resist being forced into behaviours that are not natural to us – though a surface veneer may be carried as we work in a globalized context. As Page and Bednar (2006) illustrate, we can incorporate new behaviours into our institutional rules, if not into our personal behaviour – but this takes considerable energy and an underlying willingness to change. Life in the West is often too fast to allow a long maturation time to build up trust. This is not to say that life in the East is not hectic, it can be. But initially there is a slow development of trust and knowledge as the *guanxi* network builds up its momentum, or while *nemawashi* processes are completed – then the business becomes hectic as all persons concerned with a project rush towards its completion (Kidd 1983). In contrast, the typical (fast) Western person will '… rush to pick up the ball and run with it – anywhere', but this running is undirected as it begins before full knowledge of the project target is known. So how and why should the Asian manager incline to or even mimic the Western way of quick-trusting when they have an adequate historical mode – as in Confucianism? The 'oriental' process allows the business partners to 'care for each other' in many ways that are not limited to the supplier/ buyer mode within a (Western) contract; easements are allowed between the parties, with the belief that the contract will be fulfilled eventually. A debt is incurred within the *guanxi* network that brings with it obligations to fulfil the commitment as Fu *et al.* (2006) clearly state. However, trust in this form is not universal across the globe, nor is it perceived equally between different actors in one milieu. Kidd and Li (2007) report on the changing values of 'trust' as joint ventures mature in China. They found that over time Western managers wished to disassociate from the joint venture to become an independent trader while at the same time, as they now trusted their Chinese partners, they wished to keep a strong tie with their long-term partner. On the other hand, the Chinese, thinking they were getting to know and trust their Western partner more deeply, were appalled to find they were 'being dropped'. In their perceptions the Westerner was acting unethically, not acting within in the *guanxi* framework. 'Trust' in these relationships is central – but is perceived differently.

Much earlier in this chapter we stated that Asian firms should not rush to copy a 'Western model' but try to use their own traditional elements of CSR in their respective business cultures, e.g. the old Confucian inclination to care for each other. Indeed, as we have seen above, researchers looking at the business ethics of Chinese firms from the viewpoint of a Chinese researcher, for instance Fu *et al.* (2006), have found it is possible to work within the old cultural ways of caring for *qinren* (family members); *shuren* (acquaintances or familiar persons such as neighbours, or people from the same village, friends, colleagues or classmates) and *shengren* (strangers). Understanding the roles they play in various situations helps discover and effectively utilize the different types of *guanxi*. These three types of *guanxi* have different social psychological meanings (to the Chinese personnel) and this perception is governed by different sets of interpersonal rules. It is not good enough to say those in Asia 'ought to be faster' or those in the West 'ought to be slower' as these are too simplistic and serve only to make headlines that disguise the realities that people do try to accommodate one another. But business pressures and simple personal greed may well break the learning process of 'trusting to trust', which takes a long time to mature. These actions also require several attempts at interaction so as to generate a suitable data set from which to begin the processes referred to by Möllering, since we cannot all take leaps of faith every time we have to make a decision.

Looking the other way

Of course, although trust is a vital component of our lives, we need to accept and openly address the problems it causes us – for instance, let us return to the question of manufacturing, selling and buying fakes. We understand that so-called fake clothing may be derived from contract over-runs, which are then dumped in the supply chain at a cheap price agreed by the original (local) manufacturer (having already received his official contract fee for the x-thousand goods already made for the brand owner) but now sold at a price still low enough for the grey-sellers to make their own profit on the goods that are in fact full-quality items. In fact, the customer does not suffer in this case. But some firms make fake labels to be attached to shoddy goods which are sold-on as 'originals', although also suspiciously cheap. It is really the shoddy items of clothing, accessories, mechanical parts or even fake drugs that worry honest manufacturers and customers since there is no guarantee of the quality of raw materials, of manufacturing care with respect to 'fitness for purpose' or the ultimate safety of the goods. Often these fakes are inserted into the bona fide supply chain so that forwarders have no idea they are fakes, especially as they are sold finally as full-price goods. If the goods fail prematurely the buyer immediately blames the brand, and not his/her choice of purchase at a discount in a dubious marketplace. In reality, a quickly torn or faded (fake) 'branded' T-shirt may be a simple embarrassment, but the innocent users of fake medication or aircraft parts may come to far greater harm.

The following statistics, taken from a report on the *Third Global Congress on Combating Counterfeiting and Piracy*, which convened in late January 2007 in Geneva, give some sense of the scale of the problem:

- The World Health Organization estimates that as much as $35 billion of pharmaceuticals are counterfeit; that is, roughly 10 per cent of pharmaceuticals sold globally each year are fakes.
- Estimates attributed to the US Federal Trade Commission and the Motor & Equipment Manufacturers' Association are that counterfeiting costs the global automotive spare parts industry $12 billion annually, of which $3 billion is in the US.
- The US Federal Aviation Administration estimates that 2 per cent of the 26 million airline parts installed each year are counterfeit.
- The European Commission reported that 5.2 million items of counterfeited foodstuff, drinks and alcohol were seized in 2005 at the borders of the European Union.

The International Anti-Counterfeiting Coalition (IACC), a group of brand-owning companies, said the annual global trade in fake goods has risen to approximately US$600 billion, up from $5.5 billion in 1982. That accounts for five to seven per cent of world trade, the group says, and they state clearly that China is the biggest transgressor (IACC 2008). Such concerns would seem to jeopardize calls for global convergence. However, it is important to stress, with respect to CSR, no country is immune from criticism at some point of its development.

The original congress report noted that just about anything is copied and sold regardless of its quality or its end use. The authors continue:

> Perhaps the most amazing thing about counterfeiting is the volume of its activity. By its very nature, the extent to which goods are counterfeited and pirated is unknown and will probably never be fully measurable. But nearly every profitable product is subject to immense pressure from counterfeiters. The Senior Vice President for Pfizer, Robert L. Mallet, has explained that sales of counterfeit pharmaceuticals may double in the next five years to the point where one in every five persons may use counterfeit pharmaceuticals. Senior Intellectual Property Counsel for DaimlerChrysler, Beate Lalk-Menzel, warned against buying counterfeit brake pads, transmission units and car accessories. In addition, Brian Monks, Vice President for Underwriters Laboratories, reported that cheap electrical products sold in deep discount stores, or in flea markets, carry a high risk of being counterfeit and may be dangerous (for instance, fire extinguishers which enhance fires, or electrical extension cords which burn).
>
> (*The Manufacturer US* 2007)

The UK television producers of Channel 4's *The Fake Trade* chose to highlight the same Geneva conference mentioned above (Hornby 2008). The viewers of the programme at one time saw a panel of the CEOs convened to discuss with reporters the issues following two days of presentations about the fake trade. A reporter in the audience asked:

> ... we have been reading a number of things in recent years about counterfeiting and trafficking and the name of the country 'China' comes all the time at the top of the list. This morning so many speakers spoke, but none of you mentioned China. Can I know why?" The panel members were totally silent; they offered no response.
>
> (*The Fake Trade*, Channel 4, transmitted on 3 March and 10 March 2008)

It would seem that the panel members, as representatives of major firms, were embarrassed to be associated with the fake trade, perhaps they could have insisted they were themselves untainted, but it is very difficult to be totally sure within the complexities of global supply chains – better perhaps to remain silent.

We have stressed the creation and dissemination of fakes as they represent an important part of our lives. Basically we do not know which one of our goods are fakes, though we will have bought them as though they were bona fide. Sometimes, of course, we stop to consider – why are these goods so cheap? And at other times, perhaps in a bazaar, we really do understand that fakes are being presented to us be they designer labelled clothes, watches or DVDs. We might consider them a good bargain or just a holiday purchase. We understand that underpinning these goods are a myriad of sweatshops and dubious supply chains in which the people are paid very little – in fact, they are exploited. Should we therefore buy these goods knowing the poor are perhaps near starving, or the very young are being told to make the goods or leave the factory? Or should we be happy that some, albeit tiny amounts, of our money are being paid to the workers and thus keeping them from actual starvation? We are caught in a CSR dilemma – which of many CSRs ought we to accept? Ours from the developed world, those of the supply chain operators or those of the workers themselves (if they even consider CSR)? It is no wonder, therefore, that the concept of 'fair trade' has developed in the UK (see http://www.fairtrade.org.uk), which oversees that the whole supply chain is correctly recompensed from our purchase and that the front-line workers are not exploited. To an extent this foundation assuages our angst about our own CSR – enabling our views to be matched to the alternative CSRs upstream in the supply chain. In fact, this becomes a very similar argument to that put by Pellotta in his plea (which is worth repeating) that charities ought to be professionally managed profit-organized institutions: '[charity] is an exchange between the non-needy (donors) and the non-needy (the charity workforce) to provide services for the needy. It is thus an exchange between equals to help the needy'. Both the Fairtrade Foundation and Pallotta's TeamWorks help massage our CSRs to meld with those afar holding different concepts.

Looking forward

Behavioural norms develop over many years, and these change only slowly. Hofstede (1991:13), for example, defines culture as 'the way that we behave, which is different between nations'. Therefore, it becomes reasonable to accept that we must accept differing ways of 'conforming' to CSR so it becomes not universal, but created from within a culture.

The nature of CSR in an international context becomes confused when there are laws of behaviour that are man-made and mandatory, to be applied to all branches of a global enterprise but through their application in different legislatures. On the one hand, we think these have merit, since operating branches may be compared against each other and managers, investors or customers can evaluate the branches' performance under the same set of transparent rules. But when these rules hit against the natural mode of operation of local managers, we, and they, have to consider which may be best.

> ... it is said (with apparent sincerity) that some Chinese firms keep several sets of books – one for the government, one for company records, one for foreigners and one to report what is actually going on. By contrast, international

accounting standards are built on foundations that China does not possess, such as truthful record-keeping and deep, clean, markets so that "fair" valuations can be placed on financial instruments, property, or softer assets like brands and intellectual property

(The Economist 2007)

In these circumstances we find understanding others becomes difficult, and opprobrium is easier to administer when we find, as did the IACC (2008), that China is the globe's largest manufacturer of fakes. Condemnation becomes stronger against the Chinese manufacturing regimes when we find, unfortunately, that many fake manufacturers, and even straight firms, are employing staff in less than reasonable environments that are unsafe and polluted and offer low wages. But it is too easy to proceed along the route of 'China bashing' just as many did some years ago with respect to Japan Inc., as the apparent superiority of Japanese manufacturing systems gradually dominated many Western sectors. However, Western firms are not free of blame in their policies of exploitation, but therein the 'rule of law' operates that generally aids the oppressed, as might be seen in the rapid evolution of the Fairtrade Foundation movement.

We have to take a long view. Europe blossomed hesitantly only after its seventeenth century 'Enlightenment', and the US really only came into its own after the World War I and II and can base its opinions only on its polyglot 200-year-old society of immigrants who fled from Europe. On the other hand, China has been a dominant though not coherently governed nation from about 200 bc, if not before. It developed rules of administration demanding learning and the passing of examinations to achieve promotion to higher grades; it developed the arts and the sciences. But later, as Europe struggled to find its feet, China became a closed-door regime wherein it was a law unto itself. No wonder then that CSR in China is different to that in the West, notably the US. Given China's natural acceptance of hierarchy and the 'rules according to Confucius' and that these behaviours have spread across Asia, it is not surprising that the two major financial powers, Japan and China, take a long-term view of CSR. From the old Confucian 'rules' they have developed finely tuned *guanxi* networks that the Western world does not have; at least not with the same long-term view. The West has its well-worn phrase 'if you scratch my back, I'll scratch yours' and in this vein has developed antidotes in the form of SOX or other regulatory instruments to keep, in theory, the West open, transparent and corruption-free. These rules work reasonably well, but they have no resonance with *guanxi*.

We might note the Japanese game of *Go*.

> *Go* is a strategic board game for two players. It is known as *igo* (Japanese), *weiqi* or *wie ch'i* (Chinese) or *baduk* (Korean). *Go* originated in ancient China […] is noted for being rich in strategic complexity despite its simple rules. […] In combinatorial game theory terms, *Go* is a zero sum, perfect information, partisan, deterministic strategy game, putting it in the same class as chess, checkers (draughts), and Reversi (othello); however it differs from these in its

game play. Although the rules are simple, the practical strategy is extremely complex. The game emphasizes the importance of balance on multiple levels and has internal tensions.

(Wikipedia at http://en.wikipedia.org/wiki/Go_(game))

Quite often comparisons are made between *Go* and chess as a metaphor of the differences between Eastern and Western strategic thinking. The initial *Go* board is empty and an area is captured in a holistic manner. In chess, one begins with two 'fully loaded' adversarial sides whose job is to kill off, one by one, the opposition. *Go* is quite the opposite; individual stones are only significant as part of a larger group, and the effect of those groups is determined only as the game proceeds with multiple, simultaneous battles leading to a point-based win; chess has a goal of killing one individual piece (the king).

Throughout this chapter we have alluded to the Asian way of working as a collective, in groups knowing and supporting each other with strong *guanxi* bindings. This is in contrast to the particular modes of the Western world where 'me' often seems to take precedence over 'us'. We thus come back to the dilemma that has haunted us throughout this chapter – that Eastern and Western modes of behaviour, strategic gaming and social cohesion are quite different. There are going to be different forms of CSR applied (in good faith) by the oriental and the occidental, and indeed in differentiations between each nation if we accept the notion of national differences posited by Hofstede (1991). The question is how can we draw these CSR together?

Conclusions

We have stressed 'trust' as a foundation of getting two sides to move to the basic compromise of individual ideals that initially prevent each acknowledging the other; and as Bogenrieder (2006) suggests '... actors have to search for common ground' since they do not initially in their learned, even hidden, norms of behaviour have any place for the ideals of the other. Following the creation of commonalities, we hope, as trust grows, the actors in an enterprise and those working with others in a joint venture will be able to exchange data and concepts, personal models of their world views, knowledge, and later, wisdom. But this will be a long drawn-out process as the exchange of knowledge is 'sticky' (Szulanski 1996; Huber 2000); and even in Japan Fruin (1997) found that Toyota workers were a little reluctant to tell their peers how to do tasks better. On the other hand, Nonaka *et al.* (2000) and others have pursued the Japanese concept of *ba* as a working space – conceptual, virtual or real – in which team members may relax and exchange knowledge (Nonaka *et al.* 2000; Porter 1998; Ishikura 2004). So, until the relevant actors in their enterprise more freely exchange knowledge, aspirations or hopes with others, they cannot expect those others to abide by a one-sided application of CSR, as all our 'rules' have been predicated by a knowledge base built up over many formative years.

It has to be remembered the views expressed here – whether we like it or not, and whether typical or not – are from a Western perspective, since the authors were born in the West and grew up in that milieu. Nevertheless, we recognize there ought to be universalities in our arguments, since without a common understanding between parties from different cultures there will be no progress made upon any accord, and CSR will be one of the least considered aspects as the actors stumble towards consensus in building their business goals. Such a convergence leads not towards a universally held ideal of upholding and sharing, but more towards accepting and knowing that one must compromise in order to create a new, more universally acceptable regime, and this learning depends on our embracing 'trusting in trust'.

Of course, there is no easy conclusion to draw. The overriding image is the ways of business in Asia, at least typified by China, are the ways of the long term. And despite opportunism being rife, this is has been the case in global trade over thousands of years (Bernstein 2008). In China there is a drip-by-drip approach to test out relationships in which CSR (as it is portrayed by the West) is irrelevant, or at best the Western CSR is seen as 'too fast' in its application, and possibly insincere. Asia has its honour system, but this does not necessarily support individuals uniquely, instead it looks to the collective good; and troublingly, to the Westerner, there is the lack of the 'rule of law' across Asia that normally is assumed to protect individuals, and which is a basis of Western CSR.

Thus, potentially, we reach an impasse: how can we support firms that make fakes within an industrial and commercial world that is increasingly interdependent and messily global? How indeed do we ascertain if our partner firm does or does not make fakes, or employs staff in unsuitable conditions? And who indeed defines 'unsuitable'? The 'butterfly in China' flapping it wings affects us all, and we have to accept that our world views differ. We must learn therefore to accept compromise as an initial premise, and be willing to grow together upon a mutual, trusting, learning base. Following on from this broad hope we suggest as more firms in China reach to their global markets they will better embrace the concepts of CSR as these become institutionalized by 'rubbing against CSR as practiced by more sophisticated partners'. And those so-called 'sophisticated' partners may also learn from their so-called 'junior' partners as we all have something to give to the other.

However, it is not the projection of CSR in annual reports that is important, but the acting out 'in practice' in an ethical manner – which means at least giving acceptable wages to workers (who are not under age and thus ruled out of an adequate education by being forced instead to work). We return again to our concept of *noblesse oblige* wherein the powerful really do look after their weaker dependants, to develop our 'community spirit' and to embrace philanthropic ideals. It is through globalization perhaps that convergence may be learned more quickly. The forces of 'relative advantage' (Ricardo 1911) both in production ability (China) and in financial instruments (US) will ensure the continuation of the global supply chain, notwithstanding the present financial crises.

What we must ensure is that there is a mechanism for the continual questioning of our interpretations of 'our CSR' and how it is to be applied to others who have, they argue quite correctly, their own valid CSR. Fakes may thus be accepted for what they are – opportunistic manufacturing – and their profits should recompense the intellectuals who made the originals as well as the shop-floor workers; but the manufacturers of fakes that are supplied knowing they may result in significant harm must suffer the heaviest of sanctions. Surely in this we can all agree.

Suggested further reading

Buhmann, Karin. (2008) 'Corporate Social Responsibility – A China approach'. *Asia Portal – In Focus*. <http://www.asiaportal.info/infocusblog/?p = 39>.
Chapple, W. and J. Moon. (2005) 'Corporate Social Responsibility (CSR) in Asia: A Seven Country Study of CSR Website Reporting'. *Business and Society*, 44 (4): 415–41.
Human Rights in China. (2006) 'IR 2008: Maximizing the Impact of CSR in China'. *China Rights Forum*, 3: 132–38. <http://hrichina.org/public/PDFs/CRF.3.2006/CRF-2006-3_IR2008-CSR.pdf.>
Li, Zijun. (2005) 'Lack of Corporate Social Responsibility Behind Recent China accident'. Worldwatch Institute. <http://www.worldwatch.org/node/3859> (accessed September 2008).

There is a 'pressure' to learn more about CSR: useful websites

Crossroads – Review of Corporate Social Responsibility in China at http://china-crossroads. com/about-2/.
The US-China Business Council at http://www.uschina.org/corporateresponsibility.html.

References

Bernstein, W. (2008) *A Splendid Exchange: How Trade Shaped the World*. London: Grove/ Atlantic.
Berrone, P., J. Surroca and J. A. Tribó. (2007) 'Corporate Ethical Identity as a Determinant of Firm erformance: A test of the Mediating Role of Stakeholder Satisfaction'. *Journal of Business Ethics*, 76: 35–53.
Bogenrieder, I. (2006) 'Co-operation in a System of Distributed Cognition or How to Co-operate with Diverse Knowledge', in B. Renzi, K. Matzler and H. Hinterhuber (eds) *The Future of Knowledge Management*, 205–14. London: Palgrave.
Brazelton, J. K. and J. L. Ammons. (eds) (2002) *Enron and Beyond – Technical Analysis of Accounting, Corporate Governance, and Securities Issues*. Amsterdam: CCH Inc.
Buchholz, R. A. and S. B. Rosenthal. (2005) 'Toward a Contemporary Conceptual Framework for Stakeholder Theory'. *Journal of Business Ethics*, 58: 137–48.
Carroll, A. B. (1996) *Business and Society: Ethics and Stakeholder Management* (3rd edn). Cincinnati: Southwestern/Cengage Learning.
Chen, E. (2009) 'Challenges of Chinese Philanthropy' *CRS Asia*, 5(5). http://www.csr-asia. com/weekly_detail.php?id = 11592 (accessed on 7 February).
Chen, M. (2004) *Asian Management Systems* (2nd edn). London: Thompson Learning.
Chen, X. P. and C. C. Chen. (2004) 'On the Intricacies of the Chinese Guanxi: A Process Model of Guanxi Development'. *Asia Pacific Journal of Management*, 21(3): 305–24.

Clarkson, M. B. E. (1995) 'A Stakeholder Framework for Analysing and Evaluating Corporate Social Performance'. *Academy of Management Review*, 20: 92–117.

Fang, T. (1999) *Chinese Business Negotiating Style*. Thousand Oaks, CA: SAGE.

—— (2004) 'The "Coop-Comp" Chinese Negotiation Strategy', in J. B. Kidd and F-J. Richter (eds) *Trust and AntiTrust in Asian Business Alliances*. London: Palgrave.

Fruin, W. M. (1997) *Knowledge Works: Managing intellectual capital at Toshiba*. London: Oxford University Press.

Fu, P. P., A. S. Tsui and G. G. Dess. (2006) 'The Dynamics of Guanxi in Chinese High-Tech: Implications for Knowledge Management and Decision Making'. *Management International Review*, 46(3): 277–305.

Fukuyama, F. (1995) *Trust*. New York: The Free Press.

Hofstede, G. (1991) *Cultures and Organizations – Software of the Mind*. London: McGraw Hill.

Hornby, N. (2008) *The Fake Trade*. A [UK] Channel 4 television production – written and directed by Nick Hornby. Transmitted 3 and 10 March.

House, R. J., P. J. Hanges, M. Javidan, P. W. Dorfman and V. Gupta. (2004) *Culture, leadership, and Organizations: The GLOBE Study of 62 Societies*. Thousand Oaks, CA: SAGE.

Huber, G. P. (2000) 'Transferring Sticky Knowledge: Suggested Solutions and Needed Studies', in J. S. Edwards and J. B. Kidd (eds), *Proceedings of KMAC2000, Knowledge Management Beyond The Hype: Looking Towards The New Millennium*, 12–22. Birmingham, UK: Operational Research Society.

IACC. (2008) 'GET REAL – The Truth About Counterfeiting'. http://www.iacc.org/counterfeiting/counterfeiting.php (accessed 15 February).

IBLS. (2008) 'INTERNET LAW – Beijing Puts First-Ever Piracy Criminal in Jail as Fakes Create One-Third of GDP'. International Business Law Services. <http://www.ibls.com/internet_law_news_portal_view.aspx?id = 2059&s = latestnews> (accessed 7 February 2009).

I-Chuan Wu-Beyens. (2000) 'Hui: Chinese Business in Action', in Kwok Bun Chan (ed) *Chinese Business Network*, 129–52. Singapore: Prentice Hall.

Ishikura, Y. (2004) 'Cluster as "Ba" for Knowledge Management', in J. B. Kidd and F-J. Richter (eds), *Trust and AntiTrust in Asian Business Alliances*. London: Palgrave.

Jarillo, J. C. (1988) 'On Strategic Networks'. *Strategic Management Journal*, 9: 31 – 41.

Kao, H. S. and N. Sek-Hong. (1993) 'Organisational Commitment: From Trust to Altruism at Work'. *Psychology and Developing Societies*, 5: 43–60.

Kidd, J. B. and F-J. Richter. (2002) 'The "Oppression" of Governance?', in J. B. Kidd and F-J. Richter. (eds) *Corruption and Governance in Asia*. London and New York: Palgrave.

Kidd, J. B. and X. Li. (2007) 'Trust One's Alliance Partner? Maybe – Maybe Not! Preliminary Results of Recent Research in China', in R. Chow and O. H. M. Yau (eds) *Harmony vs Conflict: Managing in a Turbulent Era*. London: Palgrave.

Kidd, J. B. and F-J. Richter. (2004) 'The Talkative Company', in C. F. Benton, F-J. Richter and T. Takai (eds) *Meso-Organisations and the Creation of Knowledge*. Westport, CN: Praeger.

Kidd, J. B. (1983) 'Potential Nemawashi – the Benefit of Long-Term Employment', in Sung-Jo Park (ed.), *East Asia*, 2: 84–105. Frankfurt: Campus Verlag.

—— (2007) 'The Great Game Evolves for Central Asia and Opportunities Beckon'. *Management Decision*, 45(8): 1224–52. A special edition by D. Lammond and R. Dwyer (eds). *Alleviating Poverty Though Trade*. For the International Trade Centre (UNCTAD/ WTO).

Kidd, J. B., S. Prabhakaran and N. Shrinivasan. (2008) 'Has Logistics Security Gone a Regulation Too Far? Guarding Against Perpetrators from the Anomic to the Fraudster'. Proceedings of the 17th International Conference on Management of Technology Creating and Managing a Knowledge Economy. IAMOT 2008, April 6–10, 2008.

Luo, Y. (1997) 'Guanxi: Principles, Philosophies and Implications'. *Human Systems Management*, 16(1): 43–51.

—— (2000) *Guanxi and Business*. Singapore: World Scientific Press.

McClelland, D. C. (1961) *The Achieving Society*. Princeton: Van Nostrand.

McNally, C. A. (2002) 'Strange Bedfellows: Communist Party Institutions and New Governance Mechanisms in Chinese State Holding Corporations'. *Berkeley Electronic Press (Politics & Business)*, 4 (1). <http://www.bepress.com/bap/vol4/iss1/art4/> (accessed 3 April 2008).

MLA. (2009) 'Responsibility': from *The MLA International Bibliography*. New York: Modern Language Association (MLA). <Dictionary.comhttp://dictionary.reference.com/ browse/responsibility> (accessed 22 January 2009).

Möllering, G. (2006) *Trust: Reason, Routine, Reflexivity*. Oxford: Elsevier.

Nojonen, M. (2003) 'The Competitive Advantage with Chinese Characteristics – the Sophisticated Choreography of Gift Giving', in J. B. Kidd and F-J. Richter (eds) *Corruption and Governance in Asia*, 107–30. London: Palgrave.

Nonaka I. R. Toyama and N. Konno. (2000) 'SECI, Ba and Leadership: Unified Model of Dynamic Knowledge Creation'. *Long Range Planning*, 33 (1): 5–34.

Page, S. E. and J. Bednar. (2006) 'Culture, Institutional Performance, and Path Dependence'. Institute of Governmental Studies, Paper WP2006–6. Berkeley: University of California. <http://repositories.cdlib.org/cgi/viewcontent.cgi?article = 1102&context = igs> (accessed 7 January 2009).

Pellotta, D. (2008) *Uncharitable: How Restraints on Nonprofits Undermine Their Potential*. Hanover, NH: Tufts University Press.

Pondel, E. (2003) 'Family Values: Nepotism Brings Trust, Stability to Farmers Insurance'. *Daily News* (Los Angeles), 3 July.

Porter, M. (1998) *Clusters and the New Competitive Agenda for Companies and Governments*. Boston: Harvard Business School Press.

Ricardo, D. (1911) *The Principles of Political Economy and Taxation*. London: Dutton.

Sachs, J. (2008) *Common Wealth: Economics for a Crowded Planet*. London: Allen Lane.

SOX. (2002) – Sarbanes-Oxley Act of 2002 (SOX). See the central resources at the US Centre for Audit Quality. <http://thecaq.aicpa.org/Resources/Sarbanes+Oxley>.

Szulanski, G. (1996) 'Exploring Internal Stickiness: Impediments to the Transfer of Best Practice Within the Firm'. *Strategic Management Journal* 17(Winter Special Issue): 27–43.

The Economist. (2007) 'They're Behind You'. 8 December: 80.

—— (2007b) 'Cultural Revolution'. 11 January: 37.

The Manufacturer US. (2007) 'Global Congress Calls for Greater Effort, Resources in Combating Counterfeiting & Piracy'. *The Manufacturer US*. 30 January 2007. <http:// www.themanufacturer.com/us/detail.html?contents_id = 5101> (accessed 28 January 2009).

Transparency International. (2008) *Corruption Perception Index*. Berlin: Transparency International.

UN. (2007) *Millennium Development Goals Report*. New York: United Nations.

UNDP. (2006) *Human Development Report. Beyond Scarcity: Power, Poverty and the Global Water Crisis*. New York: United Nations and Palgrave MacMillan.

Verbos, A. K., J. A. Gerard, P. R. Harding and J. S. Miller. (2007) 'The Positive Ethical Organisation: Enacting a Living Code of Ethics and Ethical Organisational Identity'. *Journal of Business Ethics*, 76: 17 – 33.

World Economic Forum. (2005) 'Full Survey: Trust in Governments, Corporations and Global Institutions Continues to Decline. Geneva, World Economic Forum'. http://www2.weforum.org/site/homepublic.nsf/Content/Full+Survey_+Trust+in+Governments,+Corporations+and+Global+Institutions+Continues+to+Decline.html (accessed 28 January 2009).

World Economic Forum. (2005) 'Trust in Governments, Corporations and Global Institutions Continues to Decline'. Press release, 15 December prior to their annual Davos conference. <http://www.weforum.org/en/media/Latest%20Press%20Releases/PRESSRELEASES87> (accessed 3 April 2007).

Index

Entries for illustrations and tables are in *italic*.

misunderstanding of CSR in 48–50, 57; professionalisation of CSR in 9; trust relationships in 153; and Western social paradigms 10

keiretsu 54, 153
kigyôshûdan 52–3
Korea 148

labour rights *see* workers, rights of
labour unions 54, 61, 126, 128–9, 150
law: in Asia 152; rule of 30, 32, 160, 162
LDCs (least developed countries) 121, 126–8, 131, 138
legitimacy theory 97, 113
liberal democracy 15–16, 32

Malaysia 1, 9, 13, 95, 98–9, 101–6, 110, 113–14
management, corporate 45, 47, 51, 61, 99–101
Mao Zedong 26, 30–1
media: in China 32; control of 25; freedoms 32–3; trust in 150
minimum wage 13, 68, 124, 131
Mitrphol Sugar Group 80
MNCs *see* multinational companies (MNCs)
moral development 133, 145
morality 1, 4, 18
Multi Fiber Agreement (MFA) 121, 130
multinational companies (MNCs) 4, 13, 15, 74, 82, 99, 101, 122–3, 125–31, 133–5, 143

National Annual Corporate Report Award (NACRA), Malaysia 102–3
neoliberalism 12, 23, 26–9
NEP (National Economic Policy), Malaysia 105
NEP (new ecological paradigm) 24–6, 31, 35
Nestle 79–80, 90
NGOs (non-government organisations) 45, 47, 59, 61, 123, 150
NICs (newly industrialised countries) 67–8
'nomunication' 153
non-government organisations *see* NGOs
NPOs (Non-Profit Organizations) 56

Obama, Barack 2

philanthropy 6, 48–50, 57–8, 76–7, 79, 81, 122–3, 143, 151
poverty 10, 38, 68, 73, 124, 127, 148
power elites 25, 32, 144
press, free *see* media, freedoms
Principle of Responsible Investment 61
property rights 12, 23–4, 34, 46, 149

ready-made garments (RMG) 13–14, 121–3, 126, 134–5, 146

sexual harassment 13, 71, 124–5
shareholders: accountability to 96; rights of 7, 10
SOCAM (Service Organization for Compliance Audit Management) 129
social movements 28, 34, 61
socialism 16, 26–7, 29
SRI (socially responsible investment) 47, 55
stakeholder approach 4–5
stakeholder theory 7, 97, 128
stakeholders: in Asian context 146–7; and CSR 78
strategic thinking 161
supercapitalism 3–5, 17, 19

tax evasion 124
TBCSD (Thailand Business Council for Sustainable Development) 77, 80, 82
Thailand 1, 9, 13, 67–8, 71–83, 92, 121; occupational injuries in *70*; poverty in *69*
Tiananmen Square *see* China 1989 social movement in
trade unions *see* labour unions
transparency 2, 13–14, 59, 82, 99, 101–3, 151
trust 2, 14, 17, 58–60, 142, 150–7, 161–2

water pollution 31, 72
women, in Thailand 71
workers: in Bangladesh 13, 124–6, 133, 146; children as 127–9, 142; and CSR 159; female 71, 125–6, 129; rights of 33, 77, 123, 131; in Thailand 68, 71
World Economic Forum 150–1

For Product Safety Concerns and Information please contact our EU
representative GPSR@taylorandfrancis.com
Taylor & Francis Verlag GmbH, Kaufingerstraße 24, 80331 München, Germany

www.ingramcontent.com/pod-product-compliance
Ingram Content Group UK Ltd.
Pitfield, Milton Keynes, MK11 3LW, UK
UKHW021610240425
457818UK00018B/488